From Tartan to Tartanry

From Tartan to Tartanry

Scottish Culture, History and Myth

Edited by Ian Brown

Edinburgh University Press

Edinburgh University Press Ltd
22 George Square, Edinburgh
www.euppublishing.com

Typeset in Linotype Sabon by
Iolaire Typesetting, Newtonmore, and
printed and bound in Great Britain by
CPI Antony Rowe, Chippenham and Eastbourne

A CIP record for this book is available
from the British Library

ISBN 978 0 7486 3877 2 (hardback)

CONTENTS

PREFACE

The contributors to this volume come from a wide variety of fields. Their range has allowed us to bring together a more interdisciplinary study of tartan and tartanry than is often achieved. Thanks are due to all of them. They bring fresh, often unexpected and sometimes startling insights to our topic.

My personal thanks are especially due to Hugh Cheape, David Goldie, Murray Pittock and Alan Riach for their rigorous advice to me, and for the many ways they have supported my own contributions. Thanks are also due to Cairns Craig for his early support for the development of this project. I am particularly grateful to Jackie Jones and Esmé Watson of Edinburgh University Press for their editing skills deployed firmly, yet lightly, throughout the production of this volume and to my wife Nikki Axford for her practical help and moral support. Thanks are also due to Gerard Carruthers and the staff of the Scottish Literature Department and the Library at Glasgow University where I have the pleasure of being an Honorary Professorial Research Fellow.

It would be wrong not to note that the late Professor Richard Prentice had planned to contribute to this volume. His sadly premature death in November 2008 prevented his even beginning to draft his chapter. There is no doubt that he would have brought the very particular combination of sociological, psychological, anthropological, heritage and tourism knowledge and insight to his chapter that he brought in such innovative ways to the rest of his research. He was certainly one of the most active researchers – and prolific publishers of original studies – that I have ever had the honour to know. It is a matter of regret to his many colleagues and friends that his acute insights and rigorous mind are no longer at our service.

Finally, I dedicate this volume to my brother Gavin without whom this book would not have been.

Ian Brown

Introduction

TARTAN, TARTANRY AND HYBRIDITY

Ian Brown

The essence of tartan – and tartanry – is an absence of certainty. The very design of tartan embodies constant dynamic tension between the clarity, even rigidity, of its grid and the literally endless potential for colour and variety contained within, and visually threatening to break, the lock of that grid. Its impact visually has been compared to that of a flower garden. In 1723, the author of *A Journey through Scotland* described women's wearing it 'in the Middle of a Church, on a Sunday, look[ing] like a Parterre de Fleurs'.[1] A key element in this metaphor is that the flowers are not strewn wildly: they are contained, growing within, but also out of, a formal garden. Tartan embeds carefree design carefully, a celebration both of the vitality of nature and of the interaction of human intellect, aesthetics and dynamic growth. In a *bon mot*, John Laver has presented a parallel contemporary view. A senior academic, settled in Scotland for many years, he had planned to wear morning dress to his daughter's wedding. She persuaded him he should wear a kilt like the younger men. Afterwards he commented, 'I'm glad I did or I would have looked like a penguin in a flower garden'. The vitality, even vibrancy, of tartan – the ways its interaction of potential and rigorous vigour separate it from the frozen world of the penguin – are summed up by the designer and weaver Annie Stewart:

> Tartan is an ordered way of introducing a riot of colour in a very restrained manner because the design in the warp is the same as the design in the weft. The true colour that is created by the crossing of the warp with the weft is strong, but easier to look at because of the grid design. It remains organic instead of psychedelic even when vivid colours are used.[2]

This volume seeks to explore the warp, weft and variety – organic or not – of tartan and tartanry. The first four chapters, by Hugh Cheape,

Murray Pittock, Trevor Royle and Michael Newton, provide a warp. They focus on the history of tartan, addressing various ways in which at different times and in different places it has been mythologised and seeking to bring sense to what has sometimes been a fraught discourse. Later chapters offer a weft, a variety of cultural perspectives that explore attitudes and usages with regard to tartan and the ways in which its use has led to varieties of 'tartanry'. What is true of both tartan and tartanry, however, is that they are polysemic and multi-valent, embodying meanings that cannot be contained in any single discourse. And so the 'weft' chapters of this volume address them in relation to heritage, mythopoeia and history, popular culture, popular theatre, literature and cultural translation, film, comedy, rock and pop music, sport and 'high' culture.

The etymological history of 'tartan' offers an interesting frame of meaning. The *Dictionary of the Scots Language (DSL)* derives the term from Old French *tiretaine*, 'a sort of cloth half wool, half some other yarn; stuff of which the weft is wool and the warp linen or cotton'. This origin would identify it as the form of cloth now called linsey-woolsey. The earliest *DSL* entries, indeed, could suggest that it still meant simply a form of cloth: from 1532–3, 'Ane uthir tartane galcoit gevin to the king be the Maister Forbes' and from 1538, 'For iij elnis of heland tertane to be hois to the kingis grace'. By 1561, however, an entry from Dundee suggests that colour is implied by 'tartan', not just a form of cloth, while the matter is entirely clear in an entry from 1616–33: 'warm stuff of divers colours which they call tartane'. The emphasis on diversity – indeed hybridity – can be found, if the origin is in fact French, in the Breton use of *tiretaine* for cider made half of apples and half of pears. The complexity of the word, however, extends to debate as to its actual origin. Alan Burford has made a case for Gaelic origin, linking it with the Gaelic for 'across', 'tarsainn'.[3] The problem with a Franco-Scots derivation is that it would suggest a Lowland origin for tartan, for which evidence is lacking, though Richard Grange suggests, perhaps boldly, that 'It seems that tartan – and the tartan plaid – originated in the Lowland districts and its popularity spread to the Highlands'.[4] Meanwhile, for a Gaelic derivation from 'tarsainn' the problem is that the Gaelic word used historically is 'breacan', derived from 'breac', meaning 'speckled' or 'spotted'. This complexity is compounded when James D. Scarlett suggests tartan design originates in Pictish society,[5] an ethnological speculation beyond possibility of proof. Whatever its derivation, one theme the etymology of the word foregrounds is that of hybridity or crossing, even contrariness. Meantime, the related word 'plaid' seems also to emerge as a Scots term in the sixteenth century, firstly for cloth or a garment – a shawl for women or mantle for men – and its weave, and very quickly applied to its colouring. The Gaelic 'plaide' ('blanket') the *DSL* suggests is derived from Scots, though the journey may be in the opposite direction. Tartan's linguistic roots are intercultural and elusive, but intriguingly so.

What is striking is that such an intriguing aspect of Scottish culture should at various times and in various ways have attracted the levels of hostility that it has, both from non-Scots and Scots. Sometimes the hostility has been based in political and military conflict. Daniel Defoe in his *Memoirs of a Cavalier* (1720), supposedly 'Written threescore years ago by an English gentleman', illustrates the typecasting of both the Highlander of the War of the Three Kingdoms and his dress as beyond the exotic:

> I confess the soldiers made a very uncouth figure, especially the Highlanders: the oddness and barbarity of their garb and arms seems to have something in it remarkable [. . .] their doublet, breeches and stockings, of a stuff they called plaid, striped across red and yellow, with short cloaks of the same. These fellows looked when drawn out like a regiment of Merry-Andrews ready for Bartholomew fair.[6]

The vocabulary here is of course coloured by hostility to the invading army of 1639. Key words like 'uncouth', 'odd' and 'barbarity' typify Highland dress as somehow outré, beyond civilisation, when, of course, it was an element in the Celtic civilisation of Scotland that was, and is, a source of art of considerable cultivation. The later-invented shibboleth, referred to by Ian Maitland Hume, that the kilt should not be worn south of the Highland line is, in a sense, another version of an attempt to corral the dress into some form of reservation for the eccentric. The very word 'barbarity', of course, arises from the ancient Greeks' fear of and contempt for those great civilisations around them that did not speak Greek and so were beyond 'civilisation', at least so far as the Greeks, with their own special barbarisms, were concerned. Trevor Royle in his chapter (see p. 56) refers to such perceptions, or rather typecasting, of the 'other' continuing when the Highland regiments were established:

> With the 'barbaric' allure of their uniforms Highland soldiers became an instantly recognised and widely feared element of the

British Army and their service in Africa, India and North America helped to consolidate Britain's growing mercantile empire.

Defoe's passage also includes a reading of the tartan as the patching of the costume of Merry-Andrews: buffoons or harlequins. A deal of recent resentment of tartan and tartanry has been focused on such twentieth-century comedic personae as those of Harry Lauder. Even a perceptive critic like Cairns Craig could at one time observe

> No Scottish writer could have brought myth and history together, as Yeats did [. . .] Such a conjunction was made impossible because the tartan myth was a myth of historical redundancy, and being redundant its images declined (as Yeats said the ancient gods of Ireland had declined to leprechauns) from the noble stature of Ossian and Scott's Jacobites to the parodic red-nosed, kilted, drunken, mean Scotsmen of music hall comedy and picture postcard jokes.[7]

In fact, as Paul Maloney, Margaret Munro and David Goldie in their chapters make clear, what is here presented as a degringolade is arguably more positive and certainly more complex. As Jonathan Faiers has pointed out, reflecting – presumably unconsciously – Defoe's earlier text with regard to the comedic and subversive, not to say threatening and potentially anarchic, influence of the tartan, an impact extending beyond Scottish artists:

> The great 'turns' of the nineteenth- and twentieth-century music halls, entertainers noted for their tartan costumes – for example Harry Lauder, Dan Leno, Marie Lloyd, or clowns such as Coco – donned their tartans as a masquerade that would allow them to become the transgressive characters beloved by their audiences. Their swaggering tartan costumes invested their performances with the spirit of rebellious and subversive clowning that can be traced back to the figure of Harlequin, British nineteenth-century panto-mime's translation of Arlecchino from the original *commedia dell'arte*.[8]

Paul Maloney has pointed out to the present author that staged tartan in kilt, trews, bunnet, frock-coat and other items, seen often by some critics as demeaning, can equally – or perhaps even more – be seen as celebratory, joyously conspiratorial with the audience and full of ebullient life.[9]

At particular periods, of course, the significance of tartan on stage has carried specific, and dangerous, meanings. John Jackson, the actor, playwright and, later, theatre manager, managing the Theatre Royal Edinburgh from 1781 to 1791 and launching the Glasgow Theatre Royal in 1782, had an early success playing the title role in John Home's *Douglas* in Edinburgh in 1762. As a result David Garrick invited him to join his Drury Lane company. Jackson tells of bringing his costume south, including Highland dress and appropriate weaponry, seeking to repeat his Edinburgh triumph in 1763. This was not, however, possible. Writing in 1793, Jackson explains

> Lord Bute's administration [. . .] was become so unpleasing to the multitude, that anything, confessedly Scotch, awakened the embers of dissension, and fed the flame of party. Mr. Garrick therefore put a direct negative [. . .] for even to have performed the play of *Douglas* would have been hazardous, and to have exhibited the Highland dress upon the stage, imprudence in the extreme. Could I have supposed at that period, that I should live to see the tartan plaid universally worn in the politest circles, and its colours the predominating fashion among all ranks of people in the metropolis?[10]

During the Disarming Act's currency, of course, Jackson's wearing of Highland dress, which is clearly from context intended as, at the least, including tartan plaid, would not have been illegal in London, but two implications are clear. One is that it had been worn with apparent impunity in 1762 on the Scottish stage, where it would have been strictly illegal, so perhaps paralleling the ways in which, in another artform, portraiture in tartan of society figures appears to have gone on with impunity. The other is that tartan was identified in 1763 not just with the Highlands, but the 'Scotch' as a whole, so that it could become a subject of general Scotophobia. This accords with the earlier general identification of tartan and Scottishness referred to in several chapters and demonstrated by the 1675 depiction of John Lacy in a tartan costume to portray the title character, Sauny the Scot, in his own 1667 play (see p. 95). It also appears, at least on the basis of Jackson's contemporary evidence, that, furth of Scotland, well before the 1822 royal visit and half a century before Balmorality's development, tartan was seen as widely acceptable and fashionable in British high society. Murray Pittock, for example, notes that 'in 1789 the future George IV wore tartan at a masquerade ball'.[11]

Tartan and certain aspects of tartanry have been and can still be a threat, at the very least, to critical convention and *amour propre* and often an element in direct challenge to established and even establishment values. It could also, as Murray Pittock argues in his chapter, be seen as embodying alternative traditions to those of the dominant hegemony. That it did so was, of course, a central reason for its prohibition in the 1746 Disarming Act. Tartan had, and retains within its polysemy, a capacity to bear meaning beyond many other sartorial designs. Domhnall Uilleam Stiùbhart recognises that, while the nexus of tartan and plaid might – indeed in the nature of things must – evolve, that evolution maintains and foregrounds the potential for tartan to represent an alterity that supports the unbuttoned, emotionally spirited and carnivalesque:

> by the late seventeenth century the plaid was increasingly becoming a male garment in the Gàidhealtachd, as women abandoned the traditional female plaid of *earasaid* in favour of contemporary Lowland fashions. In addition, the tartan, that clothing of brawn, vigour, and spectacular display *par excellence*, was more and more being compared to and distinguished from garments of 'renunciation' worn in the south, namely the black hat and cloak worn by Presbyterian ministers and, on a wider British stage, the rise of that most emblematic whig garment, the sober three-piece suit.[12]

Of course such potential for alterity carried a cost. One aspect of that cost was the recurrent process of stigmatisation, which in some critical discourses still continues. Another is that of appropriation by the forces that regarded the tartan as 'other'. The dimension of tartanry called 'Balmorality' is a clear case, following on from the 1822 royal visit, of the winner apparently taking over the loser's tokens. In fact, of course, two things underlie that royal visit and the later development of Balmorality. One is the process by which tartanisation of public events and personae represents an attempt at reconciliation after conflict. This is hardly a shameful process and arguably a necessary one for the future of any body politic. The second is the way in which the appropriation of tartan iconography, within the context of the dominance of Scottish cultural tropes throughout the Western world after the impact of Ossian and Walter Scott, asserts the complex of values appropriation was intended to suppress. Victoria did not bring about tartan's revival in Scotland. As John Telfer Dunbar points out, there was, as part of 1820s and 1830s Romantic Gothic revival, a continuing interest in tartan, including the Eglinton tournament of

1839,[13] which flowed into the spectacular 1842 welcome given to Victoria and Albert at Taymouth Castle. Their Balmorality can be seen as an enthusiastic endorsement of and response to this. In short, it is an open question whether George IV in a kilt and Victoria and Albert at Balmoral are appropriating and subverting a set of values, or whether they are being appropriated and subverted. Certainly one of the strong strands of Scottish nationalism in the nineteenth century expressed itself in a form of unionism that demanded the defence and assertion of Scottish rights and institutions. And arguably that process led eventually to the possibility – because sufficient specifically Scottish civic structures survived and were active – of the re-establishment of the Scottish Parliament in 1999. David McCrone makes such a case *passim* in *Understanding Scotland* (2001).[14] Such structures were energised, even embodied, by a variety of tartan identity tokens, and Ian Maitland Hume's reporting in his chapter of aspects of his ethnological research highlights the interaction of such tokens with individuals' internalised sense of identity. Indeed, as Michael Newton shows, the importance of such internalised tokens of identity for an expatriate community cannot be overestimated. However domestic Scots may regard the resort to tartan and its symbols by expatriates, they have no more right than any other home community with a large diaspora to pass judgement on what their expatriate cousins evolve in response to their own diasporic needs. The international dynamism of tartan and tartanry is not to be restrained by attempts by the home community to police an iconography that is, whatever its roots and however Scottish-focused, international. Indeed, one of the debates with Michael Newton in preparing this volume was whether the word 'tartanry' could rightly be used of North American experience or whether another word showing respect for expatriate developments such as 'tartanism' might not better be used. In the end that debate remains, so far as this volume is concerned, open-ended.

All of this is not to romanticise the ways in which the evolution and, to an extent, social standardisation of tartan in the nineteenth century proceeded. A glorification and idealisation of tartan could be used to blink at the treatment of the Highlands and Highlanders. As Neal Ascherson observes,

As the nineteenth century passed, 'Highlandism' took a firm grip on Scottish identity. Tartan and bagpipes became national symbols as the Scots proclaimed, in effect, that 'we are all aboriginals now'. [Patrick] Sellar's dismissive radicalism went out of fashion. And yet

there are those today who look at the crofting counties, those
communities which have been confirmed in the tenure of what is
so often the worst land, and wonder if they are not looking at
'Indian' or Aboriginal reservations under another name. As long as
the rich soils of Scotland remain a speculator's free-fire zone while
the barrens [*sic*] are reserved for one specific community, the ghost
of Patrick Sellar will never be laid.[15]

As the present author observes in his chapter, the development of
aspects of nineteenth-century tartanry went hand in hand with the
pan-European response to industrialisation and Improvement, the fad
for Kitsch, sentimental response to deeply painful experience, that
provided Scotland with the Kailyard. But even with this much-derided
phenomenon we have to be careful. The use of such sloganised
categories can distract even the clearest minds from seeing what is
to be seen. Cairns Craig wrote in 1982

> What Kailyard did was to turn the language of Lowland Scots into a
> medium necessarily identified with a couthy, domestic, sentimental
> world. After Kailyard it becomes impossible to give expression to a
> vernacular working class environment in Scotland without provok-
> ing those connotations.[16]

This was written after – to consider drama alone – a twentieth century
that had seen such centrally important texts in 'the language of
Lowland Scots' as Joe Corrie's *In Time o Strife* (1927), Ena Lamont
Stewart's *Men Should Weep* (1947) and John Byrne's *The Slab Boys*
(1978). All these plays and many others, especially in the 1970s
theatrical revival, 'give expression to a vernacular working class
environment' and do so 'without provoking' in any sense 'a couthy,
domestic, sentimental world'. We should not blink at the negative uses
of tartan, tartanry and such related phenomena as Kailyard, but
equally we should not let their negative potential distort our vision.
  Certainly 'tartan' has at different times become, not always in a
complimentary fashion, associated with particular cultural and literary
themes. Nineteenth-century National Drama, arising in significant part
out of adaptations of Scott's novels, created a popular drama that
explored Scottish historical themes. CRJ, writing in the *Glasgow Herald*
in 1907, calls such drama 'tartan' and argues for a different approach:

> [. . .] there is a very flourishing and distinct modern national life in
> Scotland, and [. . .] this life so far has had almost no expression in

literature of the better sort or in the drama. The stirring times of the past have their splendid and ever-increasing monument of dramatic literature [. . .] We do not, as someone has well said, want 'tartan' plays at the present moment. We want plays as true and national, though not necessarily as sordid and bitter, as Mr Douglas's [*sic*] novel 'The House with the Green Shutters'. We want modern life of Scotland, particularly I believe middle class town life [. . .] above all, the family life of Scotland with its endless jar and revolt, discomfort and affection, should yield abundance of dramatic fruitfulness.[17]

It is, then, no new thing to see tartan as backward-looking, but, as this volume shows, this is not a necessary, but rather a contingent function. Tartan's polysemy means that it has enormous potential for flexibility in use and meaning.

The point about the discourse of tartan and tartanry is that it is not easily or simply defined. When Colin McArthur tries to do this, he produces a caricature, assimilating 'Tartanry' and 'Kailyard' into one linked phenomenon when they are quite distinct:

The Tartanry/Kailyard ensemble permits and foregrounds only certain types of flora, fauna and humankind, the privileged icons being thistles, heather, stags, highland cattle, Scotch terriers, tartaned figures (often with military connotations) and a handful of historical figures of whom Burns and Scott are pre-eminent.[18]

In McArthur's *Scotch Reels* collection of essays, John Caughie observed in 1982

It is precisely the regressiveness of the frozen discourses of Tartanry and Kailyard that they provide just such a reservoir of Scottish 'characters', Scottish 'attitudes' and Scottish 'views' which can be drawn upon to give the 'flavour of Scotland', a petrified culture with a misty, mythic, and above all, static past.[19]

In fact, these discourses, as is shown by their continually developing and widespread presence – not to mention the range in topic and period of chapters in this volume – are far from frozen, rather being dynamic. As David McCrone, Angela Morris and Richard Kiely observed in 1995

A considerable literature has grown up to debunk heritage, to show that much of it is a modern fabrication with dubious commercial and political rationales. Being able to show that heritage is not 'authentic', that it is not 'real', however, is not the point. If we take the Scottish example of tartanry, the interesting issue is not why much of it is a 'forgery', but why it continues to have such cultural power. That is the point which critics like Hugh Trevor-Roper (1984) [1983] miss. As his fellow historians Raphael Samuel and Paul Thompson show, myths are no mere archaic relics but potent forces in everyday life. Myths are constantly reworked to make sense of memories and lives (Samuel and Thompson, 1990).[20]

Such an argument accords with the late Richard Prentice's concept in heritage tourism of 'endearment'. By this, he meant the ways in which memories, souvenirs and photographs become tokens by which tourists engage personally with the experience of visiting a site and authenticate their own experience of the act of visiting. In several ways Prentice's concept of 'endearment' applies to experiences outlined in Ian Maitland Hume's chapter. As Craig Beveridge and Ronald Turnbull remark in a passage David Goldie also addresses:

> meanings are never passively consumed, but always subject to selection and adjustment to other discourses [. . .] response to tartanry is not uncritical assimilation, but a complex negotiation dependent on the beliefs and values which are bound up with these other concerns.[21]

Indeed, the attacks on tartan and tartanry, particularly in the 1970s and 1980s, deny this complex negotiation and can even be said in their overstated hostility to have inhibited, and even stifled, for a time the potential for fruitful examination of that intellectual and symbolic complexity. Andrew Marr observes, 'Indeed, the deconstruction of the tartan cult is in danger of itself becoming a cult'.[22] In context, it is clear Marr uses 'deconstruction' in the sense of 'demolition', or at least 'an attempted demolition', while in fact what is required and what this volume in its modest way attempts is a critical deconstruction in order to enhance understanding. A failure to seek to understand constructively the various – and fluid – natures of tartan and tartanry is a roadblock to fully exploring many aspects of contemporary Scottish culture. For the sake of progressive discussion, therefore, it is essential that sensible, measured analysis and discussion both of tartan as a historical and cultural phenomenon and of the varied nature of tartanry, positive as well as potentially negative, be undertaken without adopting reductive, restrictive and, therefore, false definitions.

Jonathan Faiers observes 'Apparently simple in construction, tartan is also capable of staggering complexity; it is multivalent and dichotomous' and, he goes on, globally consumed.[23] He is here making a point that applies not just to the material, but to the wide range of discourses that tartan inspires and with which it engages. Just as 'contradictory elements merged to make tartan a uniquely resilient textile'[24] so the contradictory elements of the discourses of tartan and tartanry and the interactions of the two create resilient discourses which the chapters in this volume can only begin to address. These discourses may lie in the apparently superficial area of the implications of clothes themselves: whether in cultural transmission as the '[p]laid shirts of cowboys lead to US working class usage'[25] from the workwear of Scottish expatriate drovers – in some versions of history singing Burns's 'Green Grow the Rashes O' and becoming 'gringoes' to their Mexican auditors – to the working-class personae of late-twentieth-century American rock musicians and the remarkable creative working kilt products to be found on the utilikilts website,[26] or in modern high fashion:

> Talking about fashion and not mentioning tartan is like talking about fine dining and not bringing up wine. The fabric is an eclectic essential in high fashion, and Jean Paul Gaultier would agree.[27]

Beyond such international fashion-focused examples, however, the issues discourses of tartan and tartanry raise for Scottish culture, the interaction of history and myth and any concept of what is 'Scottish' proliferate and will remain unfrozen and lively for many years to come. The chapters in this volume seek to continue and develop this lively, unresolvable, flourishing and colourful debate.

Notes

1 Quoted in Dunbar, *History*, p. 97.
2 Quoted in Banks and de la Chapelle, *Tartan: Romancing the Plaid*, p. 241.
3 Bruford, 'Is tartan a Gaelic word?', pp. 57–71.
4 Grange, *A Short History*, p. 4.
5 Scarlett, *Tartan: The Highland Textile*, p. ix.
6 Quoted in Dunbar, *History*, pp. 38–9.
7 Cairns Craig, 'Myths against history: tartanry and Kailyard in 19th-century Scottish literature', in McArthur, *Scotch Reels*, p. 10.
8 Faiers, *Tartan*, p. 166.

 9 Private conversation, 29 March 2010.
10 Jackson, *History*, p. 372.
11 Pittock, 'To see ourselves', p. 298.
12 Stiùbhart, 'Highland rogues', p. 173.
13 Dunbar, *Costume*, pp. 87–8.
14 McCrone, *Understanding Scotland* (2001).
15 Ascherson, *Stone Voices*, pp. 212–13.
16 Craig, 'Myths against history', p. 11.
17 CRJ, 'A Scotch National Theatre'. I am grateful to Professor Jan McDonald for drawing my attention to this article.
18 McArthur, 'Breaking the signs', p. 23.
19 John Caughie, 'Scottish television: what would it look like?', p. 116.
20 McCrone, Morris and Kiely, *Scotland – the Brand*, p. 207.
21 Beveridge and Turnbull, *The Eclipse of Scottish Culture*, p. 14.
22 Marr, *The Battle for Scotland*, p. 28.
23 Faiers, *Tartan*, p. 1.
24 Ibid., p. 55.
25 Ibid., p. 124.
26 I am grateful to David Goldie for drawing my attention to this site.
27 http://www.fabsugar.com/Fab-Read-Tartan-Romancing-756417 (accessed 20 January 2010).

GHEIBHTE BREACAIN CHARNAID ('SCARLET TARTANS WOULD BE GOT . . .'): THE RE-INVENTION OF TRADITION

Hugh Cheape

ᘯ

The words of the poet Duncan Bàn Macintyre, in his 'Òran don Bhriogais' ('Song to the Breeks') in response to the 'Disclothing Act' of 1746, offer a robust message that tartan and Highland dress were firmly embedded in the attitude and aesthetic of Gaelic culture. Having served in the government's Argyll Militia in the recent Jacobite War, his song was borne along on an iterating note of outrage and betrayal of the Gael and of the clans who had supported the Whig cause (see below).[1] With the recent disavowal of kilts and tartan as components of the 'invention of tradition' and in a late-twentieth-century ambivalence of Scots towards them, a 'prehistory' of tartan within Gaelic culture, such as we see in songs such as this, has been lost to sight and omitted from accounts of tartan and Highland dress. In terms of the material culture of dress and textiles, the historiography has been narrow and reductionist, seeking definitions of ever-receding 'origins' and bolstering defences against the assaults of detractors. Without exception, accounts of the history of tartan have largely ignored the voice of the devisers and wearers of tartan.[2]

The 'success' of tartan since the turn of the nineteenth century has perhaps lessened imperatives to draw on esoteric evidence, but the evidence is there and adds significantly to the fuller picture. As a putative 'badge' of Scotland, widely recognised, and symbolic of nationhood, tartan's role has extended beyond the Highland dress of a post-Romantic era with its formalities of different styles to Celtic couture fashion and upholstery and decor fabric.[3] This equation may be problematical but yet it is topical as issues of nationalism and ethnicity are being aired. As an indicator of belonging, now to the larger entity of nation but also to the smaller community of kin and clan, these associations have led to an emphasis on, or more recently a fixation and obsession with, tartan as a badge or uniform of clanship. In the twentieth century, the kilt's role as garment for ceremonial and ritual use came to dominate attitudes to it. It was not fashionable for everyday wear except for a few die-hard patriots, the Royal Family or Anglo-Scots gentry, though it was worn by boys, particularly for semi-formal occasions like church-going or within school uniform codes, and of course by Scottish Boy Scouts. Now there is a new enthusiasm in Scotland for the national dress and the kilt has enjoyed a renaissance as style item. There is even a postmodern trend in kilt-wear instigated with 1970s and 1980s punk styles; we see the kilt worn with chunky socks, boots, white T-shirt and black jacket – the look is masculine with a hint of menace.

The origins of tartan have been much debated and have attracted speculation in recent literature. Controversy has confused a nation. In its least critical form, an unquestioned assumption held that tartan was a form of ancient and autochthonous dress, in other words, for example, the dress of the Picts and Scots. Those antiquarians and historians who took an interest in the subject could see the Highland dress ubiquitously in their fieldwork and researches. In *The Highlanders of Scotland*, for example, published in 1837, we have an early instance of this; the Celticist William Forbes Skene (1809–92) concluded

> the sculptured monuments which bear evidence of the existence of the Highland garb [. . .] afford complete proof of its having been the ordinary dress of a considerable part of the northern population from the earliest period of their history. There is thus distinct evidence for the remote antiquity of this dress.[4]

Such perceptions were never seriously questioned and became part of the litany of popular Scottish history or a wistful mythology of Scottish identity. In a classic of this genre, *The Clans, Septs and Regiments of the Scottish Highlands* (1908), the author concludes firmly and in terms which defy contradiction, but which have served to cloak too much of Scottish material culture: 'The origin of the Highland garb in its primitive state is lost in the mists of antiquity'.[5] This had become a comforting element in the history of a nation which had clearly suffered acculturation and attrition, and whose mists had been known to swallow much since the supposed disappearance of the Ninth Legion beyond the Roman Frontier in North Britain early in the second century AD. Indeed, claims based on such a collective conviction or myopia can be interpreted as part of what might be termed a primordial view of Scottish ethnicity in which individual and collective ethnic identity is more or less fixed and unchanging and may be defined by a list of characteristics deemed essential. But this particular touchstone of national identity has come to be denounced as national self-delusion or bespoke history, supplied by or for Scots in exile either in the cities of England or overseas. The author of the article 'Nations and their Past' in *The Economist* (21 December 1996) listed 'the things the Scots hold most dear: the kilt, bagpipes, clan tartans' as an example of 'self-delusion serving to fortify national cohesion'. He concluded briskly: '[. . .] the whole concept of a distinctive Highland culture and tradition is a retrospective invention'.[6]

This essay quoted extensively and, by now, typically the distinguished Oxford academic Professor Hugh Trevor-Roper, whose nippy deliveries on Scottish historical topics have frequently irritated Scottish academics, partly because, whatever their reliability, Scottish history from the pen of an 'Oxbridge' academic seemed to be preferred to anything home-brewed. Far from being challenged for its lack of depth and scholarly shortcomings, the tendency has been for Scottish academics to treat it with resignation or contempt (and say nothing in response) and the Scottish nation to cringe before the dismissive pen. Debate on tartan and Highland dress had been reopened in the face of a potent 'invention of tradition' thesis relating cultural phenomena such as national costume in the case of Scotland to Victorian romanticism and a love affair with the Highlands. In his contribution to the debate, Trevor-Roper delivered a smug *coup de grâce* to *soi-disant* Scottish national pride with the story that the kilt was 'invented' by an Englishman.[7] Such a debate has tended to be circular, without adding much more than value judgement to our knowledge of Highland dress. The resulting controversies in the face of this dominant paradigm have mischievously obscured simple human and historical realities like the dynamics of fashion, ancient and modern, and a liking for colour and pattern. The uses of colour and pattern in weaving cloth may be as old as civilisation itself, however defined, and is widespread throughout the world, but Scotland has made this art her own and re-exported it in its own unique style to the rest of the world.[8]

Tartan may be, on the one hand, a dress fabric highly distinctive in style, design and colour – what is generally termed 'plaid' in North America – or on the other, a design with patterns in multicoloured checks used today in many forms. Arguably the word 'tartan' for pattern and design is older than its meaning of fabric.[9] Patterns and colours may not always conform to the conventions that have emerged over the last two centuries. The worldwide demand for tartans, however, usually overrides constraints imposed by supposed rules and regulations governing what is and is not tartan and what is perceived as permissible in Highland dress. Nonetheless, uniform styles and conformity in dress conventions have emerged since the late nineteenth century and have been encoded in books and tailors' patterns; strict observance is expected and in some circles has become a touchstone of Scottishness. The perpetuation of such views, relatively recently formed, is a self-assumed role of guardians of Scottish 'ethnicity'.[10]

The fundamental simplicity of tartan suggests in fact an ancient origin and a long pedigree. It is a colourful and flamboyant fabric whose design is achieved by weaving yarn in sequences of colour in warp and weft to produce stripes and checks. While the effect is often complex, the technique is simple. Different coloured yarns are woven in plain twill to produce a check of colours and blends, in other words two colours of threads produce a three-colour combination. In detail, the dyed yarns are counted into bands of different widths when the weaver sets up the threads on the warp and this is described as the 'thread count'. The same sequence of yarns in colours and widths is then woven in the weft to achieve a check of regular pattern. The thread counts of the different coloured yarns act as a key to the patterns or 'setts' which today make up the hundreds of named clan and family tartans as well as the corpus of institutional, civic and regional tartans.[11]

As a form of 'national dress' in kilt or plaid, tartan is assumed to be 'traditional', as we have seen, originating in a distant past and invented by remote ancestors. Scots have assumed that it was the traditional dress of indigenous peoples, in this case – depending on your loyalties – the Picts of the North-East or the Gaels of the Highlands and Islands. But the art of weaving is ancient and universal and the uses of checks and stripes in patterning cloth was known in prehistory and must be almost as ancient as the art of weaving itself. Simple decorative weaving was known in all early cultures. A piece of fabric excavated from an Iron Age site at Falkirk, for example, and dated to the third century AD, shows a simple check achieved with self-coloured yarns. It is referred to as the 'Falkirk tartan' and is in the collections of the National Museums of Scotland. It incorporates natural wools from primitive breeds of domesticated sheep in darker and lighter colours that have been separated out in spinning into yarn and woven together in regular patterns. In this instance two shades of self-coloured wool woven in simple twill produce a check of two colours and an intermediate shade.[12] The use of undyed wool was common in weaving in both the Lowlands and the Highlands and the principle survived in Scottish tradition in the so-called 'maud' or 'Shepherd's plaid' of blacks and browns on a light ground which came to be adopted retrospectively as a Lowland check not linked to any clan. Significantly, in view of Sir Walter Scott's interests, it was also adopted for the Scott tartan in the early nineteenth century, as an emblem for one of the most prominent Border families.

The quintessential image of a Scottish national dress and identity is that of the male kilted Highlander, a stereotypical and anachronistic figure adopted in the early nineteenth century in the full flood of European Romanticism. The iconography is simple and recognisable, but it masks a complex of issues. In the hands of skilful 'artists' such as Sir Walter Scott, this figure was the embodiment of what was seen as a primitive civilisation lying remotely to the north and west of Scotland's Highland line. At the time – and since – there was an evident paradox in that the kilted Highlander in the eighteenth century, despite earlier associations discussed in the next chapter by Murray Pittock, came to be equated with Jacobitism and opposition to the prevailing status quo of government and Hanoverian kingship. This was recognised by Prince Charles Edward Stuart when he landed in the West Highlands in 1745 and led a tartan-clad army south. Equally it was recognised by a vengeful government which outlawed tartan throughout Scotland in a Disarming Act which remained law until 1782.

The Disarming Act, or 'Disclothing Act', was passed through Parliament in 1746 and came into force in August 1747. It was one of a series of legislative measures designed to force the assimilation of Scotland into the greater Britain following the Battle of Culloden. The effects of the Act have been much debated by historians. According to its title, 'An Act for the more effectual Disarming of the Highlands in Scotland, and for more effectual securing the Peace of the said Highlands, and for restraining the use of the Highland dress, &c', the purpose is self-evident. Tartan and Highland dress, bracketed with weapons, had come to be regarded as an outward and visible manifestation of Jacobitism and continuing loyalty to the Stuart dynasty in exile and, so, political treachery and lawlessness. The ownership and carrying of weapons were expressly forbidden only north of the Highland Line, whereas tartan was proscribed through-out Scotland, save for military personnel serving King George. The application of the law was undiscriminating. Yet a visual paradox exists in a number of portraits of mainly Highland gentry painted in tartan and Highland dress in the 1750s and 1760s, such as Mac-Donalds of Sleat and Campbells of Lochlane and Ardmaddie. These overtly vaunt loyalty to a society whose core values of Highland and Gaelic identity seemed to transcend a narrower political agenda. Earlier, William Mosman's outstanding and intriguing portrait of 'John Campbell of the Bank' was actually painted as soon after Culloden and the Act as 1749, while Allan Ramsay portrays the Earl of Wemyss in tartan trews and plaid with his wife soon after their marriage in 1745, perhaps in 1747 or 1748. Evidently, tartan was meaningful and, outside such élite groups, some of them supporters of the Hanoverian settlement, the Act was a drastic measure and its penalties severe. Collective memory of this post-Culloden phase has reinforced anti-English feeling in Scotland, but, of course, a large part of the government army at Culloden comprised Scots. The repression was not of Scotland by England *per se*, but of one section of Scottish society by another, allied with Hanoverian England. Further, a careful reading of contemporary events shows that the draconian legislation and 'army of occupation' were the response to a conviction that the 'Rebellion' was going to re-erupt and that guerrilla warfare would continue indefinitely.[13] The British government, therefore, reacted brutally to the ongoing threat of Jacobitism as they perceived it. Indeed, recent scholars have interpreted this as a campaign of genocide against the Gaels.[14] Another reading, however, may see it as a civil conflict of Whig Gael against Jacobite, related to the imminent 'improvement' about to generate significant economic change in the Highland economy, including the eighteenth-century first phase of clearances.

Whatever the politico-economic implications, however, the legisla-tion against Highland dress and its application were deeply resented by many in Scotland and by most, if not all, Highlanders. The Gaelic poet Alexander MacDonald – Alasdair Mac Mhaighstir Alasdair – the best-known propagandist for Gaelic culture in the Jacobite cause, composed his rousing song, 'Am Breacan Uallach', celebrating the tartan plaid in about 1750. The picture given in the twenty-five stanzas and chorus is significant for how Highland dress was per-ceived within Gaelic culture; it was fìor chulaidh an t-saighdeir ('the true dress of the soldier'), the dress of the hunter, the appropriate dress for church, weddings and public occasions, the proper dress for travelling away from home, and carried a note of masculine and high social status. The song opens

> B' fheàrr leam breacan uallach
> Mu m' ghuaillibh 's a chur fo m' achlais,
> Na ge do gheibhinn còta
> De 'n chlò as feàrr thig a Sasunn.
>
> Mo laochan fèin an t-èididh
> A dh' fheumadh an crios ga ghlasadh:
> Cuaicheineachadh èilidh,
> Dèis èirigh gu dol air astar.
>
> ('Better is the proud plaid
> Around my shoulder and put under my arm,
> Better than though I would get a coat
> Of the best cloth that comes from England.
>
> My own little hero is the garb
> That would require the belt to fix it on;
> Putting the kilts into pleats,
> After rising to go on a journey.')[15]

The proscription of Highland dress was felt universally. The poet Duncan Bàn Macintyre (1724–1812) fought on the government side in the Jacobite war of 1745 but his 'Song to the Breeks' composed against the Disarming Act was omitted from the early printed editions of his work because of its anti-English language and anti-Hanoverian political sympathies. He described even the loyal Gaels as dishonoured and enslaved, and the English-style Lowland dress as unnatural, humiliating, uncouth and hideous. The tone is bitter against George II (whom the poet gratuitously exiles to Hanover), the London government and those in Scotland who supported them, such as the Campbells, and he builds a case on the betrayal of those who had joined Duke William whose only reward was to suffer the humiliating taking away of their very clothing. His conclusion was that the Act would turn the country Jacobite:

> 'S nam bitheamaid uile dìleas
> Do 'n rìgh bha toirt cuiridh dhuinn,

Chan fhaicte sinn gu dìlinn
A' strìocadh do 'n chulaidh seo.
[. . .]
Nan tigeadh oirnne Teàrlach
'S gun éireamaid 'na champa,
Gheibhte breacain chàrnaid
'S bhiodh àird air na gunnachan.

('And if we would all be loyal
To the king who was appealing to us,
We would not be seen till Doomsday
Submitting to this garment.
[. . .]
If Charles were to come over to us,
And we would rise up to take the field with him,
Scarlet tartans would be got
And the guns would be taken up.')[16]

The physical and psychological damage wreaked by the '45 crippled Gaelic society and arguably may never have been made good. The policing of the Disclothing Act became desultory in the 1750s and rehabilitation of the Gael suddenly became an expediency. Prime Minister William Pitt reversed the government policy of a generation when he began to recruit Highlanders – in his histrionic words 'a hardy and intrepid race of men' – for the burgeoning empire and to fight France in North America. Between 1757 and 1761, nine regiments were raised, more in the American War of Independence, and in 1793–4 alone, eight line regiments and a number of fencible regiments were raised in the Highlands to meet the threat from France. Basing the organisation of these military echelons on the big clans, even if the clan system was by the later eighteenth century much eroded, ensured much of their success and helped to build *esprit de corps*. It also gave birth to the stereotype figure of national identity. With this recent history, the mood of the moment was for a fierce and romantic figure deriving from a primitive civilisation of simple but marked virtues. The Gaelic narrative-poem epic of 'Ossian' displayed such virtues and revealed a native classical tradition to the outside world. James Macpherson, whether translator or creator, published his *Fragments of Ancient Poetry collected in the Highlands and Islands of Scotland and translated from the Gaelic or Erse Language* in 1760. Its success was instant. The feats of arms of kilted and tartan-uniformed Highland soldiers in the late-eighteenth-century wars of emerging empire consolidated the image of the warrior hero in tartan, although the reputation was out of all proportion to the numbers involved.[17]

This period saw the emergence of the clan tartans as we know them today and of the transformation of Highland dress from 'uniform' into 'costume'. The concept was already beginning to take form in a contemporary concern for Highland and Gaelic culture. The stated purpose of the Highland Societies of London and Scotland, founded respectively in 1778 and 1784, included research into and recovery of Highland 'Language, Literature, Music and Manners', all of which were deemed to be in crisis or on the verge of extinction. The first public gesture of the Highland Society of London was to sponsor the repeal of the Disarming Act and the legal reinstatement of tartan. The uniform clothing of the Highland regiments and their close association through patronage or command with the leading families led to questions on the designs and authenticity of tartans. The London Highland Society instigated research into clan and family tartans and in 1815 wrote to the chieftains and heads of families asking them to 'furnish as much of the tartan of their clans as will serve to show the patterns'. In his letter to one chieftain, for example, the celebrated (or notorious) Macdonell of Glengarry, the Secretary wrote

> The Highland Society of London instructed me to apply to the Chiefs of the different Clans and request them to transmit to me as much of their respective Tartans as would be sufficient to show the Pattern and to authenticate each by attaching a card having on it the impression of their respective Coat of Arms. I have to beg that you will be so obliging as to forward me about a yard of the real Glengarry Tartan – authenticated in the manner mentioned. No time is to be lost as I am sorry to say that all the Ceann Cinnidh [Chieftains] do not feel by much the Highland Spirit by which you are animated and in a few years it is to be feared that the distinguishing Tartans of some clans will not be known.[18]

The defining moment came with the celebrated visit of George IV to Edinburgh in 1822 when, stage-managed by Sir Walter Scott, the clans came to town and the capital decked itself in tartan. Even the portly figure of the Hanoverian monarch was forced into a kilt. Not surprisingly, many took exception to this 'plaided panorama' and an Edinburgh citizen spoke for many when he said with disgust: 'Sir Walter Scott has ridiculously made us appear to be a nation of Highlanders, and the bagpipe and the tartan are the order of the day'.[19] An increasing variety of patterns or 'setts' came to be woven, sometimes in minutely differentiated versions, and adopted as dress and badge by families and clans who each gave their name to a particular 'sett'. It was fashionable to discover a Highland pedigree and a tartan as badges of clanship. Most clan tartans which are woven and recognised as such today are the inventions of astute manufacturers in the nineteenth century, skilled in the marketing ploy of product differentiation, and of writers who emerged, such as the 'Sobieski Stuart' brothers, providing antique pedigree and historical explanation of named patterns as demand increased especially in the 1820s and 1830s. Writers composed histories of tartan and Highland dress for an expectant readership, and artists produced versions of medieval or early Highland dress suggesting origins in a simple untailored garment draped around the body, kilted and belted at the waist.

Scott's first Jacobite novel was published in 1814; the myth had been born before the real mythmakers arrived. The two self-styled 'Sobieski Stuarts', John and Charles Allen, arrived in London from the Continent in 1816, began to visit Scotland and settled in the Highlands in 1826 in a rustic palace made available to them by Fraser of Lovat on Eilean Aigas in the River Beauly. The brothers revealed that they were descended from the exiled Stuart monarchy and the rumour freely circulated that their father was an illegitimate son of Bonnie Prince Charlie.[20] They published two remarkable and sumptuous works, *Vestiarium Scoticum* (1842) and *The Costume of the Clans* (1845). The first of these purported to be based on a sixteenth-century manuscript discovered by them in the library of the Scots College at Douai in north-east France, together with an inferior copy of 1721 and another manuscript version of the first discovered in the Monastery of St Augustine in Cadiz. The manuscripts were already the subject of controversy before their publication in 1842, but the contemporary demand for tartans swamped the tide of accusation and refutation over their authenticity. These precise details of all the old clan tartans as provided by the Sobieski Stuarts were consumed enthusiastically and, though undoubtedly fake, accepted on face value. This important episode is still the stuff of controversy and certainly in the second half of the twentieth century was considered to have debased the notion of tartan as national symbol and the tradition of ancient origin.[21] The 'invention of tradition', by-product of European Romanticism it was said, is now recognised as the dynamic which led to the creation and proliferation of the 'setts' of the tartans and the concept of tartan as clan badge or uniform.

The counter-argument, which has not yet been effectively articulated, is that tartan is certainly ancient in some form or another and intimately associated with historical Highland dress rather than merely a latter-day notion of it.[22] In the medieval period, surviving written accounts introduce a distinction between the respective peoples and cultures of Lowland and Highland Scotland. Distinctiveness, distinctions and resultant tensions within Scottish society began to be obscured in the nineteenth century and Scott succeeded for his readership in creating an apparent homogeneity to demarcate and strengthen the distinctiveness of Scottish society in comparison with England. If we detect this syndrome in his Highland novels, we should also see his essential Highlander cast as the honoured but powerless figure in a timeless past rather than the active political agent of recent history or the victim of the Clearances. But distinctions are first particularly evident in the fourteenth-century John of Fordoun's 'History of Scotland' when he introduces the concept with 'the manners and customs of the Scots vary with the diversity of their speech'. This is taken up in greater detail in *The History of Greater Britain*, published in Latin in Paris in 1521 by the scholar and university teacher John Mair:

> Further, just as among the Scots we find two distinct tongues, so we likewise find two different ways of life and conduct. For some are born in the forests and mountains of the north, and these we call men of the high land, but the others men of the low land [. . .] The Irish tongue is in use among the former, the English tongue among the latter. One half of Scotland speaks Irish, and all these as well as the Islanders we reckon to belong to the Wild Scots. In dress, in the manner of their outward life, for example, these come behind the householding Scots – yet they are not less, but rather much more prompt to fight; and this both because they dwell more towards the north and because, born as they are in the mountains, and dwellers in forests, their very nature is more combative [. . .] From the mid-leg to the foot the men of the high land go uncovered; their dress is, for an over-garment, a loose plaid and a shirt saffron-dyed.[23]

Early writers begin to describe the plaid in this way and generally refer to the Highlanders as going bare-legged. Some such references go back to the twelfth century, for example descriptions of Scots on the First Crusade and the better known and curious account of the Norse king Magnus Barelegs.[24] This indication of a distinctive culture, clearly associating the Gaelic Scots with the people of Ireland, is also an indication of a distinctive history in which tartan later played such a distinguished part.

Some of the origins of the reputation for combativeness Mair identifies can be sought in the Lordship of the Isles in which Clan Donald achieved the status of a virtually independent kingdom within Scotland by about 1400. The Lordship, undoubtedly a cultured principality, was suppressed by the kings of Scots in the late fifteenth century. The consequent destabilisation and fragmentation of Highland society led to the rise of the 'clans' and competition for power and territory. This critical process, recognised within Gaelic tradition by the label Linn nan Creach ('the Age of Raids'), lends emphasis to the reiteration by chroniclers and historians of the fierce hostility of Highlanders. The success and reputation of individual clans would not necessarily depend on royal favour and the legitimate occupation of land by feudal charter but rather on force of arms, vigorous leadership, and dependence on and loyalty to the chieftain and his kin.

By the sixteenth century in the wider context of Renaissance Europe, changing dress sense made brighter and variegated fabrics more typical. Tartan was Gaelic Scotland's version of Renaissance fashion. A heightened dress sense in contemporary Europe led to brightly coloured fabrics being used and elaborately draped and kilted round the body. This was fashionable Renaissance man as Highland chieftain, as John Michael Wright's later 1683 portrait of Lord Mungo Murray so vividly demonstrates. The precursor of today's kilt was the 'belted plaid', a generous length of tartan arranged in folds round the body and gathered at the waist and shoulder with belt and brooch.[25] Though a male pose dominates the iconography of Highland dress, Gaelic culture preserves a female version in the subtly coloured earasaid, or plaid form.[26] To dress dramatically in an untailored garment was a particular art form beloved of all Highlanders and celebrated in poetry and song. To praise a man's and woman's appearance and dress (and therefore dress sense) of brightly coloured tartan was a natural device in conventional panegyric.[27] The language and literature of Gaelic is clear and explicit about the role of tartan in the people's dress. Tartan was developed and considerably elaborated in this period of crisis and creativity which also saw the 'invention' of Highland dress in tartan more or less as we still have it today. Colour was a strong marker of dress sense, as a typical seventeenth-century song reference to Highland troops in the War of the Three Kingdoms makes clear:

Luchd nan còtaichean sgàrlaid, chit' an dearsadh là grèine.
Luchd nan còtaichean gearra, dha maith da 'n tig fèileadh.
Luchd nan osanan ballach, 's nan gartanan gle-dhearg.

('Company of the scarlet coats, to be seen gleaming on a day
   of sunshine.
Men of the short coats, the plaid becomes them well.
Men of the tartan hose, and of the bright red garters.')[28]

Tartan's emergence as such an overt phenomenon in European terms
was due to political dynamic, though its role and reputation were
equally cultural. In the course of the seventeenth century, the Highlands and Highlanders were drawn firmly into national politics,
particularly in the War of the Three Kingdoms and the Montrose
Wars of the 1640s, and in the 1650s when a Gaelic-speaking force was
defeated as far south as the Battle of Worcester. The dramatic, though
intermittent, success of the Gaels demonstrated at the least that they
were a potent enough force to overturn a ruling regime. Still in the
north and west Highlands both a political and military system and an
ideology survived – and vigorously – the dismantling of the Lordship
of the Isles.

Highland troops also fought on the Continent, especially in the
Thirty Years War, where they were particularly noticed and singled
out for their dress and for their fearsome effectiveness. This national
and international role and reputation is reflected in a distinctive,
confident, assertive – often forceful – culture which seems to emerge
in the seventeenth century. It is still evident to us today in the form of
the poetry and song of the period, and also in the instrumental music,
particularly in the pìobaireachd ('piping') which evolved and flourished dramatically at the same time, in the genre now described as ceòl
mòr ('great music'). Such patterns of fundamental changes do not
often occur in a vacuum, and the emergence of pìobaireachd, which
tends to be described in terms of an isolated phenomenon, was a
symptom of contemporary changes such as the strategic and tactical
need for more troops on the field of battle and bigger armies (such as
the remarkable forces rapidly assembled by the Marquis of Montrose
and Alasdair Mac Colla). Fighting could no longer be the preserve of a
social élite, which anachronistically it had continued to be in Gaelic
Scotland, outliving its tradition in chivalric Europe. The warrior
aristocracy that had traditionally responded to the incitement to battle
of the bardic poet and the harp, or clarsàch, were no longer adequate

for contemporary warfare. The louder high-pitched bagpipe came in the seventeenth century to provide the incitement to battle – the brosnachadh.[29]

Highland dress was certainly a material culture manifestation of these political and cultural changes and in effect represents the Highland and Gaelic version of European Renaissance or late-Renaissance dress styles. Conspicuous consumption ensured that the smartest cloth was the most expensive, and the most expensive would usually be imported tartans in bright shades of red, since red was also the most difficult colour to establish or 'fix' evenly over lengths of fabric. Exotic dyes like cochineal were certainly preferred to quieter or more 'muted' colours obtained from local vegetable dyestuffs. Evidence, especially from the eighteenth century, suggests that Highlands and Islands weavers would buy commercial insect dyes such as cochineal in preference to locally available plant dyestuffs. The conventional praise of the various shades of red tartan in Gaelic song chimes too with early portraiture in which red kilts and plaids predominate.[30] Significantly too, Highland dress began to be articulated within Gaelic culture as a touchstone of loyalty to traditional values. Anyone seen to be moving away from these, like Highland leaders who were being lured into espousal of Lowland and English politics, would be roundly criticised. The powerful spokesman for the Gaelic and Royalist cause in the Civil Wars, John MacDonald of Keppoch – known to Scottish tradition as Iain Lom – complained of the frequent absences in the 1660s of the Glengarry chieftain, Lord MacDonald of Aros, through his visits to the Restoration court in London. This seduction became evident in his adopted dress:

> Gur fada leam an Sasann thu,
> 'S a bhith 'gad chreach le spòrs.
> B'fheàrr leam còt' is breacan ort
> Na pasbhin chur air cleoc;
> Is tu bhith falbh gu h-aigeannach
> An triubhas chadaidh clò.

> ('You seem to be too long in England,
> Being ruined by gaming.
> I would prefer you in a short coat and plaid
> Than in the cloak which fastens;
> And that you should march vigorously
> In trews made of tartan cloth.')[31]

If tartans were being abandoned by some of the leaders at home, what of its fortunes on the wider stage? The late seventeenth and early eighteenth centuries saw a remarkable national political and cultural role for tartan. Following the death of Charles II and the accession of James VII and II, the Roman Catholic monarch was challenged in Scotland by the Protestant Earl of Argyll. He arrived in Scotland from the Netherlands in 1685, was swiftly defeated and captured at Inchinnan in June, just after the parallel arrival of Monmouth in Dorset, and executed. This challenge had been briskly crushed by the Crown using the Highland clans. The Stuart dynasty therefore almost inadvertently lined up with an anti-Campbell cause in the Highlands, encouraging those clans that had been loyal to the Crown in the 1640s and 1650s to believe they still had a national, or even international, role to play. Though perhaps only briefly, a cult of tartanry flourished in the Stuart Court. The kenspeckle Ewan Cameron of Lochiel was entertained at Court, patronised as a 'tame savage' and personally branded by James VII as the 'King of Thieves'. The Stuarts came to recognise, with finally catastrophic consequences, that the clans were prepared to fight and to die for them.[32]

The success of the Gaels and of Gaelic culture was further reinforced by a rationalising of feudal superiorities after the Argyll Rebellion. Then the Earl of Argyll's forfeiture led to Campbell feudal privileges being reallocated, a move which tended to reinforce the claims to power and territory of many clan chiefs. This late triumph of 'feudalism' in the seventeenth-century Highlands is something of a paradox of Scottish history and goes some way to explaining the much-quoted and picturesque examples, such as *The Grameid* of 1691, of clan armies being assembled and paraded for expeditions. It also goes some way to explaining the creation of Jacobitism as a military and strategic force, and must be significant in terms of the post-1745 legislation aimed particularly at dismantling and destroying Highland feudalism.[33]

Though Gaelic culture was so successful, as we are claiming, and the fashion for tartan spread, there were serious setbacks. With the Revolution of 1688–9, James VII and II was dethroned and exiled. William of Orange had no loyalties or affections towards the Highland chiefs. The vengeful Earls of Argyll were restored. An immediate outcome was the suppression of Highland support for the Stuarts and the consequent 1692 Massacre of Glencoe. It is an ironic truth, however, that fashion will adopt the uniforms of revolution and rebellion. It is a significant and extraordinary fact that when Queen

Anne created her Sovereign's Bodyguard in 1713, they were dressed in an elaborate and remarkable tartan uniform.[34] At the same time, as Murray Pittock's chapter makes clear, tartan was undoubtedly a uniform of Jacobitism and also of the so-called 'Jacobite' political party which emerged after the Union of the Parliaments in 1707. Its purpose and sentiments were clearly strongly anti-Union and, for the most part, anti-English. Meantime, a number of contemporary portraits show that tartan had been adopted as fashionable outfitting by many Lowland grandees. It became fashion wear as a political statement, clearly a well-known phenomenon in any age, and some writers particularly refer to women in the towns as wearing tartan as anti-Union, pro-Stuart fashion.[35]

A significant concept then articulated in Gaelic poetry and song seems to give one version of this putative political allegiance or cause, and to unite all Scotland against England. It was a traditional belief, clearly intensified by the Union of 1707, that there could be a national uprising in Scotland against the 'Auld Enemie' in a Gaelic guise – a sort of pan-Celtic revival embracing all Scotland. Such a belief seems to emerge from the thirteenth-century prophecies of Thomas the Rhymer and, though a literary phenomenon from our point of view, its survival (for example, in Gaelic) was much more vigorous and popular than might be realised or given credit for. The Jacobite cause provided a new focus for this belief and tartan had given it an easily identifiable uniform – in effect a uniform of nationhood or nationality. A Gaelic propaganda song of 1715 expresses this concept so well in contemporary terms:

Is i seo an aimsir an dearbhar an tairgneach dhuinn,
Is bras meanmnach Fir Alban fo an armaibh air thùs.
An uair a dh'éireas gach treun laoch 'n éideadh glan ùr,
Le rùn feirge agus gairge gu seirbhis a' Chrùin.

('This is the time when the Prophecy will be proved for us,
The Men of Scotland are keen and spirited under arms and at the
      forefront of battle.
When every brave hero will rise in his splendid new uniform,
In a mood of anger and fierceness for the service of the Crown.')[36]

The denouement of this political movement and its outward and visible badge was the 'tartan army' of the '45 and the systematic attack on Gaelic culture by the government following the suppression of the

Rebellion. Highland separateness, so confident and assertive as we have seen, had become a major threat to the government as established under the new Hanoverian monarchy.

In conclusion, clearly it would be unreliable to insist on tartan as a – or the – mark of Scottish identity. This element of history, like many others, goes to show that, though ethnic identity can be reliably investigated in anthropological discourse, it must be contingent and changeable rather than fixed and scriptural, emerging from or within particular social circumstances and chronologies. The modern denunciation and disavowal of tartan mischievously draws a veil across, and therefore effectively denies, an up-to-date view of certain vital strands in Scottish history and material culture, and particularly this Renaissance rhetoric of textile. Certainly in this context, *pace* Professors Hugh Trevor-Roper and Eric Hobsbawm (the scholarly perpetrators of the 'invention of tradition' thesis), invented traditions constitute an obstacle to an understanding of the past. To categorise tartan and Highland dress as a folk or peasant costume invented in the Romantic era is, however, to lose the historical resonances and significance of tartan as social, economic, cultural and political statements. These were in particularly full vigour from about 1600 until the 1740s, and their potential power cruelly and dramatically confirmed in the perceived need for the attack on Highland culture of 1747–82. Even in this twilight period, the Gaelic poet Duncan Bàn Macintyre, quoted above, could still refer in the late eighteenth century to Highland dress as Suaicheantas na h-Alba – 'the Badge of Scotland'.

Notes

1 MacLeod, *Songs of Duncan Bàn Macintyre*, p. 14; see also Watson, *Bàrdachd Ghàidhlig*, pp. 68–71, 278–9, for songs expressing outrage over the proscription of Highland dress.
2 See Mackay, *Romantic Story*, for a historical account of Highland dress by a Gaelic speaker, which fails, however, to give significant space to the evidence of language and literature; see also Cheape, *Tartan. The Highland Habit*, pp. 11, 87, in which the significance of Gaelic literary evidence is briefly explored.
3 See Banks and de la Chapelle, *Tartan*, for a contemporary assessment of the international appeal of tartan.
4 Skene, *The Highlanders*, p. 147.
5 Adam, *Clans, Septs and Regiments*, p. 191.
6 *The Economist*, 21 December 1996, p. 56.
7 Trevor-Roper, 'Invention of tradition', pp. 21–2; the story of Thomas

Rawlinson, the English 'inventor of the kilt', seems to derive from a letter in the *Edinburgh Magazine* in 1785, sourced in McClintock, *Old Irish and Highland Dress*, pp. 150–2; see also Ferguson, 'A reply', for the inadequacy of Trevor-Roper's research.

8   See Banks and de la Chapelle, *Tartan*, passim.

9   See McClintock, *Old Irish and Highland Dress*, pp. 111–12, for a summary of citations in record sources such as the Treasurer's Accounts in which the word 'tartan' appears as an attributive; see also Bruford, 'Is tartan a Gaelic word?', pp. 57–71, for the tenable proposal that 'tartan' is indeed a Gaelic word.

10 This issue has been addressed by the Scottish Parliament in the Scottish Register of Tartans Act (2008) and the establishment of a Register based in the National Archives of Scotland from January 2009; see www.tartanregister.gov.uk

11 See Stewart, *Setts of the Scottish Tartans*, for a systematic and instructive treatment of the thread counts and setts in Scottish tartans.

12 Cheape, *Tartan. The Highland Habit*, pp. 7–9; this work emerged from exhibitions of tartan in New York (1988) and Edinburgh (1989), and takes as its premise the material culture evidence of textile and clothing in the extensive collections of the National Museums of Scotland.

13 Gibson, ' "The summer's hunting" ', pp. 153–4.

14 See Macinnes, 'Scottish Gaeldom and the aftermath', p. 72.

15 Watson, *Bàrdachd Ghàidhlig*, pp. 111–13; the author of this chapter is responsible for the translations from Gaelic.

16 MacLeod, *Songs of Duncan Bàn Macintyre*, pp. 8–15; see also Gunn, *Songs and Poems*, p. 9 for 'Òran nan Casagan Dubha' by Robb Donn, also on the side of the government, with his rhetorical trope, spòrs' air do dhìlsean ('making sport of the faithful'), against King George.

17 This perspective for a 'history' of tartan is proposed in Cheape, *Tartan. The Highland Habit*, pp. 39–55.

18 NMS [National Museums Scotland] L.1985.1 (papers and textile archive of the Highland Society of London on long-tem loan to the National Museums Scotland).

19 Fyfe, *Scottish Diaries*, p. 505.

20 Stewart and Thompson, *Scotland's Forged Tartans*, p. 13.

21 Most historians of tartan have undoubtedly drawn on the extensive original research of the Sobieski Stuarts and yet joined the chorus of denunciation. Only Stewart, *Old and Rare Scottish Tartans*, p. 58 and McClintock, *Old Irish and Highland Dress*, pp. 156–7 have recognised the brothers' worth.

22 Cheape, 'Researching tartan', pp. 35–46.

23 Constable, *History of Greater Britain*, pp. 48–9.

24 Duncan, 'The dress of the Scots', pp. 210–12.

25 The generous length of fabric is variously quoted as four to six yards of

double-width cloth or eight to ten yards of single-width cloth; see, for example, Watson, *Bàrdachd Ghàidhlig*, pp. 68, 279, for mid-eighteenth-century references to the belted plaid by the Gaelic poet John Mac-Codrum of North Uist.

26 Quye and Cheape, 'Rediscovering the Arisaid', pp. 1–20.

27 This rhetorical theme was articulated for modern scholarship in a seminal paper by Dr John MacInnes to the Gaelic Society of Inverness in 1978; see MacInnes, *Dùthchas nan Gàidheal*, p. 293.

28 MacDonald and MacDonald, *MacDonald Collection*, p. 49; for an exploration of different perceptions of colour, see Cheape, 'A' lasadh le càrnaid'.

29 This is explored in Grant and Cheape, *Periods in Highland History*, p. 129.

30 Cheape and Quye, 'Historical and analytical research of dyes', pp. 202–7; a marked absence of vegetable dyes in old surviving tartan fabrics contradicts a modern expectation that muted colours from locally sourced dyestuffs characterise ancient Scottish tartans. The influence of William Morris and the Arts and Crafts movement led to a revival of the use of vegetable-based dyes in textile production and their proliferation in, *inter alia*, tartan design and pattern differentiation.

31 Mackenzie, *Òrain Iain Luim*, pp. 124–5.

32 Stevenson, *Alasdair Mac Colla*, p. 295.

33 Stevenson, *Alasdair Mac Colla*, pp. 292–8.

34 Cheape, *Tartan. The Highland Habit*, p. 30.

35 Dunbar, *History*, pp. 97, 102.

36 Watson, *Bàrdachd Ghàidhlig*, p. 149.

2

PLAIDING THE INVENTION OF SCOTLAND

Murray Pittock

૭

In 1983, Eric Hobsbawm and Terence Ranger published what was to become regarded as a key study, *The Invention of Tradition*, with Cambridge University Press. It contained a number of high-profile chapters, including one which dealt with Scotland in the Romantic period, Hugh Trevor-Roper's 'The Invention of Tradition: The Highland Tradition of Scotland', which claimed that Macpherson's Ossian was a fake and a fraud based on a 'usurpation of Irish culture', that the modern kilt was an invention of the eighteenth century and that family tartans belonged to the nineteenth. The Trevor-Roper position became prestigious and influential, despite its author's evident lack of acquaintance with Scottish history or Gaelic scholarship (for example, the idea that 'racially and culturally' the Highlands 'was a colony of Ireland'). The view that tartan was an 'invented', pseudo-Highland Scottish identity, factitiously imposed on a trousered nation by Sir Walter Scott, David Stewart of Garth and the Sobieski Stuarts, has become a commonplace of Scottish cultural commentators. In 2008, Trevor-Roper's arguments received a new lease of life with the posthumous publication of *The Invention of Scotland*, whose title, far from being invented, was taken from my 1991 study of the same name. It makes some of the arguments of the earlier essay in more sophisticated guise, and is notably rather more detailed and cautious in its discussion of Macpherson. However, comments such as 'in Scotland alone the Celts had no claim to a native civilization. Lost in almost complete darkness [. . .] Highland society had no history' and 'Scottish culture had always been sustained by forgery' continue to remind the reader of the earlier essay on which it was based.[1]

Trevor-Roper was not alone, of course, nor was he the first scholar to express doubts about the antiquity of clan tartans (or, indeed, the authenticity of Macpherson's Ossian poems). More than thirty years earlier, John Telfer Dunbar's work inspired the high-profile 1949

Saltire Society exhibition in Edinburgh, where the notion of the clan tartan was attacked, and an argument backed by scholarship presented to the public, to the effect that the tartans of the 1745 Jacobite Rising were 'quite unlike the "clan" tartans of to-day'. Accompanying texts such as *Old Highland Tartans* and Dunbar's *Two Centuries of Highland Dress* (1951) argued for the inauthenticity of clan tartans and the changing fashion of other aspects of Highland dress, such as the fashionability of 'the large hairy sporran' from the later part of the eighteenth century (almost certainly as a thinly veiled representation of military masculinity, though Dunbar does not put it in these terms). The Saltire exhibition, visited by both the Queen Mother and Princess Margaret, anticipated in its arguments much of Trevor-Roper's case, though it was more subtly put. In the decade in which *The Invention of Tradition* appeared, much cultural commentary, from Barbara and Murray Grigor's *Scotch Myths* (1981) to John Prebble's *The King's Jaunt* (1988), also helped to sustain a climate of similar ideas by feeding the idea of a factitious tartan identity as an imposition by the Romantic period on the authentic national culture of Scotland. It was, however, the prestige of Lord Dacre as a historian that was critical in pressing this unexamined idea – which advanced claims well beyond debates over the authenticity or otherwise of individual clan tartans – into wide circulation, and with it the supposition that large swathes of the popular representation of Scottish culture were inauthentic to the point of fraudulence, and sometimes beyond it. The 1992 Canto edition of *The Invention of Tradition* owns up to which is its most important essay by placing a kilted gentleman presenting a dead stag to Queen Victoria on its cover. Trevor-Roper's essay fed into modern suspicions concerning authority and authenticity to present a key icon of Scottish culture as a charade.[2]

What could have been the motivation for such a charade? In part, Trevor-Roper bases his case – rather mischievously, perhaps – not on tartan as such, but on the introduction of one particular form of it, the fèileadh beag ('philabeg', or 'short kilt') in the eighteenth century, allegedly on the sole responsibility of the Quaker industrialist Thomas Rawlinson (in fact there is some evidence that the short kilt had been known since the 1690s). In Trevor-Roper's view, Rawlinson's innocent invention, created to enable Highlanders to function more freely in eighteenth-century commercial society, eventually became the basis for a factitious tradition invented by the Sobieski Stuarts and their allies, who gave birth to a visual fakery to which James Macpherson had been the verbal midwife. Other interpreters (particularly in Scotland) saw Sir Walter Scott as the chief culprit in the rise of tartanry, who in the interest of integrating the once loathed Highlands into a unified and modern Scottish identity, whose various traditions would be relieved of both conflict and threat thereby, elided 'the distinction between tartan's role as the public face of Scots in the British Army and its place as a native dress in civil society'. After the 1745 Rising, tartan had been banned from public use except in the army (though in practice there were many exceptions). The performance of the British Army in the Napoleonic Wars had led to unparalleled popularity for the Highland regiments and their distinctive dress (Scots and Irish made up a vast proportion of the army). This offered Scott an opportunity to publicly reconcile the long distrusted 'Highland' culture of Scotland with the 'Lowland' mainstream by presenting the country in Highland dress to George IV on his 1822 visit; so the story goes. Thus on the one hand, the charade is based on a partial interpretation – and therefore under-interpretation – of the nature and role of tartan across time, and on the other an over-interpretation of the function of tartan in a given space, Edinburgh in 1822.[3]

Such explanations perhaps appeal more than they should do to historians. They are sharp, apt and 'explode' long-cherished views with the same easy vehemence and lack of either rigour or depth as a Channel Five history programme. For twenty-five years, they have dominated the historiography of tartan at a cultural and political level. But they share a common problem: they are, in Johnsonian phrase, a good story which is far from being wholly true. Not only is it almost absurd to credit that a famous creative writer could engineer a piece of brief theatricality in one town in an age before television and thereby create a national culture; it is equally ridiculous to suppose that an English Quaker industrialist could determine the sartorial priorities of one. The Trevor-Roper argument in *The Invention of Tradition* was held to be influential and original research. Yet, the *Edinburgh Magazine* had alleged that the fèileadh beag was an 'English' invention in 1785, while Stewart of Garth viewed this claim as 'an attack on the tradition of the Highlander',[4] and so the argument from patriotism was already both old and contentious when Trevor-Roper weighed in on it in the 1980s.

That it was an eighteenth-century argument is in itself significant. The fèileadh beag began to appear in frequent use in the very age of what appeared to be the final manifestation of the Scottish patriot qualities of tartan as a rebel cloth. In the late medieval and early modern periods, John of Fordoun and Hector Boece among other historians had developed the idea of the true or 'old Scot' as being found in the North. This was the home of the country's martial spirit, the place (usually defined loosely as north of Forth-Clyde rather than the Gaelic-speaking areas as such, some of which were in any case south of Forth-Clyde in this period) where English imperial pretention had foundered in the face of implacable native valour. In 1538, James V ordered a hunting suit of Highland tartan; tartan of a sort was one of the distinguishing characteristics of the 'old Scots' and their traditional pursuits (such as the hunt), as it already was in the depiction of Scots soldiers of fortune abroad. These 'Highlanders' were the representatives of the Gàidhealtachd as an imagined space where Scots looked selectively 'in order to recapture the pristine virtue of their forebears'.[5]

At some point in the seventeenth century, this began to be an idea which forced its way visually more into the political mainstream. In 1983, Allan Macinnes, in an important essay on the Covenanting dynamic, argued that the wars of 1638–51 politicised and engaged the Gàidhealtachd to an unprecedented degree. It may have been at this juncture that tartan began to become more broadly available for adoption as the property of the Stuart party: it was on its way to becoming the rebel and not just the patriot cloth, the mark of the Jacobite who supported the ancient royal line and (after 1707) opposed the Union. At the same time, Scots as a whole began to be stereotyped in England as tartan wearers, as Ian Brown's reference in his chapter to the 1675 portrait of John Lacy playing Sauny the Scot makes vividly clear. This was clearly emplaced 'during the last quarter of the seventeenth century' and was brought to the fore by the politics of the Exclusion Crisis of 1679–82. The 'Anglo-Scots art song' created a literary space for Scotland in London, and that literary space was often coloured in tartan.[6]

In Edinburgh, there were similar developments. At the beginning of the 1680s, a 'cult' of 'tartanry' 'briefly flowered' at James, Duke of York and Albany's viceregal court at Holyrood: tartan was clearly beginning to be the cloth of the Stuart legitimist party during the Exclusion Crisis, being referred to as 'a beautiful garment' at James's court. This adoption of Edinburgh with the full panoply of a royal capital was also signified in other kinds of representation, including the Jacob de Wet portraits of the Stuart royal line, painted for Holyroodhouse between 1684 and 1686, which were a definitive statement of Scottish royalism set up in opposition to the Whiggery of the Exclusion Crisis. Similarly, James's cultivation of specifically Scots institutions (avatars of the Enlightenment) was part of a policy to set up distinct and more reliable royal centres than London in the other national capitals of the Stuart multi-kingdom monarchy. It is noteworthy, though, that de Wet's pictures do not use tartan to endorse the royal line. It had perhaps begun to become a badge of Stuart sympathy, but not yet one suitable for formal display in association with the Crown itself. Yet, sixty years later, the Stuart heir wore tartan as a matter of routine, and it is likely that his father did in 1715 also.[7]

It was during the era of the Jacobite Risings from 1689 to 1746 that tartan became confirmed as the uniform of that party. As early as 1689, it was being noted that non-Highland professionals such as 'Mr Drummond, the advocate' attached to Dundee's army were wearing 'Highland habit' as a signifier of their loyalty to 'old Scotland'. In James Philip of Almerieclose's *Grameid* of 1691, a Latin epic of the 1689 Rising written by an eye-witness, tartan garb is represented as characterising the Jacobite army's struggle to restore the 'Gloria Scotorum' in the face of Saxon pride, that glory which had stayed the pride of every invader since Rome.[8] 'Jacobite tartan' (a reconstituted sett can now once more be purchased) began to be worn in Edinburgh in the aftermath of the 1707 Union, and accessories as well as dress are known: a surviving scarf is believed to date from 1712. In 1713, the Royal Company of Archers (Jacobite leaning until the late 1740s) adopted tartan in its dress, a sartorial choice which would have been pretty well unthinkable in the Edinburgh of 1600. Jacobite gentry continued to support an explicitly patriot reading of Scottish history, and were among those requested to subscribe for new editions of John of Fordoun and similar volumes. In 1715, the Jacobite army was uniformed in tartan irrespective of its place of origin: the army at Perth on 1 October was described as 'betwixt 3 and 4000 foot [. . .] all in Highland cloaths tho mostly Lowland men'. In 1721, Allan Ramsay's 'Tartana, or the Plaid' called for its adoption as the patriot garb of domestic manufacture, 'before base foreign Fashions interwove', an oblique reference to the Union. Ramsay stresses the antiquity of tartan, the garb of the 'old Scots', and interestingly presents family-specific tartans: 'If lin'd with Green *Stuarta's* Plaid we view,/Or thine *Ramseia* edg'd around with Blue'. Colour was certainly becoming important as a means of the display of patriotic or Jacobite politics, particularly in the context of the conservative and repressive garb of Presbyterian Whig Scotland. As Domhnall Uilleam Stiùbhart notes, in a quotation Ian Brown has already drawn attention to,

The tartan, that clothing of brawn, vigour, and spectacular display *par excellence*, was more and more being compared to and distinguished from garments of 'renunciation' worn in the south, namely the black hat and cloak worn by Presbyterian ministers, and [. . .] the rise of that most emblematic whig garment, the sober three-piece suit.

Scotland had renounced the Stuarts, its independence and Episcopalianism. Those who contested these renunciations often wore the tartan, the kilt being referred to as 'am fasan' ('the fashion') even in Gaelic. Tartan was now most definitely a statement.[9]

In 1740, the Duke of Perth 'gave Charles and his younger brother [. . .] two *complete* sets of Highland dress [. . .] possibly as a gesture of thanks for the Knighthood of the Thistle which was conferred on him on 19 May 1739'. The patriot garb was thus the reciprocal gift for the patriot honour. In 1741, Charles Edward and Henry wore their tartan to a ball in Italy, while Perth himself expressed his pride in the tartan to Charles in 1744: 'I think it my greatest honour to be and to be looked upon as one of those that have a right to wear that kind of garb'. Tartan accessories may have multiplied at this date: Jacobite ladies dressed in 'riding habits [. . .] fashioned from tartan', while 'domestic furnishings such as bed hangings, curtains, shoes and various other items' were all made from the patriot cloth. Jonathan Faiers speculates that 'a woman dressed in men's riding clothes made from a cloth of insurrection' was a compelling intensifier of tartan's radical message. It was possibly more than this: the idea of the 'unnatural woman' was an important part of Hanoverian propaganda against the Jacobites, and cross-dressing was part of the unnaturalness of such women. For the women themselves, a refusal to bow to the code of eighteenth-century politesse was part of their patriotism, an irreconcilability which, as Andrew Lincoln points out, Scott explores in the character of Diana Vernon in *Rob Roy*.[10]

In 1745, Charles wore his tartan garb on campaign, by which time it was so strongly associated with him that Richard Cooper, an Edinburgh engraver, used it to the mark the Prince out in a print advertising a reward for his capture. By the early 1750s, 'Charles was being depicted in tartan on drinking glasses' and later 'fragments of tartan' allegedly worn by him acquired almost the status of relics. By 1745, the Jacobite force was regularly described in its own official despatches as a 'Highland Army', a term which posterity has found confusing. It was not clearly a 'Highland', still less a Gaelic-speaking force as the orders were issued in English. The term 'Highland Army' – always expressed in English – was rather intended to present the image of a patriot force rooted in Scottish martial valour. Jacobite leaders were well aware that they commanded thousands from the east-coast Lowlands, from Edinburgh and Haddingtonshire, from Ireland, France and England. But all alike were fighting for the patriot cause. In the Manchester Regiment 'each officer paraded in a plaid waistcoat' and girls wearing 'Plaid Breast-knots, Ribbands, and Garters' in the north-west at the time were known as the 'Lancashire Witches'. Near-kitsch items were already in evidence: for example, a tartan snuffbox was left behind at Ashbourne in Derbyshire by the invaders. The English Jacobite Sir John Hynde Cotton ordered a full tartan suit (still to be seen in the Museum of Scotland) in 1743–4 to signify his allegiance. As far away as Staffordshire, 'the Blue Coat Hunt tracked a fox dressed in red with hounds clad in tartan, while at Burton-on-Trent in 1747, a bull decorated with orange ribbons was baited by dogs garbed in plaid'. In other words, the Jacobite ethos was pictorially Highland rather than actually Gaelic. Tartan made a statement of a wider political allegiance, in which the 'honest man' code of English Jacobitism (built on the assumption that – as Mark Knights points out – 'Lying was thus claimed to be central to Whig methods' and 'also to Whig ideology') could readily represent itself in the garb of the patriot Highlander, whose preference of poverty and liberty to wealth and slavery was an undeniable mark of such 'honesty'.[11]

Tartan was certainly seen as a uniform rather than an ethnic identifier when it came to gathering evidence. The evidence given by Alexander Law, a Brechin innkeeper, at Whitehall in August 1746, states for example that James Lindsay 'wore Highland Cloaths' and that 'Buchannan was dress'd at that time in Highland Habit'. On 18 August 1746, Lord Balmerino, a Fife aristocrat, was executed wearing a tartan blindfold: 'brave Balmerrony [. . .] [i]n the midst of all his foes/Claps Tartan on his eyes [. . .] A Scots Man I livd [. . .] A Scots Man now I die [. . .] May all the Scots my footsteps trace', as a song commemorating the event put it. In December 1746, a Jacobite-clad protest was planned at Leith. Tartan here signifies patriot martyrdom: what Daniel Szechi has called 'The Jacobite theatre of death'. English cartoonists responded by wrapping all disaffected Scots in plaid, and then in the 1760s, the era of Bute and Wilkes, began to depict the careerist Scots descending on London as a tartan horde. Tartan was proscribed in its brighter variants in the 1746 Disarming Act (19 Geo. II c.39), although, as Hugh Cheape has pointed out, no action seems to have been taken against gentry-class loyalists or the widespread check plaid of the southern uplands (described by Scott as 'maud'). In addition, there were 'persistent problems in defining what constituted Highland dress', and tartan continued to be worn in the British Army: the 'Government', or Black Watch, tartan, had its roots in patterns adopted some years earlier by the Independent Highland Companies. Nonetheless, under the Disarming Act, tartan was clearly demarcated as the cloth of disaffection, a badge of the defeated traitor at worst, at best the marker of a fifth-column opportunist within the British state who secretly wished for its dissolution, a charge frequently levelled at tartan-clad Scots caricatures in the 1760s cartoons. On the basis that making fun of your enemies is the surest way to diminish them, tartan also became what Jonathan Faiers has called 'a textile of masquerade', a faintly comic and very definite way both of identifying Scots visually and diminishing them politically. This can perhaps be seen in the 'harlequin' representations of Charles Edward Stuart, where he is shown wearing a harlequin-like tartan which may be based on that given to him by the Duke of Perth in 1740 . The near-tartan of harlequin costume came into 'British pantomine in the Regency era and in dramatic renditions of Scott'. As Faiers argues, harlequin is 'a heterogenous system that allows for hyperbole and parody', and both are present in the cartoon representations of an eighteenth-century Britain relieved at the passing of the Jacobite threat. Henceforward the element of slightly theatrical exaggeration perhaps never quite left tartan, even in its future return to respectability. It had been a symbol of Scottish patriotism and then of the party that supported it, then of mockery at the defeat of that party. When it re-emerged, it was on one dimension as a Scottish patriotism of masquerade, a fancy-dress freedom which evoked the frisson of a defeated threat, a sign of Scottish virility which endorsed the process of Scotland's emasculation. In this, it was like other features of the post-Enlightenment revival of Scotland's past as a playground for nostalgic sentiment rather than serious study.[12]

This is, though, to get ahead of ourselves in this chapter. In the mid-eighteenth century tartan still retained one important sphere of representation neither private nor comic. Only in the military sphere was it a badge of incipient respectability: the Prime Minister William Pitt 'sought for Merit wherever it was to be found [. . .] I was the first Minister who looked for it, and found it in the Mountains of the North' in the Seven Years War of 1756–63. This was at the very historical moment when Scottish Enlightenment writers such as David

Hume (*History of England*, 1754–63) and William Robertson (*History of Scotland*, 1759) were overwriting this historiography of martial valour with the culturally unionist paradigm of stadialism.[13] Their history was to be in the ascendant and spawn in the nineteenth century the school of Whig history. In the 1750s and 1760s these last invocations of the school of martial valour were perhaps useful in enabling ex-Jacobite commanders like Simon Fraser, the Master of Lovat, who recruited a regiment on the back of Pitt's recommendation, to redeem themselves in the eyes of the Crown and the governing classes.

The rehabilitation of the tartan in the limited circumstances of British military engagement is dealt with in more detail by Trevor Royle elsewhere in this volume. What is interesting in the process of tartanry's growing respectability is that it appears (as was the case with Lovat) to be linked to the rehabilitation of ex-Jacobite noble families. In 1778, the Highland Society of London was founded (its first President being Lieutenant-General Simon Fraser of Lovat, who surfaces everywhere in this context). Four years later, Lovat supported the Marquis of Graham's bid to repeal the 'unclothing act' which had banned the non-military use of tartan. The Highland Society itself proclaimed that 'The Tartan Plaid is of great antiquity' and that – a sign of things to come – 'In the Highlands of Scotland, the Plaid [. . .] was made of the peculiar *set* [sic] or pattern of tartans, belonging to the Clan of the individual who wore it'. Graham was also supported in the 1782 repeal by Lovat's half-brother, Colonel Archibald Campbell Fraser. The restoration of the tartan to the public world was followed shortly afterwards by a major act of restitution to many of the Jacobite families, with the return in 1784 of the forfeited estates to their traditional owners. By the 1790s, the Duchess of Gordon – whose own tartan was only codified in 1793 – helped to introduce tartan to court, although the Prince Regent had paved the way by wearing it at a 1789 masquerade ball. By this stage too there were Highland Games and piping contests: the latter were already well established by the mid-1780s.[14]

These years then saw a clear statement of the importance of both the distinctive dress of the Jacobite era and its noble families. There was already a large range of distinctive tartans in existence (Hugh Cheape has identified twenty-three in David Morier's famous painting *An Incident in the Rebellion of 1745* alone). It is possible that the widespread and already iconic use of Government tartan in the British Army was helping to consolidate a sense of tartan as a vehicle for collective, regimental (and hence in the context of the Jacobite Rising, family and clan) identities. There are, however, some signs that individual families were associated with distinct tartans rather earlier than this. In the controversy over the 1949 Saltire exhibition, it was argued that Hunting MacLean dated back to 1587, that the Laird of Grant specified tartan colours for certain of his vassals in 1704 and that Lovat's men were probably in standard tartans in 1732; Mackintosh has also been associated with an early date. It was already clear in the eighteenth century that bright colours – such as a loud red – could symbolise wealth and status for reasons Hugh Cheape discusses, and possibly had done for quite a significant period of time before 1700. District colours, meanwhile, often obviously depended on the local availability of dyes. It is possible that MacDonalds fought at Killiecrankie in 1689 as a regiment wearing the same tartan, and Martin Martin's *Description of the Western Islands of Scotland* (1703) describes tartans as characterising districts:

> Every isle differs from each other in their fancy of making plaids as to the stripes in breadth and colours. This humour is as different throughout the mainland of the Highlands, in so far that they who have seen those places are able at first view of a man's plaid to guess the place of his residence.

Since many of those who lived on the land of a Chief of the Name or of a sept might take that name as a sign of allegiance and to secure protection, even when no blood relationship existed, it is not surprising that tartans in various districts may have begun to be associated with families. However, this also seems possibly to have been the case with landless men from clans whose names stood proscribed, such as the MacGregors. Cheape records a 'MacGregor tartan' as being current in 1787, when Joseph MacGregor wore it to celebrate the lifting of James VI's proscription of the name: yet another legal development which brought familial and dress rehabilitation into collocation.[15]

By the 1780s the Highland Society of London had started to link Highland dress to its own notions of social prestige by developing ideas on the use of tartan as a formal costume. In 1814, Colonel David Stewart of Garth could comment that there were tartans of chiefs and of country. The next year, the Highland Society began to make a register of chiefs' tartans, although it was understood (and would remain so up to the codifying exercises of the Sobieski Stuart brothers) that tartan could still be the property of more than one clan. However, if the Sobieskis were guilty of wishful thinking, there was also commercial pressure. Wilson's of Bannockburn had been producing tartan for the military for many years by the early nineteenth century. Their Pattern Book of 1819 displays the onset of a world where having a tartan associated with a family name was a matter of consumer desire as much as scholarly fidelity: the Wilsons were already long in the business, having been producing setts with family associations since the 1790s. The associations of tartan with noble Jacobite families and British military successes rendered it aspirational. By the 1820s, specific tartans were being used as prizes at Highland Games: on 8 August 1828, 'A Plaid of Drummond of Perth Tartan' was the prize for the best dancer of the Highland Reel at the Strathearn Highland Friendly Society's Muthill meeting, a custom which was by that time already several years old. The old delight in the 'newest patterns', evident in the Jacobite era, now became delight in the 'correct' patterns, as codification and commerce went hand in hand. Development of family tartans was to this degree haphazard: hence the names of neither Currie nor Turnbull possessed one as late as the 1970s, while Cochrane was also only codified after 1945, though paradoxically the Cochranes seem to have used Royal Stuart as a mark of Charles II's favour from the seventeenth to the nineteenth centuries, or so the story goes. It was this tartan that Thomas Cochrane seems to have displayed at his St Andrew's Day Dinner at Valparaiso in 1819, on taking command of the Chilean navy.[16]

Already, given its military use in the British Army and its adoption by gentlemanly clubs such as the Highland Society, the tartan was well on the way to being a garb with social prestige, not the badge of a banditti bent on the destruction of the British state. The central role played by Scottish troops in the Napoleonic Wars – not least at Waterloo – helped to reinforce this prestige. A huge tartan display – probably not seen in the capital since Jacobite times – greeted the return of the Black Watch ('The Fighting 42nd') to Edinburgh in 1816, six years before the celebrated royal visit. By then, the Jacobite credentials of tartan were ripe for rehabilitation, because Scots loyalty to the Crown and state could be seen as an extension of the love of absolutism of which the Jacobites had once been accused, now rendered more than welcome by the threat posed by radical reformers and the absence of a competing dynasty. The radical insurrection in Scotland in 1820, damp squib as it was, enabled Scott's presentation of his countrymen as 'a nation of Highlanders' during the 1822 royal visit to be an elaborately paradoxical presentation of the country as completely loyal to the Crown and the British state while being dressed in the garb which had once denoted their fiercest enemies. This was not an invented tradition: it was the reinscription of Jacobite patriotism as the discourse of Scottish particularity, a particularity circumscribed by the death of its ancient loyalties and their replacement by support for the Crown. Scott's theatrical 'discovery' of the Honours of Scotland was only one part of this process. In the era of Peterloo, Scott's presentation of the 1822 visit spoke a language of reassuring loyalty to the past, throne and altar. To counterbalance the English radical hope that 'Milton, thou shouldst be living at this hour', Scotland was arrayed in a militant if impotent sartorial reminiscence of the garb adopted by Milton's greatest enemies, the Stuarts. George IV gave an audience to Sergeant-Major Peter Grant of Lord Lewis Gordon's brigade in 1745, the last survivor of the Rising, while in 1824, the year Grant died, a number of Jacobite titles, including that of the 1715 leader, the Earl of Mar, were unfrozen.

Tartan was the stuff of loyalty to the crown and close association with it: it was thus naturally increasingly an aristocratic motif. Alasdair Macdonell of Glengarry formed a 'Society of True Highlanders': racially and socially exclusive, the emphasis was on full and formal dress. Things were moving on from the Highland Society of London's inclusive policy that 'Highland Spirit' not 'Highland Birth' was the qualification for membership, since the Highlands could not be defined 'with any degree of accuracy'. In 1822, Alasdair Ranaldson of the True Highlanders wrote a guide to formal Highland dress 'for those Chieftains and Men of Unquestionable Family', while tartans themselves began to be made on softer cloth, to drawing-room standards.[17]

The formalisation of clan tartans as solely linked with certain families and only entitled to be worn by those families was an uneasy fusion of genuine historical associations, family snobbery, marketing and the Victorian idea of the clan system, itself a means of allowing a Scottish aristocracy to differentiate itself within the British Empire without challenging it: colourful, distinctive, once disloyal, now loyal because a friend to monarchy, and always out of date. Tartan's final – and fantastic – codification by the Jacobite wannabees John and Charles Sobieski Stuart in *Vestiarum Scoticum* (1842) and *The Costume of the Clans* (1845) allowed it to be a badge of unchallengeable family and antiquity. The right to wear a tartan became a version of the right to bear a coat of arms, as the Sobieskis 'established and consolidated the clan associations of tartan and ascribed specific clan identity to nearly all setts or designs', despite having historical justification for only some 15 per cent of those identified in *Vestiarum*. As Donald Calder Stewart wryly notes, however, this book, and James Logan's earlier 1831 volume, *The Scottish Gael*, were 'sufficient to fulfil the needs of the manufacturers'. The Wilsons had in fact been producing tartan for the Sobieskis since 1829.

The ideological reinscription of tartan on a discourse of British loyalty also incorporated the Hanoverian Royal Family in a traditional Scottish identity, and even better, the Jacobite one of the Stuarts, from whom they were – though by no means by the branch nearest to the throne in blood – descended. The fact that the Royal Family had not been Scottish for centuries was rendered less important, because by focusing on family entitlement to tartan and hence Scottishness, blood descent became a more important measure of nationality than it had been before. In earlier eras, unrelated settlers on a nobleman's estates might take the name of which he was chief, while loyalty to the Scottish state was a key medieval and early modern measure of a Scot, in what was after all a multi-ethnic kingdom. Scots who rebelled against Bruce could be described as 'English', just as later those who fought for the Hanoverian Crown were. Scottishness traditionally was loyalty to a country and its institutions as well as a matter of descent and family, though these were of course important: detailed knowledge of one's descent and family was of course in itself rather socially exclusive. The new dominant emphasis on bloodline, however, not only made Scotland a particularist club, but also supported the creation of an imperial diaspora of British colonials with Scottish ancestry but no knowledge of Scotland, one aspect of which Michael Newton's chapter examines in detail. The bloodline qualification for the national dress made Scotland inaccessible to incomers: this was useful for maintaining its autonomy from its neighbour. It also made it a country that valued ethnic purity, a definition of nationality with rather unfortunate overtones. Being a Scot was limited by family lineage, which gave it charisma; that charisma was mass-produced as tartan, which rendered it kitsch. Such was the birth of shortbread-tin Scotland.

Victoria and Albert's decor for Balmoral in the 1850s reflected both their pride (or Victoria's at least) in being Stuarts and thus Scots, and their wish to display this family heritage everywhere. The 'bright red of the Royal Stewart and its green Hunting Stewart counterpart were used for carpets, and, Dress Stuart for curtains and upholstery'. It is possible that the house on Eilean Aigas, restored – once again by the Lovats – for the use of the Sobieskis as a mansion in 1838, with accessories including thrones (!) was some sort of exemplar for Balmoral. The mansion on Eilean Aigas was 'a Celtic Xanadu', full of 'antique weapons, trophies of the chase, banners, busts, and every conceivable kind of Highland bric-a-brac'. Certainly Victoria seemed to go down a similar path in making Jacobite-related images and tableaux a centrepiece of her Scotland and of entertainment at Balmoral. In a way this might show that she was in touch with primitive peoples (like Jacobite Highlanders) who had suffered defeat nobly throughout her empire, as the Scottish soldier abroad was being seen by the late Victorian period as a visible symbol of how picturesque peoples from all over the world might be incorporated into the British Empire. The 'devils in skirts' were feared troops, but also an exemplar of the futurity of acceptance awaiting those who ceased to struggle against their destiny as British subjects. A. C. MacDonell's *Lays of the Heather* (1896) (dedicated to Rupert of Bavaria, the Jacobite heir!) is a good example of this kind of subgenre. Its poem, 'The Seaforth Highlanders in Hindoostan', repeatedly emphasises the kinship in habitat between the indomitable British Highlander and their indomitable native enemy. At Bangalore, 'For well they knew the kilted lads would lead the upper way [. . .] Sure-footed as the mountain stag the swaying ladders scaled'; at Savendroog, the 'lads in tartan green' climb 'the perilous rock by dint of tufts of slippery grass', for it is the way of 'the Highland heart within to conquer or to die'.[18] The role of the Scottish soldier as intrepid mountaineer had, of course, been present since the Heights of Abraham were scaled by General Wolfe's men in 1759. Meanwhile, tartan on the home front was increasingly formal and codified for reasons both of social exclusion and commercial opportunity. It was also a visible guarantee of Scottish blood and family and a display of wealth and status reaching up to the Crown itself.

Yet the element of masquerade in tartan was perhaps never quite lost, as Harry Lauder, the Bay City Rollers – and even the Tartan Army – discussed in later chapters bear witness. Tartan in general and the kilt in particular has moved away from being a composite of bloodline and Britishness towards its original role as a mark of Scottish patriotism – not without rebellious overtones thanks to its adoption by punk – since the 1970s. However, it has not lost its masquerade element entirely: and one of the curiosities of reading the kilt and the recrudescence of Scottish tartanry through the lens of postmodern playfulness is that this element of tartanry's symbolic representation is, as Faiers points out, of far longer standing than our postmodern moment indicates. Understanding Scottish culture now – as in the eighteenth century – is not 'a simple matter of polarities, authenticity/myth, actuality/invention', but requires a more sophisticated grasp of the culture and interplays of history. The 'See you Jimmy' hat carries in its mixture of humour and aggression the legacy of harlequin masquerade and Jacobite patriotism alike, faintly 'mocking yet celebratory'.[19] So history is carried and worn in the invention of Scotland: by this I mean the legacy of the patriot and Stuart cause in the discourses of our national representation, the subject of my 1991 book, *The Invention of Scotland*, not the posthumous 2008 collection of Hugh Trevor-Roper's papers which borrows nothing from it save its title.

Notes

1 Trevor-Roper, 'The invention of tradition', pp. 15 ff, 16, 21; Trevor-Roper, *The Invention of Scotland*, pp. 192, 204.

2 National Library of Scotland ACC 12251 Box 7 (Dunbar Papers); *Old Highland Tartans* (n.p., n.d.), p. 3; Dunbar, *Two Centuries of Highland Dress*, p. 9.

3 Pittock, 'Patriot dress and patriot games', p. 158.

4 McClintock, *Old Irish and Highland Dress*, p. 54; Cheape, *Tartan. The Highland Habit*, p. 36; Dunbar, *History*, p. 14; Grimble, *Scottish Clans and Tartans*, p. 10.

5 See Mason, 'Civil society and the Celts', pp. 95–119; Trevor-Roper, *Invention*, p. 195; also Mason, *Kingship and the Commonweal* and Pittock, *The Myth of the Jacobite Clans*, p. 39.

6 Macinnes, 'Scottish gaeldom, 1638–1651', pp. 59–94; Stiùbhart, 'Highland rogues', p. 171.

7 Lynch, *Scotland*, p. 299 for cult of tartanry; Stùibhart, 'Highland rogues', p. 174.

8 Pittock, *Myth*, p. 39; Philip, *Grameid*, pp. 23, 25, 123.

9 Pittock, *Myth*, p. 121; National Archives, State Papers (Domestic) 54/9/2d ('Intelligence Report from Perth, Stirling, 1 October 1715'); Ramsay, *The Works*, p. 29; Stiùbhart, 'Highland rogues', pp. 173–4.

10 Dalgleish and Mechan, *'I Am Come Home'*, p. 8; Nicholson, *Bonnie Prince Charlie*, p. 62; Faiers, *Tartan*, pp. 87–8. For a more detailed discussion of the 'unnaturalness' of Jacobite women in government propaganda, see Pittock, *Jacobitism*, pp. 78–82; for Scott, see Lincoln, *Walter Scott and Modernity*.

11 Pittock, *Myth*, p. 40; Whitehead, *Held in Trust*, pp. 106–7; Turner,

Manchester in 1745, pp. 12–13, 16–17; Jeffrey, 'Relics of rebellion', p. 32; Monod, *Jacobitism and the English People*, p. 293; Knights, *Representation and Misrepresentation*, p. 302.

12 National Archives TS 20/88/16, 36, 38; Aberdeen University Library MS 2222; Pittock, *Myth*, 111; Boswell, *Journal*, p. 10n; Szechi, 'The Jacobite theatre of death'; Hill, 'The illustration of the Waverley Novels', pp. 73, 75–6; Harris, *Politics and the Nation*, p. 177; Faiers, *Tartan*, pp. 88, 103, 167, 170.

13 Pitt in 1766, cited in Sinclair, *An Account*, p. 3.

14 Sinclair, *An Account*, pp. 4, 7, 10; Dunbar, *History*, p. 102; Donaldson, 'The Jacobite song', p. 434; National Library of Scotland Highland Society of London Papers Dep 268 Box 15.

15 NLS ACC 12251 Box 7; Martin, *A Description*, p. 129.

16 NLS Highland Society of London Papers Dep 268/15; Cheape, *Tartan*, pp. 28, 40, 41, 43, 44, 48, 52–3, 57; Robertson, *The First Highlander*, pp. 73–7; Dunbar, *History*, p. 21; Grimble, *Scottish Clans and Tartans*, pp. 11, 53; Pittock, *Scottish and Irish Romanticism*, Chapter 10 for discussion of Cochrane.

17 Sinclair, *An Account*, pp. 5–6; Cheape, *Tartan*, p. 52; Robertson, *The First Highlander*, pp. 73–4.

18 Cheape, *Tartan*, pp. 57, 63; *Old Highland Tartans*, p. 3; Donaldson, *The Jacobite Song*, p. 110. For the implausibility of the Sobieskis, see Stewart, *The Setts of the Scottish Tartans*, pp. 22, 120, 121; MacDonnell, *Lays of the Heather*, pp. 32–7. For a more detailed discussion of these images, see Pittock, *Celtic Identity*.

19 Pittock, 'Material culture in modern Scotland', pp. 65, 67.

3

FROM DAVID STEWART TO ANDY STEWART: THE INVENTION AND RE-INVENTION OF THE SCOTTISH SOLDIER

Trevor Royle

⌒

Back in 1961 when the British public was trying to make up its mind whether it preferred Elvis Presley or Helen Shapiro the popular music charts were infiltrated by a curiously cod song, 'A Scottish Soldier', performed by the equally cod singer, Andy Stewart, whose work is discussed elsewhere in this volume by Margaret Munro. Although it never made number one, the song stayed in the charts for forty weeks and with its catchy words and robust tune it enjoyed a wide currency, not just in Scotland and the rest of the United Kingdom but in most parts of the English-speaking world.

Stewart, an entertainer in the mould of Sir Harry Lauder, was equally popular. A native of Glasgow, he had come to the fore as a jaunty leading performer on the BBC's *White Heather Club*, an all-singing and all-dancing light entertainment television programme which provided a sanitised version of the traditional céilidh. The men wore kilts with sensible shirts and ties, the women wore white dresses with sashes, and set-piece dances such as 'The Duke of Perth' and 'Hamilton House' were danced with formal precision to music provided by the accordion-led bands of Jimmy Shand or Bobby MacLeod.

The songs were equally well crafted and sung with gusto by Stewart and other performers such as James Urquhart and Robert Wilson. Many were traditional songs sung to strictly modulated tunes; others were adapted or, in the case of 'A Scottish Soldier', given new words. The tune of this particular song was a march called 'The Green Hills of Tyrol' which dates back to the Crimean War of 1854–6. In the latter part of the campaign the Highland Brigade served alongside units from the Sardinian army whose band played a tuneful march adapted from the opera *William Tell* by Rossini. It appealed to Pipe-Major John Macleod of the 93rd (Sutherland) Highlanders who re-adapted it again for the pipes and drums.[1] In time, as 'The Green Hills of Tyrol', it became a regular feature in the repertoire of the pipes and drums of most of Scotland's infantry regiments – both the Black Watch and the Argyll and Sutherland Highlanders listed it as a Retreat air in their list of duty tunes – but the words gave the medley its poignancy. Andy Stewart's dying soldier, 'with good broad shoulder', tells the story of 'battles glorious and deeds victorious' but with death close at hand and far away from home, 'his heart is crying' and he longs to leave 'these green foreign hills' because they are 'not the hills of home'.

This was sentimentality run riot. Of course, that was part of the appeal and Stewart milked it in such a way that swaggering in his kilt he became the personification of the manliness embodied in the figure of the Scottish soldier. His audience fell for the illusion too and found itself being caught up in the stirring three-four march tune and the associated heroism of words that could have come from the pen of Sir Walter Scott or William Edmonstoune Aytoun:

> And now this soldier, this Scottish soldier,
> Who wanders far no more, and soldiers far no more,
> Now on a hillside, a Scottish hillside,
> You'll see a piper play this soldier home.
> He's seen the glory, he's told the story,
> Of battles glorious, and deeds victorious;
> But he will cease now, he is at peace now,
> Far from these green hills of Tyrol.[2]

In 1961, the Scottish soldier was still a potent figure in the country's iconography and Stewart's song was very much at one with the spirit of the times. Although defence cuts had removed the names of the Highland Light Infantry and the Royal Scots Fusiliers (amalgamated as the Royal Highland Fusiliers) and the Seaforth Highlanders and Queen's Own Cameron Highlanders (amalgamated as Queen's Own Highlanders) the army still had in its order of battle eight Scottish line infantry regiments, two battalions of Scots Guards and one heavy armoured regiment, the Royal Scots Greys. Scots made up 13 per cent of the army's personnel and with National Service still in existence – the last conscript was not demobbed until May 1963 – kilted soldiers were a common sight in public places and would remain so until the following decade when the Troubles in Northern Ireland put a stop to military personnel wearing uniform off-duty.

The relationship between the public and the kilted Jock was not just illusion. In 1968, the Argyll and Sutherland Highlanders was faced with disbandment, partly as a result of continuing defence cuts and partly (it was widely thought) as a result of the regiment's robust approach in dealing with the insurrection in Aden prior to the British withdrawal and transfer of power three years earlier. The Argylls were not the only victims of the cuts. The Cameronians, a Lowland regiment with an older history and lineage, was also earmarked for disbandment, a decision the regiment accepted with commendable dignity, but a well-organised and noisy campaign was begun by the Highland regiment's supporters to 'Save the Argylls'. Over a million signatures were collected for a petition which was presented to Parliament, and although some Labour MPs, notably Barbara Castle and Tam Dalyell, criticised the regiment for alleged heavy-handedness during the Aden operation the Argyll and Sutherland Highlanders was saved. In 1970, it was announced that it would remain on the army's Order of Battle in company strength and a year later it was quietly restored to full battalion strength, as a result of the need to assist the garrison in Northern Ireland.

All this mattered to the people of Scotland. The campaign was rarely off the front pages of the nation's press, its colourful diced Balmoral cap logo was seen everywhere and in 1968, a year when revolution gripped Europe, saving the Argylls became the most widely discussed political topic in Scotland. At a time when devolution was still an impossible dream – the former SNP leader Arthur Donaldson told his successor Billy Wolfe that 'all the activists of the SNP could have been the complement on a small passenger aircraft, and had they flown together and crashed without survivors, the cause of independence would have been lost to view for many years'[3] – the kilted Scottish soldier became a handy substitute. Indeed the campaigners recognised that deep-rooted sentiment and their cause was not hindered by the success of the SNP in 1967 when Winnie Ewing won the Hamilton by-election and in 1968 the party won control of the local council at Cumbernauld. Never mind that SNP activists campaigned against the presence of the Polaris nuclear bases on the Clyde and adopted an anti-militarist stance which still divides the party four decades later, the campaigners for the Argylls recognised the potency of the Scottish military connection and played it for all that it was worth. In their view anyone who loved Scotland wanted to save the Argylls.

In fact the love affair between the Scots and their soldiers was already long established. During the First World War the Scots provided more recruits per head of population than any other part of the United Kingdom in the 18–41 age group and the casualties were correspondingly high – some 120,000 or 15 per cent of the British total, most of them infantry privates.[4] The reasons why those young men swarmed into uniform are varied and defy a simple explanation. Partly it was a result of the general enthusiasm for war, the patriotic rush of 1914, which saw the creation of a huge volunteer army, and in that respect a sense of adventure also played a part. In Glasgow alone 20,000 had volunteered by the end of August and in the following month three battalions of the Highland Light Infantry, the local regiment, had been formed exclusively from men who worked, respectively, in the corporation's tramways department (15th battalion) or served as members of the Boys' Brigade (16th battalion) or were members of the city's Chamber of Commerce (17th battalion).[5] Partly it was patriotism, suffused in many cases with peer pressure or threats from above – one landowner, the Earl of Wemyss, gave notice that every able-bodied man aged between eighteen and thirty working on his estates in East Lothian would be put on half-pay for the duration of the war, and their jobs kept open, provided they joined up. 'If they do not enlist,' continued the Earl in his offer, 'they will be compelled to leave my employment.'[6]

A further reason was provided by recent history and the creation of dubious traditions. In the middle of the previous century Scotland had been gripped by the Volunteer craze, a Victorian fancy for part-time amateur soldiering which involved some gentle shooting practice and drills and, best of all, dressing up in turkey-cock uniforms. In Scotland the recruitment figures for the Volunteer units were twice the United Kingdom average, a figure which was undoubtedly assisted by the creation of units with Highland affiliations, most of them in the central belt. With their panoply of kilts, tartan trews, ostrich feathers, ornate sporrans and pipe bands they were an irresistible attraction and everywhere men rushed to wear them. Most of these outlandish uniforms owed nothing to tradition but were invented by local colonels and they came to represent self-conscious nationalism or what the military historian John Keegan has described as 'a force for resistance against the creeping anglicisation of Scottish urban life'.[7] Nostalgia for a half-forgotten romantic past was a factor, as was the existing iconography of the Scottish soldier, which found its apotheosis in Roger Fenton's Crimean War photographs of the sternly bearded Highland soldiers of Queen Victoria's army.[8] However, there was more to soldiering than putting on fancy dress. Being a part-time Volunteer meant following an honourable calling: it was companionable, offered self-respect and produced steadiness of character, all important moral virtues in Presbyterian Scotland.

The vogue can also be traced back to the defeat of the Jacobite army at the Battle of Culloden in 1746 and to the subsequent repressive actions against the Highland regions and attacks on its Gaelic culture described in the previous two chapters. The destruction of Highland military systems, which in any case were losing force, at least in terms of a 'clan' structure, and the Clearances of the traditional clan lands, which began very soon as an effect of 'improving' landlords' preferring cattle and sheep as income generators have been described as the beginning of the end of a way of life which was barely understood by outsiders, not least Lowland Scots. And it has to be said that, at the time, the process was largely welcomed not least by the Highland élites and professional classes, who quickly became committed to agricultural improvement and its economic benefits for landlords, as well as by Lowland politicians. In the aftermath of the Union of the Parliaments and the economic benefits of 'heavenly Hanoverianism' it was thought no bad thing to have this 'lawless' area with its 'savage' population and their 'heathen' (for so it seemed to outsiders) way of life brought under control. What to do with it was another matter. Either they could accept modernity and the Union and a place in a planned fishing village like Ullapool or assisting in the landlords' kelping industry, or they could be moved elsewhere to make new lives, courtesy of landowners who regarded themselves not as destroyers but as liberal reformers. As for the soldierly instincts of their tenants, these could be offered to the British Army at a time when it was being used as an imperial gendarmerie to expand the country's growing colonial holdings.

To a certain extent the belief that Highlanders possessed superior military virtues had been conditioned by romanticism and by the contemporary notion that Highlanders were 'noble savages' but it was also backed by evidence of their conduct while fighting for the Jacobite cause. In 1715 and 1745–6, clan soldiers had demonstrated their ability to handle weapons and to make full use of what would now be called field craft. They were also amenable to accepting orders provided they came from their own superior officers and they were used to being disciplined. It is instructive to compare this belief to contemporary attitudes to the so-called 'martial races' in

British India. This was an official designation created by senior officers who, having observed that the Scottish Highlanders had the reputation of being hardier in battle than other classes of men in Britain, extended the concept to India, where they classified each ethnic group into two categories. 'Martial races' were rated as ideal warriors, held to be brave and robust as a result of their upbringing, while 'non martial races' were believed to be unfit for the rigours of soldiering because they came from comfortable backgrounds or led sedentary lifestyles.

Acting on a suggestion made by King George II during the Seven Years War, Prime Minister William Pitt the Elder opened the door for the creation of the Highland regiments, arguing that Highlanders were regarded as good soldiers and that their fighting qualities had become evident during the earlier Jacobite rebellions. Here was a ready supply of soldiers who would do their duty, and their clan loyalties would bring a sense of coherence and reliability that would translate into good military practice. As the days of the clan system were numbered after Culloden and would soon disappear, other than as a sentimental entity based on chiefdoms, tartan and yearning for a lost past, the Highland regiments became handy substitutes. In fact, it suited landowners raising regiments to exaggerate the continuation of the clan system in order to reinforce their positions as clan/regimental leaders. Their emphasis on the combativeness of the 'Highlander' led to their perception as 'natural' warriors. As a later prime minister, Winston Churchill, neatly summarised the widely held received view of the outcome: 'Pitt canalised the martial ardour of the Highlanders into the service of his Imperial dreams.'[9] In 1766, Pitt defended in Parliament his decision to raise the Scottish regiments:

I have no local attachments: it is indifferent to me, whether a man was rocked in his cradle on this side or that of the Tweed. I sought for merit wherever it was to be found. It is my boast, that I was the first minister who looked for it, and I found it in the mountains of the north. I called it forth, and drew it into your service, a hardy and intrepid race of men! men who, when left by your jealousy became prey to the artifices of your enemies and had gone nigh to have overturned the state, in the war before last. These men, in the last war were brought to combat on your side: they served with fidelity, as they fought with valour, and conquered for you in every part of the world: detested be the national reflections against them! They are unjust, groundless, illiberal, unmanly![10]

How did this work out in practice? To a great extent the figures speak for themselves. Between 1714 and 1763 a quarter of the officers serving in the British Army were Scots, proportionally more than the English. Of 208 officers who were also Members of Parliament from 1750 to 1794 56 were Scots. At the same time one in four regimental officers was a Scot and Scots were used to receiving high command while fighting in the European and colonial wars waged by Britain throughout the eighteenth century. Between 1725 and 1800 no fewer than 37 Highland regiments were raised to serve in the British Army and by the end of the period the numbers involved are estimated at 70,000 men.[11]

From the very outset the territorial links of the regiments were vital, not just for recruiting but also for maintaining group cohesion and loyalty. The system had other benefits. Landowners who had supported the Jacobites were able to demonstrate their loyalty by raising regiments as a quid pro quo. Most considered themselves to be Highland gentlemen and, if estates had been forfeited, the raising of a regiment was a useful means of retrieving family honour and making good lost ground. That was an important consideration as the creation of a regiment depended on social status and financial capacity, the going rate for raising and equipping a regiment being £15,000, an enormous sum (nearly £1.5 million today). A landowner wishing to raise a regiment had to have contacts at the highest social level as it was the king who gave authority for the regiment to be raised in his name.[12] The actual commission for the commanding officer was signed by the Secretary for War but at the time the final arbiter was King George II.

Once the order and warrant had been issued, the regiment came into being and the commanding officer set about recruiting. For the senior officers a regimental commander would look to his closest family and friends and they in turn helped to recruit the soldiers from the tenants on their estates. When Kenneth Mackenzie, Earl of Seaforth, raised the 78th Highlanders in 1778 half of the soldiers came from his own estates while the rest were recruited from Mackenzie lands in Wester Ross.[13] To make up numbers it was common practice to recruit English and Irish soldiers. Blandishments included the promise of booty and plunder from campaigns overseas and alcohol also came into play. It was also true that landlords might apply carrot-and-stick pressure either by promising reductions in family rents or longer tenancies in return for military service or by targeting workers who agitated for higher wages for recruitment. To get some idea of how the system worked positively, there is the well-attested example of the raising of the 79th Highlanders by Alan Cameron of Errachd in 1793. He was not a rich man and did not enjoy the support of a large estate; yet a combination of patriotism and the chance to make a fortune abroad encouraged him to raise his regiment of Highlanders. He had to work hard at it, for not only was recruitment a problem but he had to face the opposition of his own family. Fortunately Cameron of Errachd enjoyed widespread respect and according to local records in the Lochaber district the 79th was raised 'on the sheer strength of his personal popularity [. . .] he was a king of men in personal appearance and large-hearted and liberal handed and in their estimation an ideal Highlander'.[14] This was an important consideration – not only did Alan Cameron enjoy the respect of his men but, as a contemporary but anonymous Gaelic poet makes clear, the regiment was bound together by bonds of clan loyalty:

> Thog thu Réisimeid chòmhlan
> De spealpairean spòrsail,
> Gillean sgiolta 'nan còmhdach,
> Clis còmhnard nach clì.
>
> Fiùrain sheasmhach, làn cruadail,
> Anns gach ball ni iad buannachd;
> Bidh srann aig an luaidhe
> Dol le luas ann an gnìomh
> [. . .]
> Na h-oifigich òrdail
> Is iad uile air deagh fhóghlam;
> Clann Ghille-Eathain nan sròl leat
> Is buidheann Lòchaidh 'nan still.
> Gaisgich mhear' de Cloinn Domhnaill,
> Fial faramach còmhstritheach
> [. . .]
> So i an Réisimeid thoirteil
> Bhios ainmeil gu cosnadh

('You raised a regiment from a band of merry active men, lads smart in their dress, agile, even-tempered and unerring, steadfast young men and hardy. On every occasion they shall overcome, their lead shot shall be buzzing, swift to good effect [. . .] the well disciplined officers all well educated, Clan Maclean of the banners with you and the Company of Lochy at full speed, hearty heroes of Clan Donald, generous, boisterous and aggressive [. . .] this is the stout regiment that shall be renowned for achievements.')[15]

With the 'barbaric' allure of their uniforms Highland soldiers became an instantly recognised and widely feared element of the British Army and their service in Africa, India and North America helped to consolidate Britain's growing mercantile empire. The Highlanders who served in America and Canada played a similar role to the Hessian forces which served in the same campaigns against the French and Native Americans and in that sense they were just as much mercenaries as the Scots who used the East India Company as a kind of latter-day French Foreign Legion. (A commercial trading venture, the East India Company maintained three armies in Bengal, Bombay and Madras.) In that sense too they were following an even older tradition – that of the mercenaries who served in French, Swedish or Spanish service during the Thirty Years War. Indeed, even earlier the French king Charles VII founded the *Garde Écossaise* in 1418 as an élite royal guard. To them war was a lucrative national industry which had the added bonus that it could be exported, and the pensioned soldier could bring income to his family and so support local economies.

Scots had a reputation as good fighters and in common with many other minorities on Europe's fringes – the Croat cavalry in Wallenstein's army, for example – they sold their skills to the highest bidder, becoming soldiers of fortune who gave good value for money. At least 25,000 were in the service of Gustavus Adolphus of Sweden, and half that number fought for King Louis XIII of France, often confronting their fellow countrymen on the field of battle, neither giving quarter nor expecting to receive it. One, Sir John Hepburn, scion of an old East Lothian Catholic family, fought in the Swedish and the French armies and rose to become a Marshal of France, having raised in 1633 under a warrant from Charles I the formation which eventually became the Royal Scots, the 1st of Foot and the senior line infantry regiment in the British Army's order of battle. Yet, despite his aristocratic antecedents he too knew his price. Trusted as one of the bravest of Gustavus's brigade commanders, Hepburn had lost his patron's confidence prior to the Battle of Lützen which saw the Swedish king lose his life in 1632. Leaving his men was clearly an emotional experience for Hepburn, a contemporary account noting that 'the separation was like that which death makes betwixt friends and the soule of man'.[16] Men like Hepburn or other notables such as Alexander Leslie who commanded the Parliamentary forces at Marston Moor in 1644 during the Wars of the Three Kingdoms all learned the soldiers' trade fighting as soldiers of fortune. It is one of the ironies of

Andy Stewart's song that his Scottish soldier is in reality a mercenary and not one of the kilted heroes of later years.

However, the history of the Scots as mercenaries does not altogether explain the reason why Scotland swallowed the myth of the Scottish soldier. Their exploits took place many miles away and, while they were a matter for pride, they were only one of many components of the nation's increasingly confused identity during the eighteenth and nineteenth centuries. In any case, many of the soldiers in the Scottish regiments, as in other regiments, were Irish. (In 1838, the strength of the army was 89,000, 40 per cent of whom were Irish and only 12 per cent of whom were Scots.[17]) Following the Act of Union of 1707, they were British soldiers in British regiments with only the Highland regiments wearing kilts, while Lowland formations such as the Royal Scots wore the regulation red tunic and the other appurtenances of British line infantry regiments. It would take a king's visit and a quarrel between two Highland historians to change all that.

The monarch was King George IV and the rivals were Sir David Stewart of Garth and Alasdair Ranaldson, Macdonell of Glengarry. The King's visit to Edinburgh in August 1822 was the first to be made by a British monarch since 1651 when Charles II left the country with his Scottish army to try to win back his throne in return for imposing Presbyterianism on his three kingdoms. The attempt ended in ignominy at Worcester and Charles went into exile. On his restoration to the throne in 1660 he never visited his northern kingdom again, the memory of his last residence there being too painful – the long sermons in Falkland Palace and the endless brow-beating by Covenanting divines. In the intervening 171 years no British monarch had troubled themselves to visit Scotland and perhaps with good reason; in that time the Stuarts made two attempts to retrieve their thrones from the House of Hanover and the Parliament of Scotland was united with that of England in 1707.

By the end of the eighteenth century Scotland was becoming urbanised and with heavy industry taking root in the Forth and Clyde valleys its population was centred mainly in the central belt. The long retreat from the countryside had begun, a process hastened by improving landlords who destroyed the old ties that bound their tenants to the land by removing them and making way for modern agrarian methods in the name of commercial development. All over the country, but especially in the Highlands, people were increasingly moved off land to make way for sheep and cattle; in the first instances they were settled on the coastal fringes but later they were forced to emigrate, mainly to North America. For the rural population this was the end of an old way of life: not having security of tenure they had no voice in the matter and, as Tom Devine puts it, 'the old social order was destroyed for ever'.[18]

It was at this juncture that sentiment got the better of reality. At the very moment that a way of life was disappearing many of the men responsible for the loss began forming themselves into societies to celebrate Highland and Gaelic culture and society. Most of these were bogus, drawing on instant traditions which allowed the membership to dress up in tartan fancy dress, dance reels and strathspeys, drink copious amounts of whisky and make sentimental toasts to the grandeur of dear old Scotia. As social gatherings they were harmless enough but the members took their duties solemnly and became arbiters of taste – the Highland Society of London, whose genesis is discussed in Michael Newton's chapter, quickly assumed predominance in such matters, haughtily rebuking lesser souls for wearing the wrong button with the right tartan or vice versa. Naturally this led to altercations which were fiercely debated, friends fell out over points of precedence and dress as the different groups attempted to codify and reinvent the past. One example will stand for many. Here is a description of the annual ball of the Society of True Highlanders, penned in 1816 by its founder Glengarry, a man of uncertain temper who is best remembered for almost single-handedly manufacturing his own versions of the traditions and lifestyle of a Highland chieftain and for forcing his tenants off the clan lands:

> The guests almost to a man were in the full uniform of their regiments or the Garb of Old Gaul [tartan and kilts], and such a scene of enthusiastic and harmonious enjoyment was not perhaps to be instanced, and quite beyond description; the richer dresses of the ladies were superbly appropriate, and among the Highland costumes some were mounted with the ancient clasps of Siol Chinn in gold and silver, or hereditary buttons bearing the heads of all the Kings and Queens of Scotland. Colonel Stewart of Garth wore large round cairngorm buttons richly set. Others had the globular silver buttons of their ancestry, and the richly-finished pistols, dirks, powder-horns and other paraphernalia of the rich Milesian costume gave an air or magnificence to the whole, far more brilliant than expectation had sanctioned at their first fete.[19]

This is just plain silly but the *Inverness Journal* of the day published it unblushingly along with many other equally ridiculous and fanciful accounts written by Glengarry who was a relentless promoter of a way of life which had no basis in fact. The mention of David Stewart of Garth is interesting for at the time both he and Glengarry were united in their efforts to rewrite Highland history and to celebrate their romanticised versions of the Gaelic way of life. They might have remained on friendly terms, too, but for George IV's visit when the responsibility for organising the 'plaided panorama' which accompanied it fell not to Glengarry's True Highlanders but to Stewart of Garth's rival Celtic Society of Edinburgh. Scotland's capital went tartan-mad during the ten days that George IV graced it and under the direction of the novelist Sir Walter Scott who acted as pageant-master, an invented mythology of Highland customs, replete with clan gatherings and balls, was represented as solid historical fact. The story of the bitter quarrel between the two antiquarians makes sorry reading as they sought to gain the sartorial high ground about matters to do with the belted plaid and the shoulder plaid and the correct way to wear tartan dress.

Stewart of Garth was preferred as the arbiter of Highland taste mainly because he enjoyed Scott's confidence but also because he had just published his *Sketches of the Character, Manner and Present State of the Highlanders of Scotland, with Details of the Military Service of the Highland Regiments*. So successful had it been that three editions were published in quick succession and it laid the foundations on which all other Highland military histories have been created. Most of Stewart of Garth's soldiering had been done in the 42nd Royal Highlanders, better known as the Black Watch. His original intention had been to write his regiment's history, its records having been lost while campaigning in France and Flanders, but as he had to put that history in context the work was extended to include a more general military history of the Highland regiments. The end result was a compelling and largely accurate account.

It was also compassionately written not least because Stewart of Garth believed that the way of life of 'his' beloved Highlanders was under threat from rapacious landowners and that, unless their shameless behaviour was stopped, 'the high-spirited, faithful affectionate Highlanders will become envious, unprincipled, ferocious Irishmen'.[20] While there was a fair degree of paternalism in Stewart of Garth's treatment of the Highlanders, he proved to be an unstinting critic of those landowners and clan chiefs who were clearing their people for financial gain. Amongst the worst of the offenders was Glengarry whom Stewart of Garth castigated for ousting his tenants while masquerading as a kilted and plaided Highland chieftain. In a letter to his friend Sir John Macgregor Murray of Lanrick, written before the book's publication, he complained that while Glengarry was parading his deep feelings for his fellow countrymen he was working against their best interests: of the 1,500 souls who once worked the Glengarry farms only 35 remained in service.[21] 'Who has done more to extirpate the race so far as his power extended?' he asked.

Unfortunately, Murray of Lanrick and others then persuaded Stewart to tone down his criticism of Glengarry and other Highland landowners and pressure was put on the author to restrain his language. It was a mistake, for if the book had appeared with the critical comments Stewart of Garth might been remembered as a serious historian and a writer who was prepared to criticise Highland landlords – no easy thing to do at a time when a weavers' Radical Insurrection had taken place only two years previously and there was widespread fear of a workers' revolt. Instead his name is better known for his association with the absurd pageantry surrounding the King's visit. It was Stewart of Garth who organised the parade of Highlanders which set the seal on the ceremonial, Scott's 'great gathering of the Gael' or 'the tartan confederacy' in which clan chiefs rode or marched in triumph from Holyroodhouse to Edinburgh Castle and, despite his misgivings, it was he who connived in creating the whole Celtic fantasy.

Innocuous in itself – the Duke of Atholl dismissed George IV's jaunt as a fortnight of play-acting – the visit left a hangover from which Scotland never fully recovered. It cemented the kilt as the national dress and created a bogus tartan caricature which became the accepted and increasingly acceptable face of Scotland. The Royal Family became part of the myth and, since George's porcine figure appeared swathed in tartan, successive kings and queens and their offspring have lost no opportunity to don the kilt when in Scotland. For a country whose identity was increasingly bound up with its English neighbour and a time of encroaching anglicisation of Scottish life, tartan kilts and an imagined Highland past became a means of satisfying a deep emotional need. And in no other part of Scottish life did this put down deeper roots than in the army. Following the Cardwell/Childers reforms which created infantry regiments with territorial affiliations in 1881 even the Lowland regiments were sporting tartan trews and Highland doublets and their officers carried basket-hilted claymores, a transformation which bemused military historians: 'They lacked only the kilt and feather bonnet to resemble the sort of figure whose ancestors their ancestors had despised, feared and slaughtered but who, by 1881, had come to personify Scotland.'[22]

Stewart died a disappointed man. Attacked unceasingly by Glengarry he resumed his military career and died of fever in St Lucia in 1829 while serving as the colony's governor-general. Glengarry predeceased him by a year and with him died the Society of True Highlanders, but he achieved a curious immortality. His portrait was painted by Henry Raeburn and bedecked in tartan it became one of Scotland's great Victorian icons, providing an image which was eagerly taken up by the manufacturers of whisky, shortbread and other knickknacks. For them and their products it said 'Scotland' in a way that few other symbols could; had not Raeburn executed the portrait it would have been difficult to provide a substitute. The same thing can be said of the Scottish soldier: in his kilt and sporran, his feathered bonnet and his white spats he is a colourful yet utterly respectable figure; marching in serried ranks behind the pipes and drums he is as familiarly Caledonian as the bonnie banks of Loch Lomond or the heather-covered Road to the Isles.

And still it continues. In March 2006, as a result of further defence cuts, Scotland's remaining infantry regiments lost their separate identities when they were amalgamated to form a new 'large' regiment called the Royal Regiment of Scotland with five Regular and two Territorial battalions. Although some of the old regimental titles remained in existence in the five regular battalions, it was to all intents and purposes a new formation. Only one thing endured. All the officers and soldiers wore the kilt, whether they were Highlanders or Lowlanders, and the tartan chosen was Government Number 1A as formerly worn by the Argyll and Sutherland Highlanders. One of the reasons why the Council of Colonels representing the regiments settled on the kilt for formal dress wear was that it was 'a recognisable brand'.[23] As John Prebble put it so witheringly in his summary of the legacy left by Glengarry and Stewart of Garth: 'No other nation has cherished so absurd an image, and none perhaps would accept it while knowing it to be a lie.'[24]

And yet, Prebble's notion of a deceit being imposed on the nation is not the whole story. Long after recruiting levels declined in the traditional clan areas in the later years of the nineteenth century the Scottish Highland regiments continued to embrace tartan and complex dress uniforms to proclaim their identity. In so doing they helped to produce a potent, lasting and complex iconography based as much on authentic historical antecedents as on their own interpretation of what constituted authentic Highland dress.

Notes

1 *Myleene's Musical Tour*.
2 Andy Stewart, 'A Scottish Soldier' (EMI Records, 1961).
3 Marr, *The Battle for Scotland*, p. 116.
4 Royle, *Flowers of the Forest*, pp. 284–6.
5 Chalmers, *A Saga of Scotland*, p. 5.
6 *The Scotsman*, 12 August 1914, p. 6.
7 Keegan, *Six Armies in Normandy*, p. 168.
8 James, *Crimea 1854–1856*.
9 Churchill, *A History of the English Speaking Peoples*, vol. 3, p. 112.
10 Pitt, *The Speeches*, pp. 71–6.
11 Henderson, *Highland Soldier*, p. 5.
12 Ibid., p. 6.
13 MacKerlie, *An Account*, p. 12.
14 Pitt in 1766, cited in Sinclair, *An Account*, p. 3.
15 Anon., 'Song to the Laird of Erracht to the tune of On Falling Asleep by John MacCodrum', in Maclean, *Indomitable Colonel*, p. 118. The Gaelic original is 'Òran do Fhear an Earrachd', in William J. Watson, *Bàrdachd Ghàidhlig* (Stirling: A. Learmonth, 1959), pp. 40–5.
16 Monro, *His Expedition*, p. 203.
17 MacKerlie, *An Account*, p. 36.
18 Devine, *The Scottish Nation*, p. 178.
19 Account of True Highlanders' Ball in the *Inverness Journal*, in Prebble, *The King's Jaunt*, p. 115.
20 David Stewart of Garth, 'Concluding reflections', in *Sketches of the Character, Manner and Present State of the Highlanders of Scotland*, vol. II, pp. 440–5.
21 Prebble, *The King's Jaunt*, pp. 35–43.
22 Wood, *The Scottish Soldier*, p. 76.
23 'Soldiers are dressed to kilt', *DE&S News*, 2 (May 2007), pp. 2–3.
24 Prebble, *The King's Jaunt*, p. 364.

4

PAYING FOR THE PLAID: SCOTTISH GAELIC IDENTITY POLITICS IN NINETEENTH-CENTURY NORTH AMERICA

Michael Newton

ᘒ

The use of tartan to symbolise a pan-Scottish identity rooted in antiquity – referred to as 'tartanism' in North America – was neither inevitable nor obvious to early immigrants. In fact, during the peak of eighteenth-century migration of Scottish Highlanders[1] to North America (1770–6) civilian males were banned from wearing tartan or kilts, even if the law was not well enforced. Previous scholarship about the mythologisation of tartan has concentrated on how the élite tailored this iconography for their own benefit and how heritage and tourist industries have subsequently retrenched and exploited it. The reactions of Gaelic communities to this cultural asset stripping and its effects on them have not been adequately explored, especially in North America.

Tartanism's rise coincided with Gaeldom's unparalleled crises of survival in the nineteenth century. Gaels who escaped repressive conditions in Scotland were confronted by similar prejudices in North America.[2] Whatever else it may be from other perspectives, tartanism is a phenomenon which reflects Gaeldom's subordinate status in the British polity and corresponding inability to maintain its own cultural resources or participate equitably in its own self-representation. This chapter discusses aspects of resistance to and participation in the ascendancy of tartanism as a normative form of Scottish identity and its corresponding effects on Gaelic identity in nineteenth-century North America, especially regarding language.

TARTAN AS IMMIGRANT CLOTHING

In 1736, the Trustees for the Colony of Georgia established the first planned settlement of Highlanders in North America to act as a buffer between British and Spanish settlements. The Trustees provided military gear and sent an order to Inverness for '300 yards of Tartan [. . .] for short Coats and short Hose & 1200 yards of Tartan [. . .] for Plaids'. General James Oglethorpe went to meet the Highland recruits, arrayed in 'their Plaids, broadswords, targets and firearms', after their arrival. Oglethorpe himself wore a plaid, knowing they expected this of their leader.[3] The next planned settlement was to New York Province in 1738. Lauchlin Campbell of Leorin, an Islay laird, was promised several thousand acres near Wood Creek (between Albany and Crown Point) for himself and several hundred Highlanders. According to his son, this location was chosen because the local Native Americans, 'who were taken with his Highland dress', had welcomed him.[4] From their first engagement in the Seven Years War (1756–63) to the end of the American Revolutionary War in 1783, tens of thousands of Highland soldiers fought in British regiments in North America wearing the fèileadh mór.[5] Their clothing made an impression on people in America: some Native Americans adapted items of Highland clothing (such as tartan, sporran and glengarry bonnet) for their own use.[6]

Highlanders who had settled in the Mohawk Valley of New York resettled in Glengarry, Ontario, after the American Revolution and their relations joined them into the early 1800s. Patrick Campbell wrote during his visit to New Johnstone (now Cornwall, Ontario) in 1792 that he 'saw between fifty and sixty Scotchmen [. . .] Some were dressed in their Highland plaids and bonnets.'[7] Nineteenth-century Gaelic poet Alasdair Mac Eòghain of Glengarry was never seen without his red tartan kilt.[8] Iain Mùilleir, driven by the Sutherland Clearances to Pictou Country, Nova Scotia, lived to the age of 107 and was nicknamed Bodach an Fhèilidh ('Old Man of the Kilt') because he always wore a kilt.[9] Alasdair Bàn MacDhomhnaill, who drowned in 1833 at the age of nineteen soon after arriving in Cape Breton, is depicted wearing a kilt in his elegy.[10] A few immigrants wove their own tartans as late as the third quarter of the nineteenth century. Three plaids were amongst the local textiles on display at the Antigonish Fall Fair in 1863, and a tartan woven in Inverness County, Cape Breton, in the 1870s was worn as a kilt.[11] Nevertheless, it was unusual for early Highland immigrants or their descendants to continue wearing tartan or the kilt in their daily lives by the second half of the nineteenth century. Those who did were noted because of their unusual devotion to it.[12]

EMERGENCE AND MIGRATION OF TARTANISM

What remained of formal, secular, native Gaelic institutions in Scotland after a century and a half of the assimilationist policies of the centralising British state were dismantled and replaced after the 1745–6 Jacobite Rising. Thereafter, anglocentric institutions increasingly set the standards for, and monopolised the means of, social and material advancement and success. In a state of subservience, its internal reference points violated and compromised, Gaeldom derived an increasing amount of validation from anglophone society according to the degree to which Highlanders complied with the roles and stereotypes of the loyal soldier and the noble savage. Highlanders came to be valued primarily as military assets, as most lacked English or training suitable for urban industries. Highland élites promoted the image of the kilted warrior for their own benefit, particularly the financial and political dividends of military recruitment.[13] The conspicuous part played by so many tartan-clad Gaels in British military enterprises, especially in North America, transformed their image from Jacobite rebels to staunch defenders of the Crown.[14] Pre-existing military strains within Gaelic tradition itself were sublimated into the British imperial mission.[15]

While anglophones held other aspects of contemporary Highland life in contempt, the tartan and kilt were virtually the only stable 'cultural capital' that Gaels had to bank on in the nineteenth century. Notwithstanding the alteration and commodification of these items, the need for external approval was too great to discard them altogether, especially for Gaels within the orbit of the élite or anglophone communities. Debates over Macpherson's *Ossian* offer significant parallels:

> During the nineteenth century, it is difficult to find any native Gaels who were also Gaelic-speakers and who were prepared to reject outright the authenticity of *Ossian* as published [. . .] *Ossian* became a literary and ethnological yardstick, a mark of the True Gael, which was not to be surrendered easily. In the eyes of their Gaelic admirers, the poems of *Ossian* – particularly in their Gaelic guises – imparted a new grandeur and dignity to the Highlands and to Gaelic culture.[16]

It was exactly the collapse of the credibility of *Ossian* that motivated the Scottish élite to plunder Gaeldom again in search of an ennobling

past: 'the cultural capital that had been threatened by the insubstantiality of Macpherson's Ossianic discoveries had to be redeemed and
reinvested in a more secure symbolic structure'.[17] Tartan was a
convenient substitute, as it was independent of linguistic concerns
and offered colour and mystique without representing explicit threat
to the social or political order. Protest against the Lowland co-opting
of Highland dress, however, began in the immediate aftermath of the
spectacle created for King George IV in 1822:

> They neither speak the language, nor know how to put on correctly
> the garb of the 'Gael'; and yet, without possessing the blood or the
> manly frame of that interesting race, or any other ostensible cause
> whatever, they barefacedly masked themselves in the Highland garb
> [. . .] I never saw so much tartan before, in my life, with so little
> Highland material.[18]

The author of this complaint, Alasdair Macdonell of Glengarry,
whose contradictory motivations Trevor Royle has outlined, understood that the event signalled a threat to the monopoly that the
Highland élite enjoyed over the military clout invested in the symbol
of the tartan.

Civil societies also advanced tartanism. The Gaelic Society of
London was founded in 1778 to preserve 'the Martial Spirit, Language, Dress, Music and Antiquities of the Ancient Caledonians'.[19]
The society established annual competitions at the Falkirk Tryst in
1781 for the best bagpipe performance and original Gaelic poetry.[20]
Nineteen of the twenty-five original members were Gaelic speakers;
meetings were held in Gaelic. In 1782, soldiers returning from the
American Revolution, mostly Lowlanders who did not speak Gaelic,
flooded the society's membership. Gaelic was put aside, the society's
name changed to 'the Highland Society of London' and, after 1783,
the Falkirk Tryst competitions stopped patronage of Gaelic poetry.
After some founding members failed to re-establish the use of Gaelic,
they formed an alternative organisation.[21] The society's agenda
turned to tartan. In 1782, members promoted a Parliamentary bill
to repeal the Disarming Act.[22] An effort to collect samples of tartan
from old Highland families was initiated in 1815, resulting in about
forty patches by 1820.[23]

Meantime, the Highland Society of Scotland was established in
Edinburgh in 1784 stating goals similar to that of the original Gaelic
Society of London, except that Improvement, particularly agricultural,

was listed as its highest priority. The weakness of its commitment to Gaelic was apparent as early as 1804, and abandoned by the 1840s.[24] The agenda of these organisations and the image of the Highlander which they promoted were subordinate to the objectives of the British Empire, rather than concerned with Gaelic culture itself on its own terms. The physical prowess, romantic aura and military potential of Highlanders were emphasised to the exclusion of their intellectual, artistic and political achievements and potential. The will to intervene on behalf of Highland communities in practical matters was similarly undermined.[25]

The Gaelic Society of Inverness was founded in 1871, the first organisation to make Gaelic language and literature the focus of its remit and activities. Its inaugural proceedings confirm that all of the work of 'Highland' societies over the previous century had done little to reverse the stigmas which plagued Gaeldom in its own homeland:

> Highland interests and ideas have not had adequate expression in previously existing organisations [. . .] between the indignation and the ridicule thus brought to play upon the sentiments of our people, it is no wonder that some of them shrank from declaring and showing that either Celtic sentiment or patriotic fervour had any existence in their bosoms.[26]

In comparison to the athletic and social associations, however, it had few imitators and the small number of Gaelic scholars had little impact on popular discourse. Modern Highland Games display a similar set of shortcomings. Although Highland communities had long held local social gatherings and athletic competitions, these were co-opted and reinvented by the élite in the late eighteenth and early nineteenth centuries.[27] The first Highland Games was held in 1818 in St Fillans, Perthshire, when the area was still strongly Gaelic-speaking. About a dozen competitions appear in the 1822 programme; one was for the best new Gaelic song and another for the best Gaelic singer. All competitors wore Highland garb. Local gentry presided over the event and inexorably shifted the emphasis away from Gaelic. Others followed their precedent. In the second half of the nineteenth century, Highland Games were successfully established in North America, but confusion about how to judge the popular 'best-dressed Highlander' competition led the North American United Caledonian Association to formulate explicit rules in 1884, rules more exacting than even those for dancing and bagpiping competitions.[28]

Competitions and events which featured Gaelic were sporadic, short-lived and of lower priority than the exhibition of tartanism and athleticism.

North Americans were keen on imaginative literature featuring Highlanders, like Macpherson's *Ossian* (1760) and Walter Scott's *Waverley* (1814). Indeed, the early and pervasive influence of such fiction often makes it difficult to separate folklore from 'fakelore'.[29] Most immigrants and their organisations regarded practices in Scotland to be the touchstone of 'authenticity' even after the wellsprings had been transmogrified by the aesthetics and 'improvements' of urban Lowlanders. Continuing connections between Scotland and North America, especially those involving the élite or formal organisations, encouraged innovations reinforcing the paradigm of tartanism to be imported into New World celebrations of Highland (or Scottish) identity with little dissension.[30] Queen Victoria's embrace of aspects of Highland life, including tartan, furthered their clout and appeal to the mainstream across the British Empire.[31]

NEGOTIATING IDENTITY

Perceptions of immigrant Highland communities, and internal discussions about the role and significance of tartan, cannot be determined accurately without analysing Gaelic texts. Such sources – song-poems, articles in periodicals, oral narratives transmitted in céilidhs, and so on – must be handled judiciously. When Highland garb appears, one must take into consideration whether an actual event is being described, or a conventional literary conceit with a long poetic lineage is being reiterated. Literary tradition might prescribe a rhetorical flourish containing an allusion to Highland clothing that is in fact missing. Adherence to or divergence from literary conventions suggests other cultural continuities or departures. Luchd nam breacan ('plaided-people'), for example, was a kenning for Highlanders in the Gaelic song-poetry of the seventeenth and eighteenth centuries, most of which celebrates involvement in national and international conflicts. Such songs have been sung as long as Gaelic has been spoken in immigrant communities. Many new songs in North America, especially those arguing for group solidarity, were based on the airs and choruses of older, especially Jacobite, songs. Oral literature sustained the communal memory of the kilted warrior even as such clothing ceased to be worn in daily life, while one of the first poetic statements in North America is one whose author, place and time are uncertain. 'Dèan Cadalan Sàmhach' was probably composed by a female native of Argyll as a lullaby to her daughter while her husband fought in the Seven Years War.[32] It contrasts the elegant kilt and hose of the Highlands with the homely hats, cloaks and trousers of colonial America. Gaelic literary tradition thus already contained elements that could be highlighted and creatively pressed into the service of tartanism, which was especially likely in military contexts.[33]

Some Gaelic advocates and scholars in Scotland were unabashed tartanophiles. John Francis Campbell of Islay and Alexander Carmichael, native Gaels and arguably the most important folklorists working in the nineteenth-century Highlands, were dedicated kilt-wearers.[34] The problem, some argued, was that tartan had become disassociated from Gaelic society. Rev. Archibald Farquharson, Gaelic activist and minister of Tiree, argued in the pamphlet *Address to Highlanders* (1868), which was quoted in British and American newspapers,

> There are many Highland proprietors going about through the country, dressed in the Highland garb, who cannot speak one sentence properly in Gaelic. Were I to meet any one such, I think I would be disposed to give him the following salutation: 'I am glad, sir, to see you in that dress, but how dare you wear that kilt without speaking the Gaelic?'[35]

As long as the Gaelic language itself seemed resilient, North American Gaels on the other hand did not necessarily perceive a conflict between their allegiance to it and the wearing of tartan and kilts. Gaelic organisations established in North America deferred to standards and precedents set in Scotland and to the cultural and class interests and biases of their leaders. The Highland Society of Canada, for example, was established in St Raphael's, Glengarry County, Ontario, in 1818 after a commission to form a Canadian branch of the Gaelic Society of London was obtained from the Duke of York; Simon MacGillivray, a vice-president of the London society, presided over the inaugural meeting.[36] As in Scotland, Highland and Gaelic societies with few exceptions offered little tangible or enduring support for Gaelic in the nineteenth century and were generally unwilling or unable to convince state institutions to protect it.[37] Nevertheless, Gaelic odes to associations in Glengarry, Ontario (1870), Toronto (no later than 1872), Montreal (1883) and Antigonish (1899) all stress

the importance of the language and its intergenerational transmission.[38] Individuals were encouraged to foster their mother tongue
informally in the home, in religious practices and at community
gatherings.[39] This means of survival became increasingly ineffective
as formal institutions, endowed with greater prestige, reach and
economic leverage, came to assert themselves in the daily life of
immigrant communities and had a larger impact on their relations
with the outside world and their perceptions of themselves and their
ancestral culture.

While some Gaels were expressing their concerns about Gaelic's
condition, others took comfort in the cachet afforded by tartan and
the military tradition. Gilleasbuig MacKillop of Megantic, official
poet of the Celtic Society of Montreal in the late nineteenth century,
won a competition sponsored by the Canadian Highland Society in
1859 for a Gaelic poem praising the military victories of the Highland
Brigade by playing up the clichés prescribed by tartanism. An article in
the Gaelic periodical *Mac-Talla* based in Cape Breton argued in 1894
that since Gaels were beginning to value their language and their
culture, they should also reconsider the kilt.[40] The author[41] sum-
marises the kilt's history and quotes Gaelic songs composed by
popular poet Donnchadh Bàn Macintyre, one lamenting its proscription and another celebrating the repeal of the proscription. The
reunion was difficult to arrange: tartan was no longer an organic
element in immigrant life and the preponderance of Gaelic speakers in
the lower rungs of the economic ladder could scarce afford tartan
commodities.[42] By the late nineteenth century many Gaelic advocates
came to see tartanism as competing for scarce resources or irrelevant
altogether in the struggle to sustain Gaelic culture and identity.[43]
Conflicts over competing visions of Highland identity – the Gaelic
language and oral tradition on the one hand, and the wearing of tartan
and kilts at ritual events on the other – fractured immigrant social
organisations, as happened to the Gaelic Society of London in 1782.
This pattern was repeated as associations were hijacked, or threatened, by members promoting a tartanist vision at the expense of
Gaelic.

The Scottish Celtic Society of New York exemplifies these tensions.
It was the first organisation in North America to hold a Mòd (Gaelic
song competition) in 1893, only a year after they were begun by An
Comunn Gàidhealach in Scotland. The next year, when the second
annual competition should have been held, an alternative organisation
was formed, Comunn Gàidhlig New York (Scottish Gaelic Society of

New York).[44] A correspondent commented on the divisions and warned that tokenism threatened the survival of more important aspects of Highland culture:

> Bu mhithich do na Gàidheil anns gach cearn do'n t-saoghal a bhith a' toirt fainear gur h-i 'Ghàidhlig an ite as airde tha 'nam boineid [. . .] Is bòidheach an sealladh Gàidheal sgeadaichte an éideadh a thìr, ach as eugmhais na Gàidhlig cha bhi ann an cosg bhreacan is bhiodagan ach adhbhar mhagaidh. Ma dhìobras sinn ar gràdh do'n Ghàidhlig, cha bhi fada 'na dhéidh sin gus am faic sinn deireadh eachdraidh ar sluaigh [. . .] Tha Comunn Gàidhealach New York a' coinneachadh uair 's a' mhios, ach tha móran Ghall 'nam measg, agus mur dèan sibh luaidh air, tha barrachd foghluim anns na casan aig móran diubh na tha 'nan cinn. Tha Gàidheil thuigseach a tha eudmhor a thaobh math a' Chomuinn a' bruidhinn air Comunn ùr Gàidhlig a chur air chois a chumas suas cànain, ceòl, agus cleach-daidhean ar sinnsir anns an dòigh as cubhaidh do Ghàidheil.[45]

('It is high time for Gaels in every part of the world to recognise that the Gaelic language is the tallest feather in their bonnets [. . .] A Highlander arrayed in the garb of his country is a gorgeous sight, but without Gaelic wearing kilts and dirks makes him a laughing stock. If we abandon our love for Gaelic, it will not take long before we see the end of the history of our people [. . .] The New York Highland Society meets once a month, but there are many non-Gaels amongst them, and if you don't mention it, there is more training in many of their legs than there is in their heads. The knowledgeable Gaels who are zealous about the well-being of the Society are discussing establishing a new Gaelic Society that will sustain our ancestor's language, music, and traditions in a way which is most befitting to the Gaels.')

Despite many achievements – Gaelic classes, Gaelic sermons, public platforms for Gaelic songs, and so on – they too succumbed to tartanism. In 1908, the society's annual Highland Games included competitions for the best dressed Highlander and the bagpipe championship of the Eastern States, whose award was named after Walter Scott. In that same year Harry Lauder, the stage-Highlander (whose various personae including a stage-Irishman are discussed in Paul Maloney's chapter) was imported as the feature attraction of their annual concert and made an honorary member of the society.[46] His popularity amongst native Highlanders may seem incongruous now, but these humorous exaggerations defused the potential threat of ethnic difference at a time when immigration into the United States provoked violent 'nativist' reactions. Parodies of other ethnic groups striving to attain 'whiteness' in the nineteenth century were popular on the stage for similar reasons. The ability to both don and remove a gaudy ethnic caricature, and to parody it self-consciously, highlights the ability of a group to assimilate to other norms and distance itself from its past. The society's Highland Games and its attendant tartan-ism began as secondary activities meant to support their primary aim of sustaining Gaelic language and culture. The tartan tail, however, ended up wagging the Gaelic dog.

Tartan became a successfully marketed product in North America in the nineteenth century, reinforcing the idea of a pan-Scottish identity. An article printed soon after the creation of Toronto's kilted regiment in 1891 illustrates how regiments and persons of prestige boosted it as a cultural commodity. Associations with the Highlands remained, but the real profit went to urban commercial enterprise:

> Now that clan tartans are again in high favor, there is among those familiar with this class of goods, much discussion about everything pertaining to the unique fabric; and many stories relating to Highlanders, visits to the Highlands, costumes, and kilted regi-ments and their traditions are listened to with interest, even by those whose associations lie far away from the rugged hills and glens which are the home of the noblest peasantry in the world [. . .] These tartans can only be procured in the finest colors and textures from first class establishments and ladies would do well to go only to those.[47]

CASE STUDY: NOVA SCOTIA

By the mid-nineteenth century the most robust Gaelic communities in North America were in Nova Scotia, in Colchester, Pictou, Anti-gonish and Guysborough Counties and on Cape Breton island.[48] Antigonish County is of interest for two reasons: first, it was some-thing of a buffer zone between Nova Scotia's Gaelic communities in the east and anglophone communities in the west; second, it had three organs through which ongoing discourse about Gaelic identity was articulated and negotiated in Nova Scotia, namely, the Anti-gonish Highland Society, the Antigonish Highland Games and the *Casket* newspaper.

Highland garb appears in early emigrant poetry but is used to varying rhetorical ends. One of the most celebrated settler-poets in Nova Scotia was Iain mac Ailein MacGilleathain ('John Maclean', 1787–1848), who in Scotland held the honorary title 'Bard Thigh-earna Chola' ('poet to MacLean of Coll'). Iain, who was literate in both Gaelic and English and lived in relatively comfortable circumstances in Tiree, decided to emigrate to Nova Scotia in 1819, despite the protests of his kinsmen and patron. His first and best-known poem, 'A' Choille Ghruamach', documents his difficulties clearing the virgin forest, although his discouragement was short-lived. MacGilleathain implies the wearing of tartan at a social event held in Merigomish in 1826 to which only Gaelic speakers were invited,[49] but whether this is realism or literary convention has not yet been determined. A poem he composed in support of a political candidate opens with the formulaic refrain 'Deoch-slàinte luchd nam breacanan' ('A toast to the plaided-people') and emboldens the Highlanders to vote in a body against antagonists by enumerating Gaelic virtues and military victories.[50] MacGilleathain's extensive deployment of tartanist rhetoric is indicative of his social class, his connections with the élite and his endorsement of British imperialism.

A portrait (c. 1811) was made of Iain MacGilleBhràth (c. 1792–1862) in Highland garb while he was piper and poet to MacDonald of Glenaladale in Scotland. He emigrated in 1818 and settled in Antigonish County. He composed a poem resounding with tartanistic motifs, influenced by MacGilleathain's 'Deoch-slàinte luchd nam breacanan', when his son refused to buy tartan clothing (no later than 1851). This suggests that rifts were emerging between emigrants and their Canadian-born children in their self-images and sources of cultural validation and may perhaps represent a North American version of the value-laden 'tartan' portraits and imagery of the mid-eighteenth century discussed by Cheape, Pittock and Brown elsewhere in this volume. Iain Sealgair MacDonald, a native of Lochaber, arrived in Cape Breton in 1834 to face an unusually harsh winter. He composed a song comparing America unfavourably with the Highlands, recalling MacDonald kinsmen arrayed in kilts. His poorer cousin, Ailean 'the Ridge' MacDonald, in Cape Breton since 1816, responded to each of his grievances, reminding him that the splendour of tartan was irrelevant to their overall well-being.[51]

Despite constituting a majority of Antigonish County,[52] Gaels were conscious of their culture's fragility and constituted the Antigonish Highland Society in 1861. Its highest priority was 'preserving the martial spirit, language, dress, music, games, and antiquities of the Caledonians'; membership was restricted to Highlanders, their descendants or husbands of Highland women. Members must have been allured by tartanism: they resolved on 19 September 1862 to begin holding Highland Games and 'that every member provide for himself a plaid and bonnet to be worn as the uniform of the society'. After a motion that 42nd Regiment tartan be worn, it was decided that members could wear the tartan of their choice. Amongst those members inducted at this meeting was Gilleasbuig MacGilleBhràth, son of the Piper Iain. The Antigonish Highland Games adopted the standard Games formulae (a delegation sent in 1864 to the Caledonian Gathering at Charlottetown ensured uniformity). Members of the 78th Regiment, stationed in Halifax, visited the Games and conferred validation. The first and apparently only patronage for Gaelic literature was in 1871, when a competition for original poetry was awarded to two local poets. The one surviving poem describes the building of St Ninian's Cathedral and contains no hint of tartanism.[53] A few local Gaelic poets endorsed and responded to the spectacle of the Games with tartanistic verse. An oral variant of 'Gillean glùn-gheal nam breacan' ('White-kneed lads of the plaids', an epithet implying high social status, that is, not a manual labourer) appeared in the *Casket* the day before the decision to hold the Games in 1862. Uilleam Mac a' Phearsain of Giant's Lake was so inspired by the 1871 Games that he composed a lengthy song employing the tropes of tartanism. Surviving nineteenth-century photographs display local worthies in baroque tartan outfits. Further Gaelic songs survive in Nova Scotia about clothing, but they rarely mention tartan: more common is the complaint that the youth, especially girls, are importing alien fashions and affecting the trends of the urban, anglophone world, distinguishing themselves from the rest of their community who could not afford such items.[54]

At the same time that the Games fortified tartanism, Gaelic was increasingly endangered. Without a prestige culture to validate it or an institutional framework to sustain it, economic and demographic trends delivered a lethal blow:

> The generation which came of age in the years between 1880 and 1910 was the first to leave home in large numbers, and those who came back bore the scars of the negative stigmatization of their language and culture [. . .] By the outbreak of World War II, socialization of children in Gaelic had effectively ceased.[55]

Members of the Antigonish Highland Society and the local community rallied forces intermittently. An ode to the Antigonish Highland
Society composed by Gaelic scholar Rev. Alexander Maclean Sinclair,
a native of Antigonish Co., was printed in the *Casket* in 1899,[56]
devoting itself to praising the language and culture and abstaining
from tartanism. It is inclusive of the Irish and the embrace of folk
beliefs (such as fairies and the Fian, the legendary warrior-band led by
Fionn mac Cumhaill) generally condemned by ministers. The poem
validates Gaelic culture not through tartanism but the science of
philology, especially as expounded by German scholars. Entreaties
were made about Gaelic to the provincial government, Highland
societies and local newspapers. The Antigonish Highland Society
made several attempts to galvanise St Francis Xavier University in
Antigonish into supporting Gaelic; despite being established in 1853
by local Gaelic speakers, it taught English, Classics and French but
only started offering occasional Gaelic classes in 1891.[57]

Tartanism was adopted as a marketing tool for promoting tourism
in Nova Scotia from the late 1930s onwards, but such appeals to
stereotypes further obscured the relationships between distinct linguistic communities and cultural traditions. In the opening speech of
the 100th anniversary of the Antigonish Highland Games in 1963,
Nova Scotia's Lieutenant Governor reiterated the clichés of tartanism
which overshadow the Gaelic legacy of the original Highland immigrants:[58] 'These Games are symbols of Nova Scotia's Scottish
heritage. Along with other characteristics including romanticism, love
of learning, sense of humour, and patriotism, the love of combat,
whether physical or mental, is inherent to the Scot.'[59] Meantime,
Gaelic survived in Cape Breton settlements a generation or two after
its extinction as a community language on the Nova Scotian mainland
and, to a degree, to the present day. Cape Breton Gaelic poetry seldom
indulges in tartanism, even in contexts where we would expect it:
songs commemorating regiments in the Crimean War, the Boer War
and the two World Wars, and elegies to soldiers. Poems celebrating
events and organisations focus on activities and cultural content
relevant to Gaels: songs, fiddle and bagpipe music, dancing and
a self-conscious awareness of the importance and vulnerable state
of the Gaelic language. Cape Breton poets were generally more
interested in representing their local communities in a realistic manner
than in pandering to tartanistic stereotypes expected by an external
audience.[60]

CONCLUSIONS

The anglocentric hegemony of the nineteenth century did not promote the ideals of multiculturalism as understood today: linguistic
and cultural difference was actively opposed. Tartanism offered a
symbolic compensation for the attrition of language and culture, a
badge of identity into which energies could be safely sublimated.
Unlike other immigrant communities in North America for whom
language is a conspicuous feature of identity, tartan has almost
totally eclipsed the role of Gaelic in the popular representation of
Highland heritage and become a broader symbol of Scottishness or
Celticity.[61]
    There was nothing inherently incompatible between these two
salient markers of Highland identity, nor could Gaels have predicted
that tartan would be commandeered by agents of Highlandism and
British militarism who, despite offering one form of external validation, were indifferent, if not hostile, to their language and culture.
'Tartanism exploited Gaelic as one of its raw materials. It did not
sustain it.'[62] The kilted soldier was valorised when he defended and
advanced the interests of the British Empire, but as a Gaelic-speaker
true to his native culture and language, he was a figure of contempt
and/or pity, an alien to the standards of polite anglophone society.
Contemporary authors such as the American tourist Frederic Cozzens
admitted as much in his 1859 travelogue of Nova Scotia:

> If I had formed some romantic ideas concerning the new and strange
> people we found on the road we were now travelling, the High-
> landmen, the Rob Roys and Vich Ian Vohrs of Nova Scotia, those
> ideas were soon dissipated. It is true here were the Celts in their wild
> settlements, but without bagpipes or pistols, sporrans or philabegs
> [. . .] I have a reasonable amount of respect for a Highlandman in
> full costume; but for a carrot-headed, freckled, high-cheeked ani-
> mal, in a round hat and breeches, that cannot utter a word of
> English, I have no sympathy.[63]

Between 1746 and the late nineteenth century, anglophone society
increasingly monopolised the means of production and signification of
tartan to serve its own purposes. Some Gaels happily played up to
tartanistic expectations; others dismissed tartan as irrelevant to their
culture and identity; still others condemned it as an unwelcome
distraction that would ultimately undermine fundamental differences

between Highlands and Lowlands. Whether Gaels collaborated or resisted, they were incapable of controlling the processes that ultimately divested them of proprietorship of their cultural assets. The historical development of Highland clothing, the meaning and associations of tartan and kilt in Gaelic tradition and literature, and the very existence of the Gaelic community became increasingly irrelevant as a new symbolic system evolved around and enveloped tartan in anglophone society. These phenomena mirror those of other marginalised peoples whose cultures have been harvested for profit, with or without the aid of native brokers.[64]

People of Highland descent furthest removed from the living Gaelic community – those unable to participate in the primary content of Gaelic culture – are most likely to resort to this iconography today. Tartanism seems to play an important role in Nova Scotia not among Gaelic speakers but among those English monolinguals with Highland ancestry. For them, the trappings of tartanism enable them to feel that they have not been cut off from their heritage.[65]

Although the tartan and kilt were derived from genuine Highland folk culture, many Gaels became alienated from them to the point of assuming them to be artificially imposed. The idea that the Gaelic community is poorly represented in Nova Scotia, if represented at all, may seem counter-intuitive in a province where tartanistic imagery has been promoted intensively in the interests of tourism. It may seem similarly surprising that some Gaels feel that their identity is as obscured as that of other minorities in the province by the parade of kilts and tartans. Yet, when an African-Canadian film-maker complained in 1994 that 'Scottish' history upstages the histories of other peoples in Nova Scotia, a leader in the Gaelic community responded:

> I asked her what history she was referring to. Immediately I sensed my question was not politically correct as a puzzled Hamilton [the film-maker] implied that Scottish history is what we see around us. Her apparent version being the tourism variety promoted by the provincial government [. . .] I tried, unsuccessfully, to explain that the history she was referring to is one that she is uninformed on, and that she was using stereotypes of those descended from the Gaels in the same way they are used in defining the black community. I said there was a linguistic minority within the 'Scottish' community suffering from a similar lack of accurate institutional media repre-

sentation as are those in the African-Canadian community. My assertion, however, was dismissed simply because no one had a clue as to what I was talking about. And, I guess, that was my point to begin with.[66]

It was dissatisfaction with the visual representations of Gaelic culture in Nova Scotia that led to the design of a new official image, unveiled by the newly created Office of Gaelic Affairs in May 2008. The image features a stylised salmon whose body forms the letter 'G' and whose movement sends ripples through the current: there is no allusion to tartans or kilts.[67]

Organised Scottishness in Canada has been argued to be a means 'to empower immigrant communities, to reinforce class power, or to exert cultural influence, but [it] could also have the ability to marginalize and exclude'.[68] This chapter argues that Gaels were amongst those marginalised by the tartanism promoted by such organisations. It offered little for the language or culture of the people from whom tartan was appropriated; it was in fact representative of the anglocentric hegemony that sought to delegitimise and assimilate them.

ACKNOWLEDGEMENTS

Thanks to the Angus L. Macdonald Library of St Francis Xavier University for access to sources; to Danny Gillis for the loan of Antigonish Highland Society records; to Electric Scotland for past issues of the *Scottish Canadian*; to James Cameron for his essay on St Francis Xavier University; to Ian Brown, Hugh Cheape, Jonathan Dembling and Sister Margaret MacDonell for comments on earlier drafts of this chapter.

Notes

1 To the late nineteenth century Gaels understood 'Gaelic' and 'Highland', and ethnonyms 'Gael' and 'Highlander', as synonymous. In Gaelic to this day Gàidheal is both 'Gael' and 'Highlander' and the adjective Gàidhealach is 'Gaelic' and 'Highland'. See Newton, *Warriors of the Word*, pp. 52–4.

2 Dembling, 'Joe Jimmy Alec visits the Mod', pp. 40–1; Newton, *We're Indians Sure Enough*, pp. 223, 241–3; Kennedy, *Gaelic Nova Scotia*, pp. 30–9.

3 Parker, *Scottish Highlanders in Colonial Georgia*, pp. 39, 43, 54, 64.

4 McGeachy, 'Captain Lauchlin Campbell and Early Argyllshire Emigration to New York', p. 25.

5 Newton, *We're Indians Sure Enough*, pp. 104, 107, 108–9.

6 Calloway, *White People, Indians and Highlanders*, pp. 136–8.

7 Campbell, *Travels in North America*, p. 231.

8 McMillan, 'The first settlers in Glengarry', p. 176.

9 Sinclair, *Clàrsach na Coille*, p. 166.

10 Rankin, *As a' Bhràighe / Beyond the Braes*, p. 108.

11 *Casket*, 22 October 1863. Thanks to Jocelyn Gillis of the Antigonish Heritage Museum for this information.

12 Dembling, 'Joe Jimmy Alec visits the Mod', pp. 32–3.

13 MacKillop, *'More Fruitful than the Soil'*.

14 Clyde, *From Rebel to Hero*; Newton, *We're Indians Sure Enough*, pp. 103–62; Newton, 'Jacobite past, Loyalist present'.

15 Newton, 'Jacobite past, Loyalist present'; MacInnes, *Dùthchas nan Gàidheal*, pp. 360–4.

16 Meek, 'The sublime Gael', p. 41.

17 Craig, 'National literature and cultural capital in Scotland and Ireland', p. 48.

18 Cited in Osborne, *The Last of the Chiefs*, pp. 32–3.

19 Black, 'The Gaelic Academy' p. 2; M., 'The Gaelic Society of London', p. 355.

20 MacLeod, *The Songs of Duncan Ban Macintyre*, pp. 512–14.

21 M., 'The Gaelic Society of London', pp. 353–4.

22 Clyde, *From Rebel to Hero*, pp. 132–3.

23 Cheape, *Tartan: The Highland Habit*, p. 48.

24 Black, 'The Gaelic Academy', pp. 2–3.

25 Jarvie, *Highland Games*, pp. 56–8; Kennedy, *Gaelic Nova Scotia*, pp. 163–72, 175–6.

26 'Introduction', Transactions of the Gaelic Society of Inverness 1 (1872), pp. ix–x.

27 Jarvie, *Highland Games*, pp. 5, 10, 35, 58, 65–7, 76.

28 Berthoff , 'Under the kilt', pp. 10–11.

29 Ray, *Highland Heritage*, pp. 30–1, 42–4, 49–52, 187–96; Newton, 'The fiery cross'.

30 MacDonald, 'Putting on the kilt', p. 137; Ray, *Highland Heritage*, pp. 25, 196; Kennedy, *Gaelic Nova Scotia*, pp. 176–9, 183, 208–10, 217, 244; Dembling, 'You play it as you would sing it', pp. 182–3.

31 Cheape, *Tartan. The Highland Habit*, pp. 62–7.

32 Newton, *We're Indians Sure Enough*, pp. 175–8; Newton, 'In their own words', pp. 14–20.

33 See Newton, 'Jacobite past, Loyalist present'.

34 Shaw, 'The collectors'.

35 Quoted in *Scottish-American Journal*, 14 November 1868.

36 McMillan, 'The first settlers in Glengarry', p. 170.
37 Kennedy, *Gaelic Nova Scotia*, pp. 232–4; Newton, ' "Becoming cold-hearted like the Gentiles around them" ', pp. 92–107; Newton, 'Gaelic literature and the diaspora'; Linkletter, 'Bu dual dhà sin', pp. 140–2.
38 I am currently editing these poems and others mentioned but unreferenced.
39 Shaw, 'Brief beginnings', pp. 352–3; Dembling, 'Joe Jimmy Alec visits the Mod', pp. 44–8; Kennedy, *Gaelic Nova Scotia*, pp. 35–8.
40 *Mac-Talla* 3 (8 September 1894).
41 Ian MacKenzie of London, England, using the pen-name 'Cabar Féidh'. See Linkletter, 'Bu dual dhà sin', p. 256.
42 Dembling, 'Joe Jimmy Alec visits the Mod', pp. 32–9, 52–7.
43 Newton, ' "Becoming cold-hearted like the Gentiles around them" ', pp. 109–12; idem 2005b, pp. 18–21.
44 Newton, ' "Becoming cold-hearted like the Gentiles around them" ', pp. 121–2. There are discrepancies in the English and Gaelic names of these societies, probably due to ambiguities noted in note 1.
45 *Mac-Talla* 3 (1 December 1894).
46 *Scottish-American Journal*, 29 July 1908, 10 November 1909.
47 *Scottish Canadian*, 27 November 1891.
48 Kennedy, *Gaelic Nova Scotia*, pp. 21–7.
49 Sinclair, *Clàrsach na Coille*, pp. 134–5.
50 Ibid., pp. 143–5.
51 Macdonell, *The Emigrant Experience*, pp. 80–3, 88–91; Rankin, *As a' Bhràighe*, pp. 29–30, 76–7.
52 Kennedy, *Gaelic Nova Scotia*, pp. 23–4; Cameron, 'The university contribution to Canadian multiculturalism'.
53 Matheson, *O Cheapaich nan Craobh*, pp. 73–7.
54 Dunn, *Highland Settler*, pp. 118–22; Newton, *We're Indians Sure Enough*, p. 242; Matheson, *O Cheapaich nan Craobh*, pp. 36–8.
55 Dembling, 'Joe Jimmy Alec visits the Mod', p. 47.
56 *Casket*, 14 December 1899; Sinclair, *Clàrsach na Coille*, pp. 174–7.
57 Kennedy, *Gaelic Nova Scotia*, pp. 55–7; Cameron, 'The university contribution to Canadian multiculturalism'; Linkletter, 'Bu dual dhà sin', pp. 202–7, 216–32.
58 Newton, 'My bard is in the Highlands'.
59 Quoted in Cheska, 'Antigonish Highland Games', p. 63.
60 Shaw, 'Brief beginnings', pp. 345, 350, 352–4.
61 Ray, *Highland Heritage*, pp. 94–8, 157–62.
62 Mckay, 'Tartanism triumphant', p. 34.
63 Cozzens, *Acadia*, pp. 199–200.
64 Whitt, 'Cultural imperialism and the marketing of Native America', pp. 141–3; Craig, 'National literature and cultural capital in Scotland

and Ireland', pp. 44–5; Dembling, 'You play it as you would sing it', pp. 190–1.

65 Dembling, 'Joe Jimmy Alec visits the Mod', p. 38. See also MacDonald, ' "Putting on the kilt"; Newton, ' "This could have been mine" '.

66 Maceachen, 'What history?'.

67 From the official website of the Office for Gaelic Affairs: http://www.gov.ns.ca/oga/gaelicimage.asp

68 Vance, 'A brief history of organized Scottishness in Canada', p. 97.

5

TARTANRY INTO TARTAN: HERITAGE, TOURISM AND MATERIAL CULTURE

Ian Maitland Hume

୧୨

Tartan provides an intriguing example for the study of contemporary material culture, particularly in relation to the expression of identity. There have been many academic attempts to define the discipline of material culture. This chapter seeks to link it specifically to the growing debate about the contemporary understanding of the meaning and impact of tartan and its larger cousin, tartanry (or, following Michael Newton, the differently inflected term, tartanism). We now understand that there can be as much positive assessment of their nature as there has been past negative criticism. This arises because there is growing awareness that tartan is endowed with a large range of complex meanings, depending on its use and the circumstances in which it is found. Likewise, tartanry itself, rather than just representing a romantic, kitsch interpretation of the past, now embraces whole spectrums of different meanings beyond relatively simple publicity often associated with the tourist industry. It is also clear we must also pay more attention to its role in the interpretation of Scotland's heritage for the worldwide diaspora of people who look to Scotland as the home of their forebears.

This picture is further complicated by the clearly observed changes that have been happening in Scotland over the last thirty or forty years. These accelerated during the 1990s, particularly following internal political changes, but also through the complex, though often over-simplified, influence of films like *Braveheart* (1995) and the growing awareness of a hitherto relatively ignored dimension, the growing visibility of the Scottish-American identity (not to be confused with that of the expatriate Scot). The first Tartan Day, celebrated in the USA in 1997, gave this a formal context. It opened out the debate between those who would still view tartanry as irrelevant to modern Scotland and those who perceive that it now embraces other cultures and traditions as well as the domestic ones. Finally, we must take account of how these different influences have affected the domestic perceptions of tartan in Scotland. In particular tartan may be beginning to detach itself from close association with perspectives hitherto embraced by tartanry. Thus, it properly comes to be viewed as an integral cultural element of contemporary Scottish (as opposed to Highland) identity – the material cultural component – freed from upwards of two centuries of misplaced or misdirected interpretation.

Material culture can today be described in different terms. Daniel Miller states that artefacts (such as a tartan item might be) are 'a means by which we give form to, and come to an understanding of ourselves, others, or abstractions such as the nation or the modern'.[1] We might say tartan is a means by which we give form to abstractions like heritage. Miller's general description of material culture is an attractive one:

> If culture is understood not in the narrow sense of some particular element of the human environment, but in the more general sense of the process through which human groups construct themselves and are then socialised, then material culture becomes an aspect of objectification consisting in the material forms taken by this cultural process.[2]

Pierre Bourdieu wrote that 'our cultural identity is not merely embodied but literally objectified'.[3] As we wrestle with the fact that material culture and the mind are inextricably intertwined, Augustus Lane-Fox Pitt-Rivers aptly observed over a hundred years ago that material culture could be seen as the 'outward signs and symbols of particular ideas in the mind'.[4] Thomas Schlereth's view was that material culture is a process by which an attempt is made to see through the objects to establish the cultural meaning which is relevant.[5] There are many other interpretations of the meaning, but for our purposes these help us identify the complex inter-relationship between the object, in our case tartan, and its meaning.[6] Material culture, then, is probably a useful peg on which to hang our hat as we attempt to explore the nature of tartan as symbol and extricate it from the 'tartanry' in which it has become enveloped. This raises the question of how best to interpret individual views of the relationship between tartan and identity, between tartan and heritage, or even between tartan and tourism, as well as how to distinguish differences between tartan and tartanry.

As an ethnologist, my preferred approach has always been to conduct direct interviews. Material gained by this method is generally highly informative as well as surprisingly revealing in terms of helping discern the meaning behind the object. I shall continue this part of the discussion by instancing views accumulated during two different periods of research. The first was a study of people wearing the kilt in contemporary Scotland, who did not necessarily have to wear it because their employment demanded it, but chose to wear it to mark an aspect of their identity.[7] The successor study examined the role of the kilt and tartan in the construction and expression of Scottish-American identity.[8] Together, these two studies go some way to answering the question of where tartan stands today in perceptions of the material culture of identity. They also set the scene for examination of the wider influences affecting heritage and tourism.[9]

Let us look first at the Scottish-American take on tartan. Anyone who has attended a United States Highland Games will be familiar with the surprisingly large number of people wearing the kilt to these occasions. The larger games, like the Grandfather Mountain Highland Games in North Carolina, held annually since 1954, can attract up to 40,000 people over the weekend. The same goes for the Stone Mountain Highland Games in Georgia. The Caledonian Club of San Francisco holds its Scottish Gathering and Games in Pleasanton and can attract even more attenders; these last games have been held for over a hundred years. Generally speaking, the vast majority of people wearing the kilt on these occasions do so to celebrate the Scottish part of their heritage. Some have impeccable ancestry in that they can trace their forebears to the precise glen of origin and know exactly where their families were first established in America. Gaston Macmillan told me in Pleasanton

I'm the direct descendant from the first Macmillans of this line of Macmillans that came from Lochaber in Scotland, whose ancestry we can trace and we own the farm that was first owned by them in North Carolina, so it's just a lot of family pride, I guess.[10]

At the time he was thirty-six and had joined the Macmillan clan society, having just started a family. He was now their representative at these games and glad to be wearing his kilt again. He really represented the 'traditional' Scottish-American, but one who has, like so many others, taken an active part in promoting not only his own clan and tartan, but Scotland's heritage too, the latter being an inextricable element in his perception of the 'Scottish' part of his identity.

At the other end of the spectrum we can readily find a good example of the 'new' Scottish-American in another Pleasanton interviewee, Ian Kirk. With uncertain Scottish roots, or at least no really traceable ones, he was first attracted to the Scottish dimension when he and a group were piped into church on Founder's Day at his university by a full pipe band. From then on his interest grew. He was wearing a kilt in the United States St Andrews tartan because 'it encompasses both identities and since as far as I can tell the Kirks aren't a clan, it was the only tartan adequately to represent who I was'.[11] Interestingly the films *Braveheart* and *Rob Roy* (1995) had also had a great influence on his feelings for Scotland. The significance of the tartan, in terms of the choice he had made to best reflect his vision of a Scottish-American identity, was time and again borne out amongst the many people who offered views, both on this and other occasions. It is a paradox that one of the new dimensions associated with the influences of current tartanry, the kilt made in cloth other than tartan, widely publicised in the fashion world and some Highland dress outfitters, often generates considerable antipathy amongst those looking on themselves as Scottish-American. On the other hand, if they are questioned on this point whilst being served dinner by waiters in plain black kilts at a Prestonfield House Scottish entertainment evening, that dress code they generally accept as being derived from the hotel's house style rather than having any personal element.

In terms of material culture, it is personal identification with the specific combination of kilt and tartan that is significant for Scottish-American identity expression. There are many other examples that reinforce the strong representation of Scottish-American identity and which, interestingly, sometimes take domestic Scots' own safeguarding of the culture of kilt and tartan to task. One informant had no hesitation in saying, 'You have to come to America to see how we protect the Highland heritage, because you fail to do it sufficiently in Scotland'.[12] Here we see evidence of occasional Scottish-American identification of Scotland with 'Highland heritage'.

If we now look at the situation in Scotland, it is clear that – at least in so far as the kilt and tartan are concerned – there appears to have been a fundamental change over the past three or four decades in public perception of the kilted. Following the 1747 proscription, domestic weaving effectively came to an end, thereby putting the price of the cloth beyond the reach of the man in the street for the next two hundred years. Much is made of George IV's visit to Edinburgh in 1822 and its endorsement of the tartan kilt as Scotland's national dress (as opposed to its previous predominantly Highland association). Outwith the military and certain employments, the kilt remained substantially the dress of the Highland gentleman, both formally and informally, children and certain school and Boy Scout uniform codes until the emergence of the kilt-hire trade in the early 1970s. Since then, it has become the formal wear for many Scots for evening wear, graduation ceremonies, twenty-first-birthday parties and particularly for weddings, to such an extent that a photographer in the Borders – never previously a kilt-wearing region – reckoned that 95 per cent of young men now wore the kilt in ceremonies he photographed.[13] Additionally, the Tartan Army, discussed by Hugh O'Donnell in this volume, and other groups have popularised the kilt in less formal environments so that, perhaps for the first time, we can affirm that the kilt is Scotland's male national dress in practice as well as in conception.

Inevitably the gradual journey as marker from Highland to Scottish identity has caused some discomfort to the group we might call 'traditional' kilt-wearers. For them, the breakout of Highland dress beyond the Highland Line has been a difficult situation to come to terms with. Alexander Stewart expresses this sentiment well:

> The kilt is a Highland thing, I mean that is the reason I wear it [. . .] I regard myself as a Highlander and I think it is an expression of your family and the clan you belong to and if it is to have any meaning at all, it really should be tied to the name you have. I think it would be the end of the kilt in the way it is now used, if anybody could wear it regardless of what their name was.[14]

This view, which non-ethnologists might wish to suggest embodies a false historical consciousness, clearly expresses an internalised personal value system. Recorded fourteen years ago, it would now seem even more dated than it was in 1996, but Stewart represented the in-between generation; another contemporary, the late John Macleod of Macleod, referred to his father's generation thus:

> My father had very strong views about the kilt [. . .] he said you should never wear it south of the Highland Line for any reason

whatsoever. He felt that the wearing of the kilt as national costume or something you put on only for special occasions was absolutely ridiculous and contrary to the whole cultural feeling of himself and Scotland.[15]

The kilt has come a long way since those days and the 'new' wearers have no such reservations. Martin Watt from West Lothian, who first wore the kilt at his wedding, offered an interesting view as 'new' kilt-wearer:

> Well, you see, we've all seen people wearing kilts and we've all thought various thoughts about that, but as soon as you put it on, thoughts change. When you see yourself in a kilt, you think there's some sense of tradition and there's some sense of surprise – how comfortable you feel in it, because it doesn't necessarily sit well with your conditionings. You feel encouraged to wear it more, not just for special occasions [. . .] I think it's as much about the traditional feeling of it, being in that tradition with a whole load of other folk.[16]

Furthermore, the idea, derived from various classification attempts in the early nineteenth century, that only the principal clan tartans could be 'authorised' and worn has also disappeared. Now there has been an explosion of new tartan design at the behest of football clubs, corporate entities, and commercial and social organisations, as well as many private family designs. Martin Robb mentioned that he had no kilt and decided that

> it would be nice to have one of our own [. . .] as I see it tartan is there to reflect the personality of the wearer [. . .] one or two people have said that it's not a real tartan and I am not quite sure what they mean by that [. . .] if it's been developed in the last 150 years it must be a *'nouveau riche'* tartan, but as far as I can see, tartans are alive and kicking.[17]

As if to confirm the point Robb makes, the Scottish Register of Tartans (now part of the Scottish National Archives) has well over 4,500 different tartan designs. In just one week in November 2009, tartans were registered for a remarkably varied number of registrants; these included a Rabbinical tartan (for use by rabbis), a defence tartan (former servicemen), a tartan for an Ayrshire primary school, and tartans for an Irish pub proprietor sponsoring a pipe band, an

American commercial company (for advertising its products), the University of Missouri, a Texan football team, a tartan for druids and three private family tartans.[18] Clearly some of these tartans are perhaps less likely to be worn with Highland dress, thus marking the way tartan is continuing to move into an altogether different sphere from the more usual Scottish one, generally associated with formal dress. They are, nonetheless, now fully authorised on the Register. Tartanry, the exploitation of tartan and its iconography in Scottish-related contexts, has seen, since at least the nineteenth century, dramatic extension of tartan design into many uses other than just for making kilts (and dresses). It would now seem that tartan may be leaving Scottish-focused tartanry behind, as it reaches out into an extraordinarily varied number of users, although these new users might well have strong Scottish connections or affiliations.

Visitors to Scotland today, especially if they come from Canada, the United States and perhaps also Australia and New Zealand, will possibly have a sense of tartan, a sense certainly re-enforced through visits to the VisitScotland websites. VisitScotland organises three websites to attract people to the country. The VisitScotland[19] website aimed essentially at the UK market does not, interestingly, feature tartan at all; there are no pictures of pipers and kilts and the emphasis is on the look of the country and the activities available. This contrasts strongly with the ComeToScotland website,[20] which is clearly aimed at the 'homecoming' visitor, with a revolving display of traditional scenes, pipe bands and Highland dress. Aimed at the large market that is looking for 'its' heritage, it is rather more general in flavour than the ancestral website (clan and family orientated), the third run by VisitScotland.[21] Many visitors are quite clear that one of their priorities is to see the land of their forefathers, even if they do not know precisely where they came from. The gut feeling of finally coming 'home' is one that many people wish to experience. There is little doubt that, if they have been exposed for some time to elements associated with Scottish heritage, whether it be a local Highland Games, the local use of tartan, the wearing of kilts in the family, or just the trawling through the multiple websites featuring clans, clan associations, family and clan tartans, the incentive to identify is there. For the serious overseas adopter of a Scottish national identity tag, the chances are that membership of a clan society will have been taken out and they will be well versed in much of the more dramatic, even sensationalised, history of the country before they arrive. The impact of *Braveheart* and *Rob Roy* and even a film such as *Mrs Brown*

(1997), featuring John Brown in his kilt, should not be underestimated. These paint a picture of a Scotland that they might aspir-
ationally search for, but to be able to participate actively in their
heritage search is often fulfilling enough, whatever the reality.

Paul Basu has given us a useful summary of the sort of Scotland
many in the diaspora have in mind:

> This Scotland is above all a Highland country with a wild and
> rugged landscape of mountains, lochs and rivers. It is a place of
> great scenic beauty, but also wet and cool. It is an historic land of
> castles and clans, of traditions and Gaelic language and lore. Its
> people are proud and fiercely independent, loyal to clan and family,
> but also hospitable to strangers. They are industrious, inventive and
> value education highly.[22]

Indeed this aspirational view is one to which, as Ian Brown suggests,
Colin McArthur would reduce all tartanry. This composite view,
gleaned from many informants, bears little relation to the Scotland
most of its urban population lives in. Nevertheless it is this imagined
Scotland that so often forms an image of 'heritage' carried in people's
minds and which ultimately has to be experienced physically for that
journey 'home' to be complete. Charles Edwards, from Vermont,
described it well, recounting his first visit: 'I drove up to Glenshee and
it grabbed somewhere in the very depth of me [. . .] being up in that
wild country. Something resonated and I don't quite know what it
was.'[23] In one sense, this sort of experience goes well beyond a normal
touristic one and VisitScotland cannot yet quantify the heritage
element in the overseas visitor figures. Nonetheless, it does break
down UK visitor interests in some detail, telling us that 23 per cent of
UK visitors in 2008 came for heritage, architecture or literature
interests. The United States provided the greatest number of overseas
visitors that year with 14 per cent, followed by Germany and Ireland,
with 10 per cent each, Canada 5 per cent and Australia 4 per cent.[24]

So far, this chapter has glimpsed different aspects of 'Scotland',
tartan and Highland dress and their meanings for both the diaspora
and, in a limited way, those Scots who wear the kilt today. The
attempt to consign the kilt and tartan to the 'other', especially during
the 1980s following Tom Nairn's 'tartan monster',[25] Trevor-Roper's
theories concerning the origin of tartan and Highland dress and the
invention of tradition[26] and David McCrone's expansion on these
themes in the 1990s, viewing the 'mythic structure of tartanry' as part

of our 'vain search for the true image because none such exists, nor indeed should we be looking for it in the late twentieth century',[27] now appear dated. McCrone does recognise the significance of the myth of tartan in *Scotland – the Brand*:

> Using the term 'myth' might seem to apply value judgement, as if the whole thing was a fraud, but myths provide guides to the inter-pretation of social reality and if we want to know what tartan means today, that is where we have to begin.[28]

Indeed, through our exploration of the reasons people wear a tartan kilt today, the myth is revealed as involving a complex series of different individual interpretations of identity, using the convenient symbol of a material culture artefact. The artefact itself is not only extremely expressive visibly, but also perceived as peculiarly a sum-mation of history and heritage, both real and imagined. Randi Storaas, the Scandinavian ethnologist, has given us a useful inter-pretation:

> Symbols are created which express their ideas. These re-enforce intra-group solidarity and contribute to legitimising their ideas and also show an ideological fellowship. Here a re-vitalisation phenom-enon may arise.[29]

Where tartan is used as symbol, particularly in Highland dress, whether by wearers in the United States or other parts of the Scottish diaspora, or those who wear the kilt in Scotland for varied reasons and occasions, what emerges is evidence of a potent symbol. Tartan provides instant linkage to a past and a probably-forgotten, possi-bly-imagined heritage for some, to a clear expression of Highland identity for others, to Scottish identity for many, both in Scotland and overseas, or even simply to a means to identify visibly with a collective of people with whom they share common feelings. In the same way tartanry (and tartanism) is now evolving not only to include the whole spectrum of kilts and clan societies in America and expressions of tartanised identity in Scotland, but also the way heritage is depicted for those 'roots' visitors seeking the origins of their forebears. The extraordinary explosion of interest in tartan, which has also encour-aged the Scottish Government to legislate for the adoption of the Scottish Register of Tartans,[30] now seems to express the preferred method to express collective cohesion by many diverse groups of registrants. They all wish to incorporate the symbolism of tartan in their own specific social cultures because of the inherent qualities attached to the symbol. Perhaps it has an even more mystic than mythic quality, one that allows it to draw their interest, and in turn embody these social cultures.

Notes

1 Miller, 'Artefacts and the meaning of things', p. 397.
2 Ibid., p. 399.
3 Bourdieu, *Outline of a Theory of Practice*, p. 42.
4 Pitt-Rivers, *The Evolution of Culture*, p. 23.
5 Schlereth, 'Material culture in material life', p. 240.
6 For a fuller interpretation of the relationship between material culture and the wider study of culture, particularly in the context of tartan, see Maitland Hume, 'The contemporary role of the kilt and tartan', pp. 42–6.
7 This study was condensed into an essay in *Review of Scottish Culture*, no. 12 (1999–2000, pp. 59–67) and the interviews are available in the University of Edinburgh School of Scottish Studies Sound Archives.
8 These interviews formed the material used in my unpublished doctoral thesis (2001) and are also available in the University of Edinburgh School of Scottish Studies Sound Archives.
9 In addition to these two studies, an extensive range of views and material has been accumulated over the past ten years through the writer's activities as a lecturer and professional tour guide leading specialist groups from the United States throughout Scotland, with particular emphasis on the contemporary and historical as well as the heritage aspects of tourism.
10 University of Edinburgh School of Scottish Studies: Sound Archives [hereafter SSS: SA] 1999.3.
11 SSS: SA1999.37.
12 SSS: SA1999.37.
13 SSS: SA1997.1.
14 SSS: SA1996.41.
15 SSS: SA1996.44.
16 SSS: SA1996.48. This interview formed part of the original research, some of which was used in *ROSC*, 12; see note 7, above.
17 SSS: SA1996.46.
18 Details of these registrations made during 18–24 November 2009 can be found at the Scottish Register of Tartans, National Archives of Scotland, HM General Register House, 2 Princes Street, Edinburgh, EH1 3YY.
19 www.visitscotland.com, aimed principally at the UK and European visitor.

20 www.cometoscotland.com, primarily for the New World visitor.

21 www.ancestralscotland.com; this site features clans, surnames, ancestors and roots, as well as the www.homecoming2009.com websites. These websites have different URLs and are kept discrete from each other.

22 Basu, *Highland Homecomings*, p. 67.

23 SSS: SA.1998.57.

24 For a detailed breakdown of incoming tourism, see www.visitscotland.org/research_and_statistics; the interesting detail, however, refers only to UK visitors. Annual reports are available from 2008, 2007, 2006 and 2005 in pdf format.

25 Nairn, *The Break-Up of Britain*, p. 165.

26 Trevor-Roper, 'Invention of tradition', pp. 12–13.

27 McCrone, *Understanding Scotland* (1992), pp. 184–7.

28 McCrone, *Scotland – the Brand*, p. 52.

29 Storaas, 'Clothes as an expression', p. 148.

30 Launched 5 February 2009; www.tartanregister.gov.uk

6

MYTH, POLITICAL CARICATURE AND MONSTERING THE TARTAN

Ian Brown

ॐ

Perceptions of tartan as a cultural phenomenon (and the developing concept of tartanry) raise issues of the relationship of historical evidence and mythmaking. This relationship develops in the historic context of the processes by which in the eighteenth century tartan, clan and regimentation interacted and of later perceptions of that inter-action, particularly those of contemporary cultural commentators. In interrogating the assumptions underlying recent critical attitudes to tartan (and tartanry), this chapter draws on Mary Douglas's summary of Claude Lévi-Strauss's view of the nature of myth:

> the function of myth is to portray the contradictions in the basic premises of the culture. The same goes for the relation of the myth to social reality. The myth is a contemplation of the unsatisfactory compromises which, after all, compose social life. In the devious statements of the myth, people can recognise indirectly what it would be difficult to admit openly and yet what is patently clear to all and sundry, that the ideal is not attainable.[1]

The stance underlying this chapter is that myths, including tartan mythologies, are not false or inauthentic history, although they may have historical roots. As thinkers like Roland Barthes have suggested,[2] they are rather embodiments of often rich contradictions that demand exploration, analysis and understanding, and cannot simply be dis-missed as 'backward' or substituted ingenuously by new 'progressi-vist' mythologies.

One of the key tartan myths involves its role as an identifier of clan or family membership. Recently, Colin McArthur has described the attachment of tartan to clans or families as 'delusion', a 'grotesque act of mythmaking'.[3] It may be worth considering the ways in which tartan appears to have come to be linked to clans or families in order to see whether such words make sense. Certainly it is common ground that the process of linking specific tartan setts to specific families was systematised only in the early nineteenth century, particularly in the context of the 1822 royal visit to Edinburgh discussed in previous chapters. It would be odd, however, if such a process of linkage emerged from the ether without any precedent. Of course, it did not. There is evidence, as we shall see, of earlier linking of families and setts.

An incidental aspect of the mythology of the royal visit is that somehow it imposed tartan on the Lowlands. It is clear from written, material and portrait evidence since at least the sixteenth century that tartan, though not what is now thought of as Highland dress, was worn throughout Scotland. Based in Edinburgh, the Royal Company of Archers wore a tartan uniform from 1713 at least. John Telfer Dunbar reports sixteenth-century ministerial condemnation of women's wearing of colourful tartan in church.[4] He also quotes Thomas Morer, an English clergyman who, in 1689, describes the use of the plaid by Lowlanders:

> Their habit is mostly English, saving that the meaner sort of men wear bonnets instead of hats, and pladds instead of cloaks; and those pladds the women also use in their ordinary dress when they go abroad, either to market or church.[5]

That we are not talking here of a plaid as a simple check is borne out by another of Dunbar's witnesses. The author of *A Journey through Scotland* (1723) in a quotation already cited in the Introduction observes that the effect 'in the Middle of a Church, on a Sunday, looks like a Parterre de Fleurs'.[6] Indeed the wider identification of tartan with Scots in general may be deduced from the portrait, dated to 1675, of the Yorkshire-born actor/playwright John Lacy in the title role of his 1667 play, *Sauny the Scot*, based on *The Taming of the Shrew*. In this, Lacy wrote dialogue that is plainly intended as his version of Scots, with no hint of Gaelic or Highland origin, and – characterised as a cunning servant in the mode of Roman Comedy – is clearly dressed in tartan trews and plaid.

Dunbar's influential *History of Highland Dress* (1962) offers eighteenth-century evidence of some identification of specific tartan setts with some individual families – and perhaps, through that link, the beginning of regimental tartan identification. The evidence may

Figure 6.1 The Yorkshire-born actor/playwright John Lacy (1615?–1681) in three of his most famous roles including, on the left, Sauny the Scot, painted by John Michael Wright probably in 1675. The Royal Collection © 2010 Her Majesty Queen Elizabeth II

suggest that it was rather through regimental identification that setts began to be linked with families, although this may perhaps be the less likely interpretation. Of the foundation of the Black Watch in 1740, Dunbar observes

> the tartan in use by the [earlier] Independent Companies continued to be used when they were regimented and later became the recognised Military or official government tartan. This tartan, which would become more standardised under mass production, we know to-day as the 'the Black Watch Tartan'. It has also become known as the Campbell clan tartan, which is reasonable enough when one considers that three of the six Independent Companies were commanded by Campbells. Likewise it is claimed by the Grants and Monros as *their* clan tartan on similar grounds.[7]

James D. Scarlett analyses the same evidence, observing that, though suggestions exist that the tartan was newly designed in 1740, it is on balance likely that the regimental tartan was based on the constituent companies' existing kilts – not least because this would be more economical than a new design with associated costs.[8] He suggests that the present pattern was actually a development of the 1740 sett, not brought in until perhaps 1747 or even 1757, but he observes 'When it came, the new design showed very little real difference from the old'.[9] Earlier, in 1950, Donald Calder Stewart was sceptical about a definitive Campbell link, noting that 'In a collection made about 1815 the same design, in four different sizes, is variously denominated Sutherland, Campbell, Munro, Grant, Black Watch and Government'.[10] Hugh Cheape is of the view that the process here moved from family sett to regimental: 'An old Campbell tartan in green was adopted as the uniform of the Black Watch in the 18th century'.[11] James D. Scarlett adds that the possibility of a Campbell sett being used may alternatively have arisen 'because the Earl of Crawford, the Regiment's first Colonel, had Campbell connections'.[12] This would accord with the practice at the time of landowners' raising regiments from tenantry and dependants, leading in some cases in this period to regiments being named after their colonels. It is a small step from naming a regiment after its colonel to adopting – if only in the case of the Campbell-led Black Watch – a family token as a uniform feature, although such tokens were at the time more commonly some form of badge. In any case, whether family sett became regimental or vice versa, linkage of some families with specific setts appears to have existed from at least the mid-eighteenth century, although there was still, as Dunbar's final sentence implies, no necessary exclusivity about the identification of a clan sett.

Certainly, the evidence is often confused, but an earlier study by M. M. Haldane may offer a way of understanding such confusion. His 1931 article attacks 'The Great Clan Tartan Myth', while noting that in 1704 the Laird of Grant ordered all his tenants 'to provide themselves by the 8th August with Highland coats, trews and short hose of red and green tartan'.[13] While this is evidence of a particular clan being required to wear a particular tartan, he suggests that the very fact attention is drawn here suggests it was an unusual event. Later he observes of the Black Watch tartan that, while three constituent companies were led by Campbells, the other three were led by, respectively, a Grant, a Munro and a Fraser. He questions whether, if clan tartans meant much, the other three company commanders would have acceded to a Campbell tartan being used. He goes on to say that in his view the Black Watch tartan is the basis of 'Campbell, Forbes, Lamont, Gordon, Athole, Farquharson and many others'.[14] One explanation of the confusion as to whether clan tartans existed and how they might have led to regimental tartans is surely provided by Martin Martin's description of tartans as characterising districts, already cited by Murray Pittock (see p. 41). If there is a practical material basis for tartans in given districts being in common because of local textile factors and weaving traditions, then clearly local families will tend to wear similar tartans. But Haldane is clear that at least in 1704 one clan tartan was being defined, however vaguely, while, whatever the complexity of the Black Watch tartan issue, it is soon identified with the Campbells. And in 1793, when Alan Cameron raised the 79th Cameron Highlanders, there is clear evidence of clan tartan being an issue. The existing Cameron and Keppoch tartans were largely red and it was considered that they would 'not look well with the regulation scarlet tunics'.

The matter was at last settled by old Mrs Cameron of Errachd, Alan's mother, who suggested that by blending the tartan of the Clan Mac-Donald (which contains more green that that of Keppoch) with the yellow lines of the tartan of Clan Cameron, the difficulty would be solved, and that not only would the kilt and plaid harmonise better with the doublet, but the sentiment of both clans would be respected.[15] (It is a piquant reflection of the complexities of politics and change in eighteenth-century Highland society that Mrs Cameron was sister of Alexander MacDonald of Keppoch who died on the Jacobite side at

Culloden.[16]) Whatever the underlying basis for tartan ascription to families it is clear from this case that before the end of the eighteenth century certain clan identifications existed and were seen as a matter of pride, or at least 'sentiment'. It is also clear that design issues were to the fore and could lead to the devising of modified or new tartans. In fact, the phenomenon of identification with specific setts for some families seems to precede the establishment in 1778 of the Highland Society of London, which arguably began the process of attempting to systematise the relationship of clan and sett, and well before the 1822 royal visit. The intertwining of clan and regiment can be seen to be further reinforced by the way such a commentator as David Stewart of Garth 'explicitly linked recruitment in the 1750–1810 period to clanship'.[17]

Of course the royal visit is something of a *pons asinorum* for detractors from the tartan. Hugh Trevor-Roper in a notorious chapter uses it as a stick to attack the authenticity of tartan and its identification with clans and so, somehow, its historicity.[18] Trevor-Roper's assertion that the kilt in its modern form was 'invented' by an English Quaker, Thomas Rawlinson, is based on Dunbar's citation of a journalistic publication in 1785 of a private letter of 1768, written itself some fifty years after the 'invention'.[19] The evidence for 'English' invention is confused: Dunbar also quotes Sir John Sinclair as writing in 1795 (although it was not published until 1830), 'the phillibeg was invented by an Englishman in Lochaber about sixty years ago'.[20] Indeed, in tailoring terms, if the story of invention in about 1718 is taken as true, the conception may have been Rawlinson's, but the actual invention in this story was by an anonymous Inverness tailor. In any case, as Murray Pittock notes in his chapter, there is evidence of the short kilt from the 1690s, while a costume drawing by Inigo Jones for Davenant's *Salmacida Spolia* in 1639–40 shows his perception of the 'ould habites of the 3 nationes' ('Inglish Irish Scottes'). In this drawing the 'Scotte' appears to wear a short kilt to halfway down his thighs and a separate plaid, certainly not a belted plaid, though it is impossible to discern what, if any, tartan is intended.[21] It is improbable that Jones would represent Scots in a short kilt for a stage presentation unless the garment were known. The alternative may, of course, be to backdate the 'English' invention of the short kilt to a stage designer in the first year of the War of the Three Kingdoms.

Trevor-Roper's evidence in his *The Invention of Tradition* chapter, however, is notoriously shaky. William Ferguson analyses the weakness of Trevor-Roper's discussion in the same chapter of the so-called Ossian myth. He shows Trevor-Roper to have done little more than lazily appropriate Samuel Johnson's ignorant challenges to Macpherson, apparently failing to understand the working of oral tradition as it enters the written – and revising – record. Trevor-Roper asserts that

> Indeed, the whole concept of a distinct Highland culture and tradition is a retrospective invention. Before the later years of the seventeenth century, the Highlanders of Scotland did not form a distinct people. They were simply the overflow of Ireland [. . .] Their literature, such as it was, was a crude echo of Irish literature.[22]

Ferguson points out in substantial detail that Trevor-Roper's 'account of Highland illiteracy and cultural deprivation echoes, albeit without acknowledgement, Samuel Johnson's views'.[23] Such appropriation of Johnson arguably marks Trevor-Roper's apparent desire to roll logs rather than cast light. For reasons that are unclear, he appears to want to twit the – in his own antique phrase – 'Scotch' with the emptiness of their vaunted history in a chapter which, while at times witty, is often historically risible. Yet the impact of his chapter on later journalists and commentators, already referred to by Hugh Cheape, has been misleading. Colin McArthur is ensnared enough by Trevor-Roper to talk of 'tartan's dubious history', when its history is well researched, though complex, as we have seen, and it is Trevor-Roper's methodology that is dubious.[24] Even Jonathan Faiers in his comprehensive study of tartan[25] appears to swallow Trevor-Roper hook, line, sinker and fishing rod, with the result that late in his volume he talks of the 'English little kilt'.[26] Here one of the central flaws of Trevor-Roper's thesis is reduced to absurdity. He appears to argue that, if the Rawlinson story is true, and given that Rawlinson was English, therefore the kilt is an English invention. Such essentialism holds no water. If the Scottish national identity can be said to have a core at all, it is hybridity and migration. Even if an English worker in Scotland 'invented' the kilt, that would scarcely mean it was 'English', rather than an evolution of the Scottish belted plaid. In any case, there is evidence noted earlier of the pre-existence of the short kilt. Trevor-Roper's essentialist, almost racist, logic seems odd, intellectually insubstantial and leading to his historical mythmaking. Faiers argues interestingly that the chav's favourite, the Burberry check, is in fact the English tartan, but his so-called 'English little kilt' is hardly English: it is not, for example, widely worn in Essex. His term arises from Trevor-Roper's imaginative chapter, which in Essex argot might be said to be 'having a laugh'.

Unquestionably the issues of the prevalence of tartan as opposed to tartan-in-Highland-dress (of whatever form, whether plaid or kilt) is separate from the history of the kilt. Part of the reason that the two are to an extent identified lies in the history of tartan in military uniform. This identification grew, in the Highland regiments, out of particular economic, social and political contexts, all of which impinge on the ways in which tartan came to be perceived and the values with which it was later identified. As Andrew MacKillop observes,

> Perceptions of the Scottish Highlands as an area characterised by social disorder were a constant feature of attitudes within early modern Scottish and post union governments. Recent studies of the later seventeenth century have highlighted the trend whereby these perceptions of disorder were manipulated and consciously fostered by successive administrations more concerned with the intricacies of national politics than any objective reality on the ground.[27]

The identification of the tartan kilt with the 'disorderly' Highlands was reinforced by the impact of the 1745 Rising: MacKillop notes

> Outwith the Highlands, the [1745] uprising was seen as a final proof of the innate bellicosity of the population, and it is ironic that Jacobitism was, in effect, the advert for Highland society that stimulated its involvement with the empire in the specialised form of proprietary regiments.[28]

In the age of industrialisation and improvement in Scotland, the initial placing of the Highlands beyond these developments, not to mention the impact of the Disarming Act, set the costume markers of Scottish Highland identity outside areas of 'enlightened' civilisation. This reinforced economic and social distinctions between the Highlands and the rest of Scotland:

> Highland recruiting was linked to the wider perception of the unimproved nature of the area [. . .] with hindsight these arguments can be shown to be based on both [sic] a misunderstanding of the Lowlands and Highlands. To contemporaries and observers in the 1750s, a clear division existed between commerce and military activity [. . .]
> In these circumstances, the entrenched and accepted perception of the idle and unimproved Highlander meant that their recruitment brought no real damage to Scotland's wider economy [. . .] In

essence, economic growth in the Lowlands, allied to the example of 1745, helped to confirm the potential of the region as a military reservation that would complement the wider needs of society.[29]

Such social and economic processes could lend support to 'crude whig propaganda' which 'equated clanship with perpetually non-industrious and disorderly behaviour'.[30] This was in spite of the fact that

> the raising of men by late eighteenth century Highland landlords was as much a matter of revenue as the large capitalised black cattle farms, and was as modern an estate practice as sheep farming.[31]

It is such underlying factors that provide the drivers for the creation of the myth of the Highland soldier, what Trevor Royle calls in his chapter 'martial races'. Diana Henderson observes that 'in the wild country and equally wild climate a tough, self-reliant and warlike people survived, who were accustomed to battle and skilled in arms',[32] while in his 'Foreword' to her book Brigadier James A. Oliver says

> There was a time when Highlanders, owing to instinct, tradition and necessity, were warlike but this time is long past now. Field Marshal Lord Montgomery, however, [. . .] repeatedly said that he fully realised that the clan instincts and regimental pride of his Highland soldiers required and justified very special attention.[33]

The idea that clanship – or indeed martial qualities – can be instinctive rather than socialised is of course dubious, but it is not difficult to find further examples of such romantic intertwining of clan and regiment. And of course, as we have seen, identification of clan and regimental tartan has roots at least as early as the 1740 foundation of the Black Watch.

The development of the identification of tartan and clan became systematised particularly through the marketing of William Wilson of Bannockburn. In the mid-1760s, this firm cornered the market in tartan production, initially for the army, through establishing industrial rather than the prevailing cottage-craft weaving. Wilson, based a few miles south of the Highland Line, participated in his period's processes of industrial enlightenment and improvement. His pattern books began with market-researching public perceptions of local or family identification with particular tartan setts. Unsurprisingly, initial results seem to us confusing and indeterminate. In such cases, the entrepreneurial and pragmatic Wilson chose a classification to suit his customers. Gradually over the next half century, culminating in and further sustaining the fashion for clan tartans inspired by the royal visit of 1822, Wilson's pattern books moved beyond vague and ambiguous family attributions, locality titles and simple pattern numbers to more formal identification of setts with specific family names. Sometimes these processes have been described as fraudulent or spurious, and Hector MacMillan in his play *The Royal Visit* (1974) has some fun with the process of tartan attribution, which he links to Walter Scott's stage management. In fact, though, such a process of systematisation of setts and titles flows logically out of industrialised processes and a national craze for improvement. Standardised setts make identification and sale simpler: creation of individualised brand identity for customers is good retail practice. By 1831 Wilson could respond to a request for information by James Logan, who was seeking to publish standardised setts, by saying he was 'sorry to observe that you have allowed several Fictitious and Fancy patterns to get amongst the Genuine Clan Tartans'.[34] Of course Wilson's had a commercial interest in asserting the genuineness of their own patterns, but the point here is that by then a clear standardisation was in place, and a process for adding setts to the standard record. Others might want to romanticise the 'antiquity' of setts, but here the industrialist was simply establishing product benchmarks.

It seems bizarre that such a process of, in effect, trademarking should be seen as somehow spurious or corrupting in itself. It is, however, certainly fair to say that this specifically commercial process became confused with the mythmaking of the Sobieski Stuarts and a wider process of romanticising and intermingling 'Scotland', tartan and Highland culture with Scottish history, militarisation and imperialism. Diana Henderson asserts, for example,

> As a result of history, literature and culture, soldiering was widely looked upon as a respectable profession in Scotland. The close links with bagpipe music, whose development in the nineteenth century was largely fostered through Army pipers, the Gaelic bardic tradition of an heroic romantic culture, the works of Walter Scott, the influence of the Highland Societies and the active support of a Monarch who came to associate herself with Scotland and in particular with the Highland Regiments, all affected Scottish attitudes to the Army and recruiting.[35]

Yet, of course, underlying such positivistic identifications of disparate elements were a variety of more complex factors. Edward Spiers identifies and undercuts the optimism of Henderson's vision. Considering the distinction between the army as agent of imperialism and as career choice, he observes

> The high esteem of the army as an instrument of imperialism contrasted sharply with the low regard for the army as a career, a reflection primarily of the limited appeal of army pay, terms, and conditions of service [. . .] On 19 August 1893 the *Highland News* [. . .] focused upon the recruiting dearth in Inverness-shire and ascribed the lack of recruits to 'the increase of legitimate labour, the dawn of better social arrangements at home, and a growing self-respect' which had diminished the appeal of ' the least desirable and worst paid of employments [. . .] Is it not a fact that all over the north and west, for a man to enter the army has always been regarded as equivalent to throwing himself away?'[36]

Much recent anti-tartanry discourse seems to lack sufficient, or sometimes any, historical perspective on phenomena like that outlined concerning links between tartan, clan, regiment, centralist conceptions of the 'Highlands' and the implications of the military-fiscal-improving state for the century and a half after the Black Watch's foundation. Colin McArthur, editor of *Scotch Reels* (1982), a *locus classicus* of anti-tartanry, has more recently defined this complex phenomenon in simplistic terms:

> Tartanry [. . .] constructs Scotland as a mist-shrouded land of lochs, mountains, shaggy cattle and alternatively warlike or gentle natives clad in tartan and living 'close to Nature' It is this latter quality which – the discourse runs – makes Scots particularly attuned to the supernatural. It is a discourse in which marginalised peoples throughout the world will recognise themselves.[37]

The absence of adequate historical understanding that lies behind such a statement is highlighted when McArthur later says

> It is not widely known that tartan – particularly as a set of distinctive patterns assigned to named clans – is shot through with falsity and invention, part of that (primarily) nineteenth-century phenomenon associated with the manufacture of national identities which Eric Hobsbawm and Terence Ranger have called 'the invention of tradition' in their edited collection of that title.[38]

One would want to tread softly here, but it is simply not the case that tartan is shot through with falsity. This is to misunderstand the nature we have outlined of its systematisation. And of course invention – or better re-invention – is scarcely something to slight, but a natural part of evolution. McArthur, like others before him, appears to fall into the trap of taking seriously Trevor-Roper's misguided contribution to Hobsbawm and Ranger's volume. Further, it is somewhat simplistic to describe phenomena that existed in a variety of forms at least from the sixteenth century, Dunbar indeed offering evidence of tartans from 1440[39] and bare-legged dress from 1093[40] as a nineteenth-century phenomenon associated with the manufacture of national identities.

It is certainly true that the nineteenth century saw tartan associated with the commercial exploitation of family feeling and the aggressive creation of military *esprit*, and it surely has significance in terms of perceptions of what modern varieties of 'Scotland' may be. In the nineteenth century, however, even the latter aspect of its role is complicated by its function in celebrating British imperialism. Spiers offers a specific example of how the use of tartan iconography might be developed and establish itself in the popular consciousness through placement in militarist events and popular theatre. He describes the ways in which Piper George Findlater, who won a VC with the Gordon Highlanders in 1897 at Dargai Heights in Afghanistan, became engaged in promotion and publicity partly by the state and partly on his own account. On recovering from his wounds, Findlater

> found himself in immense demand, playing the pipes in the Military Tournament, where royal personages and generals shook his hand, and at the Alhambra music hall, Charing Cross Road, where he performed several times nightly. Although the adjutant-general deplored his music-hall activities, Findlater acquired agents to manage his tours of the music halls in Ireland, England and Scotland until his public acclaim began to diminish over a breach-of-promise suit.[41]

The use of the piper in this way, including his symbolic induction by the imperial state and military élite through the quasi-democratic shaking of hands, suggests a far more complex nature and process for tartanry than Scotland's construction as 'a mist-shrouded land of lochs'. And Findlater's fall from grace, later resolved by an out-of-court settlement, suggests more the modern perils of image management for public 'heroes' than a simplistic vision of tartan as helping 'manufacture of national identities'. Meanwhile, when Edward VII helped form the Entente Cordiale in 1904 a French cartoon showed him shaking the hand of the President of France and wearing a kilt as part of full Highland dress under the heading 'Angleterre'.[42] Tartanry's complexities and ironies proliferate.

Part of the difficulty for some Scottish commentators has been a tendency to see tartan and tartanry in terms simply of Scottish culture. Both must be seen in wider terms and in the context of international phenomena. The late Angus Calder chid the present author for not seeing the Highland Clearances as 'just' a Scottish element, however harrowing, in a Europe-wide process of agricultural 'improvement'. Certainly the roots of tartanry (and the Kailyard, which is often coupled with it) should be seen in such wider contexts. One of these is the prevalence of Kitsch as a politico-aesthetic movement in the later nineteenth century, perhaps as a response to industrialisation, urbanisation and imperialism. Cairns Craig highlights the danger of failure to adopt a wider view:

> And the consequence of accepting ourselves as parochial has been a profound self-hatred. It is not our personal self that we have hated, but that self when seen moulded to the physiognomy of the group, a group whose existence has no significance in the eyes of the world: to escape the parochial we borrow the eyes of the dominant culture and through those eyes we are allowed to see the 'the world'. But we are also forced to see how close that parochial group-self stands to us – Hyde behind Jekyll – ready to claim again the self we have invented. We must distance the group-self, see it projected in the comic Scotsman of the tartan kitsch, the parodic versions of working-class Scotland, that the gap between it and us will be so wide no observer could reunite us with our cultural origin.[43]

Even here there is a suggestion that somehow there is a distance between being a modern Scot and embracing the Scottishness bound up in a tartan identity. Rather than distancing oneself from this, one might seek to understand its roots, explore its riches (and poverties) and recognise its role in any development of a modern identity for Scots and Scotland.

In doing so, it may be valuable to consider the value of terms like 'tartanry', which have become often simply hand-me-down terms of abuse. The difficulty of such terms is that they become slogans rather than concepts and, so, unexamined. Even a brilliant commentator like David McCrone can fall into this trap:

It is [. . .] no coincidence that those identities diagnosed as arche-
typically Scottish by friend and foe alike – the Kailyard, tartanry
and Clydesideism – have little place for women [. . .] there is no
analogous 'lass o' pairts'; the image of tartanry is a male-military
image (and kilts were not a female form of dress); and the Clydeside
icon was a skilled, male worker who was man enough to 'care' for
his womenfolk.[44]

There is certainly a case that the archetypes as defined by McCrone tend
to the exclusion of women, but, if there is no such thing as a 'lass o'
pairts', what is one to make of Barrie's Maggie Wylie, or Grassic
Gibbon's Chris Guthrie? And what is one to make of a definition of
Kailyard that does not include the subtle reaction to that genre
embodied in *Sunset Song*? It is sure that one aspect of tartanry is
male-military, but, as other chapters in this volume demonstrate, it is a
far broader phenomenon than that, with military tartanry demanding
direct attention in only one chapter out of fourteen. Meanwhile, subsets
of tartanry like Balmorality, defined by Jonathan Faiers as the widespread use of tartan for domestic decor, is hardly military. The
identification of tartan and kilt is also a false steer in this debate.
The kilt may have been male attire (though not in modern practice:
many pipe bands, for example, now have female members who wear
the kilt without demur), but tartan is not. From its use in the earasaid
and attraction of sixteenth-century ministerial condemnation through
to the work of contemporary designers like Vivienne Westwood, tartan
has had a constant role in female fashion. The use of limited perspectives may surely, as Craig observes, lead to forms of 'profound self-
hatred'. It has even led in the past to narrow and somewhat parochial
assertions of the kind this volume addresses, such as Colin McArthur's

Interpellated within an armature of discourses of which Tartanry
and Kailyard are the most important at the level of popular
consciousness, both we (and our hearers in other lands) can find
no alternative meaningful discourses within which to construct our
native land and our own identity.[45]

In such statements the danger is that jargon obstructs thought.

In *The Break-Up of Britain*, Tom Nairn does seek to provide, *inter
alia*, a wider context for his discussion of tartanry and other stereotypes of Scotland and its cultures. He discusses, for example, the
phenomenon of military tartanry within a wider European context:

It is not unusual for Empires to try and exploit the more picturesque and *Völkisch* sides of their provinces, to pander to petty/local vanities and precious traditions (particularly military ones). The Hapsburgs and Romanovs used the technique for centuries, and Bismarck raised it to a new pitch of perfection in Germany. What is remarkable in the Scottish case is its success and solidity, and the degree to which it was self-administered.[46]

As Trevor Royle and other contributors to this volume make clear, however, there is nothing very remarkable in this 'self-administration'. In the first case, the formulation Nairn adopts runs the danger of excluding the Scots from direct complicity in the imperialist enterprise or even denying that complicity so clearly described by more recent historians like Tom Devine and Michael Fry. It was not that the Hanoverians as British Hapsburgs or Romanovs imposed the Highland regiments, but that Scots offered them as part of their share of the imperialist adventure arising from the 1707 Union. Second, regimental foundation was based on specific pre-existing traditions and practices within the Highland region. The complementary work of Andrew MacKillop and Edward Spiers highlights this. Third, the intertwining of the developing regimental cultures, raised by landowners to whom perhaps local loyalty and certainly local dependency was felt, led directly or indirectly to the establishment by the mid-nineteenth century of close links between clan and tartan. These factors help explain both the success and solidity Nairn notes.

Nairn's critique tends, however, to move from broad intellectual sweep to interesting language usage. For example, in considering the significance of Scotland and Sir Walter Scott in the general mythology of European romanticism, he observes

> And we are also conscious of the importance in Scotland itself of a kind of pervasive, second-rate, sentimental slop associated with tartan, nostalgia, Bonnie Prince Charlie, Dr Finlay, and so on.[47]

This energetic and entertaining use of emotive language is followed two pages later by one of Nairn's more famous metaphors:

> the great tartan monster [. . .] is a sub-cultural creature rather than a performer in the elevated spheres we are concerned with [. . .] this is a popular sub-romanticism, and not the vital national culture whose absence is so often lamented after Scott.[48]

Nairn introduces this image as he asserts the elevation of his spheres
and argues that tartan manifestations became a sub-cultural substitute
for what he calls 'normal' nineteenth-century national behaviour:

> The new Scottish working class, in its turn, was deprived of the
> normal type of 19th-century cultural 'nationalization': that is, such
> popular-national culture as there was (vulgar Scottishism, or tar-
> tanry) was necessarily unrelated to a higher romantic-national and
> intellectual culture.[49]

The attack becomes more sweeping:

> Cramped, stagnant, back-ward looking, parochial – all these and
> others are the epithets traditionally and rightly ascribed to modern
> Scottishness. But deformed as they are, these constitute none the less
> a strong, institutionally guaranteed identity. It is true that political
> castration was the main ingredient in this rather pathological
> complex (such was the point of the Union), and that intellectuals
> have been unable to contemplate it for a long time without in-
> expressible pain. Still, there it was: the one thing which the Scots can
> never be said to have lacked is identity.[50]

The direction in which Nairn is heading in these comments becomes
clear in a subsequent passage:

> The relationship between civil society and State in [nineteenth-
> century] Scotland precluded a fully national culture [. . . Scotland]
> produced something like a stunted, caricatural version of [a 'nor-
> mal' national culture]. The best title for this is perhaps 'cultural sub-
> nationalism'. It was cultural, because of course it could not be
> political; on the other hand this culture could not be straight-
> forwardly nationalist either – a direct substitute for political action,
> like (e.g.) so much Polish literature of the 19th century [. . .] It could
> only be 'sub-nationalist', in the sense of venting its national content
> in various crooked ways – neurotically, so to speak, rather than
> directly. [Cultural emigration and the Kailyard School are 'espe-
> cially prominent' strands in 'the neurosis' and] connected in a way
> which permits one to focus much more clearly upon the significant
> popular-cultural reality underlying both of them: vulgar tartanry.[51]

In order to force his case, Nairn separates 'cultural' and 'political' in a
way that is as fallacious as it is hair-raising.

Not only is Nairn's charge that the use of tartan is 'neurotic', but that what he calls tartanry is vulgar, presumably beneath his elevated spheres. His outrage at such vulgarity becomes almost amusing as he proceeds. He talks of the 'tartan monster' as represented in a London pub on International night or in the crowd at the Edinburgh Military Tattoo:

> How intolerably vulgar! What unbearable, crass, mindless, philistinism! One knows that *Kitsch* is a large constituent of mass popular culture in every land: but this is ridiculous![52]

After this flurry of exclamation marks, he goes on to reveal the snobbish basis of this part of his argument:

> The latter's [sub-nationalist culture's] thirst for harmless sentiments and sub-romantic imagery found perfect objects in the debris of a ruined, alien society. On a higher plane, from *Waverley* onwards [. . .][53]

The words 'vulgar' and 'on a higher plane' begin to make clear the basis on which the argument is being developed. Not only is the language snobbish, but it also scarcely comprises, to use his own word, 'normal' discourse. The over-strained vocabulary is revealing: in the rest of the section from which the last two passages are taken, Nairn repetitively, even obsessively, uses words like 'mawkish', 'crass', 'vulgar' and 'brainless'.[54] In another text, McArthur offers an apologia that might explain such language:

> Sick of the kind of critical writing which celebrates mindlessly every manifestation of the popular, I use the term 'vulgar' consciously and polemically as a blunt instrument for making distinctions of quality between one instance of popular art and another.[55]

But 'vulgar' is not a quality word: it is a class word. In refusing to address the nature of tartan and tartanry, but making it a scapegoat or symptom for other aspects of Scottish life of which he disapproves, Nairn's over-excited argument loses force – and, on reflection, credibility. The point about much of the complexity addressed in this volume is that Scots use of tartan has been – since at least the period discussed by Paul Maloney in this volume – very often knowing, ironic and reflexively self-satirical. Above all, it is frequently humorous and, more than that, good-humoured. Nairn may have a polemic purpose:

the ultra-patriotism of tartanry is accompanied by a tradition of sentimentalized savagery which reflects Scotland's participation in two centuries of Great-British exploits, in the subjugation of many genuine 'subject nations'.[56]

But his argument would be better served by recognising the greater complexity of the phenomenon, and perhaps that tartanry is not simply sentimentalisation. Wilson of Bannockburn exported tartan for the clothing of slaves owned by transatlantic Scots. Faiers notes

> The inexorable logic of the slave system, where a process of dehumanization is necessary to make people into commodities, which then become part of a larger economic system of exchange, makes the contingency and mathematical logic of tartan the perfect textile of oppression.[57]

Yet, this is not an oppression Nairn seems to notice, and certainly 'oppression' is not a complete description of the potential and meaning of tartan and tartanry.

The negative, often hyperventilated, stances taken by commentators like Nairn can be seen to march with the flawed 'history' of Trevor-Roper. They also illustrate a point made by Craig Beveridge and Ronald Turnbull:

> The view that popular consciousness is dominated by tartanry, that the populace is sunk in ignorance and irrationality, accords perfectly with the governing image of Scotland as a dark and backward culture. This reflection allows us to locate the real significance of the discussion on tartanry, namely as another instance of the Scottish intelligentsia's readiness to embrace damning conceptions of national culture – in other words as an expression of inferiorism.[58]

Such an identification of Scotland, of course, is an extension of the stigmatisation of the Highlands as a wild place already discussed in this chapter. It is also arguable that misunderstanding and misanalysis of tartan and tartanry as politico-cultural phenomena sustain an agenda that claims to know what is best for the 'vulgar'. MacArthur makes clear such an agenda when he says

> Clearly the traditions of Kailyard and Tartanry have to be exposed and deconstructed and more politically progressive representations constructed, circulated and discussed.[59]

Here the intellectual casts himself as he who will construct other 'politically progressive' representations for the rest of society. Such arrogance may be based on a view of the leading role of the intelligentsia, but that role is altogether theoretically and practically more complex than sloganeering, excited vocabulary and the elevation of exclamation marks. As Duncan Petrie observes

> It is instructive that both Nairn and McArthur should end up relying heavily on metaphors of psychopathology and an attendant conception of the Scottish national psyche as irredeemably neurotic. The only apparent possibility of curing the patient was for Scottish writers and film-makers to self-consciously throw off their collective tartan security blanket and summon the necessary courage – and the appropriate intellectual resources – to create a more purposeful, self-reflective and progressive cultural engagement with Scotland and the world.[60]

In their defence, it may be that some of the impetus for the anti-tartan arguments associated with Nairn and McArthur are related to events leading up to and following the 1979 referendum debacle. As Petrie comments,

> The intellectual engagement with Scottish culture sparked by the events of 1979 led some critics to attack the deficient ways in which Scotland had not only been represented by others but, more seriously, had (mis)represented itself. Such debates became fixated on the pernicious effects of the pervasive discourses of tartanry and Kailyard, mythic structures that were fundamentally regressive, elegiac and symptomatic of a national inferiority complex.[61]

What Petrie describes as fixated debates are themselves regressive and inferiorist. Beyond them, as he observes, 'it has been possible to identify countervailing traditions to tartanry and Kailyard'.[62]

Indeed, tartan and tartanry contain, as this volume shows, countervailing traditions within their own discourses and those are much richer and more immanent than regressive critics like Nairn and McArthur seem to allow. As Faiers says,

> If not intentionally deceptive, much tartan history has a quality of excess, an excess in terms of symbolic meaning and perception. This has enabled it to be manipulated by a number of its most passionate promoters. Scott, the Sobieskis, Jacobite sympathizers, Hanoverian

monarchs and many others have recognized its possibilities for adaptation, and assimilation. This chimerical quality, far from reducing its popularity, has in fact ensured its longevity, and allowed it to maintain a prominent position in both popular and 'high' culture. Tartan [. . .] functions as cultural lodestone, universally recognized and with a constantly developing legendary status.[63]

In fact, the complex richness of tartan and tartanry discourses can allow even Faiers to be taken in by Trevor-Roper's mythology-as-history so that he foresees its being somehow disengaged from Scottish culture and identity:

[With the collapse and amalgamation of regiments and decline of interest in the Royal Family] two of tartan's chief symbolic functions as a military and regal textile are in decline. Similarly the establishment of an independent [sic] parliament has meant that for many Scots, tartan's other central function as a symbol of 'Scottishness' should be dispensed with as being primarily an English nineteenth-century construction.[64]

Yet, as we have seen, tartan as a 'symbol of "Scottishness"' is neither an English invention – though little harm if it were – nor one of the nineteenth century. Tartan continues in Mary Douglas's words on Lévi-Strauss 'to portray the contradictions in the basic premises of the culture'. And it does so despite attempts to caricature its varied history and meanings.

Notes

 1 Douglas, *Implicit Meanings*, p. 156.
 2 For example, passim in Barthes, *Mythologies*.
 3 McArthur, *Brigadoon*, p. 49.
 4 Dunbar, *History*, pp. 91–2.
 5 Quoted in Dunbar, *History*, p. 97.
 6 Ibid., p. 97.
 7 Ibid., p. 159.
 8 Scarlett, *Tartan: The Highland Textile*, pp. 26–30.
 9 Ibid., p. 30.
10 Stewart, *The Setts of the Scottish Tartans*, p. 28.
11 Cheape, *Tartan. The Highland Habit*, p. 74.
12 Scarlett, *Tartan: The Highland Textile*, p. 25.
13 Haldane, 'The great clan tartan myth', vol. XV, no. 6, p. 457.

14 Ibid., vol. XVI, no. 1, p. 49.
15 Drummond-Norie, *Loyal Lochaber*, p. 358.
16 Ibid., p. 354.
17 MacKillop, 'Military recruiting', p. 3.
18 Trevor-Roper, 'The invention of tradition'.
19 See Dunbar, *History*, pp. 12–13.
20 Ibid., p. 13.
21 The drawing may be found reproduced opposite page 254 of Bartley, *Teague, Shenkin and Sawney*.
22 Trevor-Roper, 'The invention of tradition', pp. 15–16.
23 Ferguson, 'Samuel Johnson's views on Scottish Gaelic culture', p. 183.
24 McArthur, *Brigadoon*, p. 47.
25 Faiers, *Tartan*, p. 65.
26 Ibid., p. 142.
27 MacKillop, 'Military recruiting', p. 62.
28 Ibid., p. 365.
29 Ibid., pp. 42–3.
30 Ibid., p. 152.
31 Ibid., p. 274.
32 Henderson, *Highland Soldier*, p. 4.
33 Ibid., p. iii.
34 Dunbar, *History*, p.153.
35 Henderson, *Highland Soldier*, p. 44.
36 Spiers, *The Scottish Soldier and Empire*, p. 113.
37 McArthur, *Brigadoon*, p. 18.
38 Ibid., p. 47.
39 Dunbar, *History*, p. 14.
40 Ibid., p. 23.
41 Spiers, *The Scottish Soldier and Empire*, p. 126.
42 Broadcast in *Edward VII – The Prince of Pleasure*, BBC 2, 23 March 2010.
43 Craig, *Out of History*, p. 12.
44 McCrone, *Understanding Scotland*, 2nd edn, p. 142.
45 McArthur, 'Breaking the signs', p. 21.
46 Nairn, *The Break-Up of Britain*, 2nd edn, pp. 152–3.
47 Ibid., p. 114.
48 Ibid., p. 116.
49 Ibid., p. 123.
50 Ibid., p. 134.
51 Ibid., p. 156.
52 Ibid., p. 162.
53 Ibid., p. 168.
54 Ibid., pp. 162–9.
55 McArthur, *Brigadoon*, p. 5.

56 Nairn, *The Break-Up of Britain*, p. 167.
57 Faiers, *Tartan*, p. 272.
58 Beveridge and Turnbull, *The Eclipse of Scottish Culture*, p. 14 (cf. MacKillop, 'Military recruiting', p. 62).
59 McArthur, 'Breaking the signs', p. 25.
60 Petrie, *Contemporary Scottish Fictions*, p. 8.
61 Ibid., p. 17.
62 Ibid., p. 19.
63 Faiers, *Tartan*, pp. 71–2.
64 Ibid., p. 289.

7

TARTANRY AND ITS DISCONTENTS: THE IDEA OF POPULAR SCOTTISHNESS

Alan Riach

ॐ

In 2006, my parents hosted their golden wedding party at a big hotel in Ayrshire, swanky-homely, gas fires like coal fires, dark wood panelling and bars, heavy flowers in big vases on ornate mantelpieces, tartan carpets, tartan wallpaper and tartan-covered furniture (or so it seems in retrospect). A few weeks before the event, my father asked me, half-wistfully, half-mischievously, 'I wonder whether your boys would like to wear the kilt?' I asked them. 'Yes, Dad,' they said. 'We like kilts. Kilts are cool.'

So I took them to the kilt-hire shop and the assistant asked me about tartan. 'As far as I know,' I told him, 'we're entitled to wear my mother's family tartan, Cunningham, and the Riachs are associated with the clans Farquharson, MacDonald and MacLean.' Sorley Mac-Lean once told me there were Riachs who were hereditary child-minders and poets to the MacLeans and I was also informed that at a certain census, many Riachs switched their name to MacLean, so there were various options. The assistant smiled and said he was afraid there was not such a big selection available in children's sizes, but what they had was hanging on two rails over by the wall. 'Well, it's a party,' I told James and David, 'so just go and choose colours that you like.'

In a few moments, David held up a smart, bright but not garish, predominantly blue tartan kilt. Simultaneously, James held up a smart, bright but not garish, predominantly green one. 'We like these ones,' they said. I took a closer look: *Ancient Dress Rangers*, said one label. *Ancient Dress Celtic*, said the other.

Sensitive to subtexts, I went back to my parents and told them this. 'It's your party,' I said. 'I don't want to cause any family trouble.'

My father laughed. 'Go ahead,' he said. 'Whatever they like. It's a party. It's dressing up, for fun. It'll be nice to see them in kilts.'

And they looked smart and wore them well and enjoyed the occasion.

And there were two comments.

A particularly stern, tight-coiffured aunt approached me, mouth pursed, and asked tensely, 'Are those tartans what I think they are?' I admitted they were. She shook her head and walked away, 'Tsk, tsk,' under her breath.

And a particularly ebullient, jovial uncle came over, arm outstretched, hand open: 'Put it there, Alan,' he beamed. 'That's a major step on the road to world peace!'

A domestic anecdote, but it illustrates well the continued potency of tartan to register as a badge of loyalty, whether or not intended by the wearer. Innocence may be tender but ignorance is no excuse in a sectarian world where flags are valuable because they come at a cost. In certain places in the United Kingdom, certain folk respond with bloody violence to such badges or flags. On that lasting currency, an important component of Scottish identity continues to trade, whether through the dispositions of those whose inherited and fostered bad beliefs approve and promulgate the violence, or in those whose good humour is open enough to accommodate kitsch as simply an indissoluble part of the story.

In this chapter, I would like to take a speculative journey through some examples of that currency in active transaction, and consider its practice as generating a complex dynamic that seems central, indeed unique, to what the word 'Scotland' means. That should not be understood as sanction or praise, but it seems to me that the story of how tartan has acquired its meanings and how these meanings function is exceptional to Scotland. No other country I know of has a distinctive, almost infinitely variable (and therefore undefined) cloth pattern as a national badge. It endorses a recognition of difference, an inclusiveness that is sensitive to qualities of character, liabilities of preference, strengths and weaknesses that anyone can see at work in any family.

The myth of Scotland as a nation in which diversity is an essential characteristic (of geography, languages, cultural habits and preferences, and so on) has its own history. Tartan is central to it, primarily because – as the story goes – after the dispersal of the clans in the wake of Culloden in 1746, and after the Highland Clearances in the late eighteenth and early nineteenth centuries, Scottish Highlanders were relocated from the Highlands of Scotland to other parts of Scotland, east and south, and to other parts of the world. Emigration from Scotland after the Second World War, through the 1950s and 1960s and on to the twenty-first century, carried the same story into the contemporary world.

Globally now, tartan is a fabric in neon, a bridge back. That bridge is not, now, exclusive to the Highlands, nor to any specific Highland region where a specific family may have lived and be buried, or whose descendants may still live there, with their own social prejudices and material conditions of living, but rather to a mythic identity. The rainbow bridge to Valhalla at the end of *Das Rheingold* shimmers no less brightly and alluringly as Wagner's old gods tramp across it. They too are all one family: doomed, of course, but to anyone hooked by Wagnerian sensitivities and grandeur, unforgettable.

Hugh MacDiarmid (Christopher Murray Grieve) opens his autobiography *Lucky Poet* (1943) by discussing his surname, Grieve, then asserting, 'Murray is the oldest name in Scotland' and continuing, 'As boys, my brother and I wore the Graham tartan. Our mother was Elizabeth Graham.' But he continues by noting that while his mother's folk were agricultural workers, his father's people were mill-workers and 'My alignment [. . .] was always on the side of the industrial workers.' Nevertheless, he says

> from the steadings and cottages of my mother's folk and their neighbours in Wauchope and Eskdalemuir and Middlebie and Tundergarth, I drew an assurance that I felt and understood the spirit of Scotland and the Scottish country folk in no common measure, and that made it at any rate possible that I would in due course become a great national poet of Scotland.[1]

Behind the hyperbole, it is the bringing together of a multitude of different specific identities evident in the placenames and the association of this with a rightful claim to tartan, thus linking Lowlands and Highlands, ancient history and contemporary technology, that animates this proposition. And it invokes the potency of myth to nourish the claim. Implicit here is the comprehensive summation of Scotland – Highland, Lowland, industrial, agricultural – that the 'national poet' would be required to embody. There are truths in this account of his ancestors, but MacDiarmid's claim is mythic creation.

The myth is evident too in the famous 1928 photograph of the founding members of the National Party of Scotland. There are no men in kilts and not a trace of tartan but the myth of national identity as something overwhelming or accommodating class difference, prioritised against it, is paramount. The Duke of Montrose, Compton

Mackenzie, R. B. Cunninghame Graham, MacDiarmid, James Va-
lentine and John MacCormick are in line: aristocrats, landed gentry,
writers, journalists, lawyers: upper-, middle- and working-class backgrounds and loyalties all represented, and with MacDiarmid, former
member of Keir Hardie's Independent Labour Party, future member of
the British Communist Party, and Cunninghame Graham, founding
member of what would be the British Labour Party, men of both
practical and idealistic political commitment.[2] The legacies are long-
lasting: in the early twenty-first century, the Scottish National and the
Labour parties are the two most powerful political groups in Scotland,
at loggerheads with each other because of conflicting commitments to
constitutional national identity. Yet both parties are allied in social
democratic values. Photographs from the 1950s and 1960s show
MacDiarmid in tartan kilt visiting East European countries in the
Communist bloc, reading his poems and taking part in festivals as an
unofficial ambassador for an imagined socialist republic of Scotland,
broadcasting an undelivered possibility given actual promise by the
cross-class group in the photograph from 1928.[3]

The artist-ambassador offers revisioning of the old icons. The music
historian and poet John Purser visiting New Zealand in 1993 had this
to say in response to a radio interviewer's opening gambit, 'When I
think of Scottish music I think of bagpipes':

> Well, I've come here on a kind of anti-bagpipe crusade! Don't get
> me wrong – I love the bagpipes – they're a terrific instrument and in
> fact I've met some very fine pipers in New Zealand and one of the
> best pipers in Scotland is a New Zealander, Murray Henderson. But
> we've been stereotyped with this and there is a hell of a lot more to
> Scottish music than bagpipes. I frequently lecture in the kilt with the
> deliberate intention of confusing people, because they see me
> coming up in the kilt and they think it's going to be haggis and
> heather and bagpipes and tartan and so on, and what they hear
> instead is a Columban plainchant, for example.[4]

So the emblem of the tartan kilt might work internationally, both
confirming and subverting conventional expectations. It might work
effectively to endorse the myth of a diverse and undefined Scottishness, an identity characterised by potential that is not simply unful-
filled but still undiscovered. The mission – evident in MacDiarmid's
work as it is in Purser's – is not conquest but exploration, self-
discovery, self-expression and education in unfamilar resources.

The gambit of this mission is predicated on foundational faith in a reciprocity of value in different identities confirming, rather than competing against, each other. This is why it can be described as mythic, rather than actual: who would deny that the ideal society of friendly neighbourliness suggested here is utopian? Yet it is worth emphasising that some myths are more enabling, less constricting, than others, and therefore worth investing in: as Lévi-Strauss said, myths embody necessary contradictions. Myths are always part of the human fabric and we are richer for them. They may arise from historical realities but there is no guarantee that they will produce utopia, rather the opposite. Any close reading of a week of twenty-first-century news about Scotland can demonstrate racism, sectarianism, violence, advocacy of economic and military over cultural authority, rampant managerialism and the usual circus of dire practices. But perhaps all this only means that the tartan myth, with its long history and basis in family fact, has been decoyed and misdirected, rather than exploited to advantage. It has evidently often enough been exaggerated *ad nauseam* and to an extent that made it weigh as an exclusive marker of Scottish identity, shoving industrial, post-industrial or city life to the margins in the national iconography. In this respect too, it shows a familiar Scottish characteristic. Consider the extent to which, nationally and internationally, Robert Burns is known as the national poet of Scotland, to the virtual extinction of all knowledge of any other Scottish poet, writer, artist, composer or creator of works of art.

I would take as the key literary foundation of tartanry Walter Scott's *Rob Roy* (1817) because pre-eminently here established is the connectedness of two main divided areas of Scotland: Highland, outlaw, country-based, clan-based, tartan, and Lowland, lawful, city-based, commercially defined, commercial, sartorially subject to fashion. Rob Roy stands for the former, Bailie Nicol Jarvie for the latter. But, of course, they are cousins, connected irrevocably by blood. So if the commercial Hanoverian succession is the material future in the ethos described in the novel, the tartan fabric of multiple, singular but related identities is the deeper and longer-lasting future, extending beyond fashions as a deep myth of what constitutes an identity different from one defined exclusively by commercial priorities and material gratifications. Ian Duncan describes the proposition succinctly:

> The opposition between Rob and Jarvie, cousins after all, articulates a relation of complementarity and complexity fixed in the

blood, rather than a binary antagonism in which one (Jarvie) must supersede and cancel the other.[5]

Having said this, however, Duncan then suggests that the transitional moment Scott describes does represent the formation of the modern world:

> Both of them constitute the new kind of world of which modern Great Britain is a part – an imperial, immanently global political economy in which jaggedly uneven times and spaces, from commercial hub to wild hinterland, are bound in a complex web by trade and military force.[6]

It is not that *Rob Roy* opens a window onto the past but rather that it shows the presence of the past in the present and future. So what we are reading in the novel is an ambiguous validation of an ethos of complex identity that is – or may be – in effect subversive of the imperial ethos to which it contributes. And this calls to mind the Nigerian writer Ben Okri's description of his visit to Scotland in the 1980s:

> It is another country. The air is sharper. The hills, stark in their solidity, sheer out in the lights. It is a country in which history breathes from the landscapes [. . . While culture,] during a time of political impotence, can become kitsch, it can also function as continual declaration and resistance.[7]

This is a valuable reminder of the positive potential for the progressive political development tartanry might embody. But it needs to be balanced against not only the destructive, regressive, limiting function tartanry has had, but also the context in which tartanry arose, developed and found global mass media representation, especially through the last half of the twentieth century and into the twenty-first century. This may be briefly sketched: begin with the visit of George IV to Edinburgh in 1822, which Walter Scott effectively choreographed, when the British monarch sported the kilt in public, over his pink tights. This completed a process, begun by the military, that rehabilitated tartan from being outlawed into a state-sanctioned garb, an acceptable badge of Scottishness within the British comity. If Ben Okri's note suggests a different reading of that episode, in which Kitsch is more subversive of British authority, then the political

relations of power between Scotland and England are no less emphasised – Okri's word 'impotence' is appropriate in both readings. In
one, impotence is subservient; in the other, it masks subversiveness.
Sometimes, it is suggested, nineteenth-century Hanoverian royalty
appropriated and endorsed tartan. Arguably, as Ian Brown suggests
in his Introduction (p. 7), the traffic was in the other direction.

Different readings of familiar things might be applied selectively
elsewhere. In nineteenth-century Scottish poetry, in Gaelic, Scots and
English, there is a plethora of patriotic and usually unionist work that
is conventionally read as endorsing a sentimental view of Scotland for
an international readership requiring superficial comfort and pious
assurance. Such cultural markets, of course, occur in many cultures,
not just Scottish and not just then. The BBC series *Lark Rise to
Candleford* (2008–) is in fact contemporary English Kailyard, with the
same underlying commercial imperatives and couthy features: eccentric characters, religiosity, village politics and jealousies, family
misunderstandings and secrets, class consciousness, cosy moralities,
the postmistress replacing the minister for spiritual communication, a
lad – and a lass – o' pairts and so on (though presumably the more or
less permanent sunshine is a specifically English feature).[8] And indeed
there is an international audience for such texts today, just as in the
nineteenth and twentieth centuries there was an international readership eager for stories, songs and poems about the Gàidhealtachd and
Scotland generally, misty-eyed, glowing in golden light, fostering a
vision of how things might have been, once upon a time. If the liability
of that tartan-clad vision was to infuse supine nostalgia for a never-
land of benevolent, happy clans, the other, militant aspect that vision
fuelled was inspired by the sense that the Gàidhealtachd – and Scotland generally – was being broken down and its people dispersed. In
this perspective, rapacious mendacity and the rise of industrial cities as
Scotland's population-centres were destroying the values of kinship,
hospitality and familial support. One of the most popular songs for
generations through to the twentieth century was Malcolm MacFarlane's Scots translation of 'The Thistle of Scotland' by Evan MacColl
(1808–98):

> Its strength and its beauty the storm never harms;
> It stan's on its guard like a warrior in arms;
> Yet its down is as saft as the gull's on the sea.
> And its tassles as bricht as my Jeanie's blue e'e.

MacFarlane also translated Dugald MacPhail's lastingly popular 'Isle of Mull':

> The Isle of Mull is of isles the fairest,
> Of ocean's gems 'tis the first and rarest;
> Green grassy island of sparkling fountains,
> Of waving woods and high towering mountains.[9]

Paradoxically, the valorisation of the Highlands and Islands as a kind of utopian – to a modern taste, sentimentalised – heaven-on-earth or lost Eden may also have endorsed militant resistance to imperial oppression, such as that enacted in the Battle of the Braes in Skye in 1882. This led directly to the Crofters' Act of 1884 and the drive to establish better legal rights for Gaelic-speaking people. A similar paradox can be observed in the religious Gaelic songs and hymns of the period. While these ostensibly adhered to church convention that might approve the rule of law and Establishment authority, they might also invoke a Biblical sense of justice and a religious conviction that could find the moral force to stand against unjust authority.

However much the clan system was eroded by the nineteenth century, the conflicts involved in a sensibility committed to loyalty to locality and kinship confronted with the evident insults of absentee landlordism, remote and ignorant political power and ruthless economic exploitation found expression in poems of different genres and perspectives. There has been some criticism of nineteenth-century Gaelic poetry as less impressive than that of the preceding era, yet reading it in this way, the field becomes richer and more complex. It is connected intricately with the politics of the time, the processes of industrialisation, colonialism and imperial expansion, and thus closely connected with what was happening in contemporary Scottish literature in English and Scots. The heroic patriotism of Walter Scott's 'Land of the Mountain and the Flood' and the domestic stability of the humble family gathered around for a communal reading of the Bible depicted in Burns's 'Cottar's Saturday Night' are only two of the most resonant examples of literary influence. At their worst, they give sanction to unionist militarism and reactionary pieties. Yet even those need to be read in this complex context.

Elsewhere in this volume Trevor Royle discusses the wearing of the military kilt in Scottish regimental uniforms in the British Army throughout the nineteenth and twentieth centuries. This is perhaps most movingly memorialised in the many statues throughout Scotland, in small towns and villages, full-figure sculptures of kilted Scottish solders. Ostensibly these were erected in memory of the cause for which the Scottish soldiers in the First World War lost their lives. Then again, further names were added to many of the memorials in memory of the cause for which Scots lost their lives in the Second World War, and indeed in other military conflicts. In this sense, they may seem to be monuments to the virtues of the cause of British imperialism and its significant, distinctive Scottish component. But another reading is possible: what is most profoundly moving about these figures perhaps is not that cause. (In any case, was there ever a single 'cause'? What fired young men to go to the trenches in the First World War was not the same thing as determined a later generation to oppose Nazism, and, besides, conscription overcast individual motivation.) Rather, they might be seen as lasting monuments to the loss of the generations suffered by the communities of people who lived and continue to live in those small towns and villages. In other words, they may be seen as monuments to the potential of a Scotland from which a fearful number of young men were simply subtracted. The tartan kilt interweaves generations of the dead from the Borders to the Highlands and Islands in a terrible statement of absolute loss.[10]

This is to measure a true value, an actual cost, which it is easy to neglect when we are caught up with evaluations of the myth of tartanry and its representation in lighter media modes. Yet material fact and media representation are never entirely separate, distant as they might seem at times. As modes of representation changed and developed, that distance opened up like a slow wrench to an ankle that might require a surgical operation and a bolt installed to bring the bones back to a co-ordinated strength that would carry the owner's weight. Examples abound, from written descriptions (Walter Scott's popularity is only the most frequently cited indication – there are many other writers of variable quality engaged in this work). These run through theatre productions making the visual spectacle even more familiar, to oil paintings, which were then used as templates for engravings that could be reproduced on an industrial scale internationally and as book illustrations, on to postcards, of which surely the most familiar is that of John Brown and Queen Victoria, the Queen mounted and her tartan-kilted Scottish supporter standing in a posture of unchallengeable loyalty before her. One contrast worth noting, in terms of how far apart the wrenched bones in that ankle had become by the late nineteenth century, is that between the artists Edwin Landseer (1802–73) and William McTaggart (1835–1910).

The former created instantly recognisable images of a Scotland defined by tartanry; the latter was one of the major artists in oil painting, depicting a populated, working, Gaelic-speaking Scotland. Here he evoked historical and mythic aspects – from Columba to the Clearances to the fishing industry related in Neil Gunn's great novel *The Silver Darlings* (1941), and the children who will inherit it all. Landseer remains familiar in international iconography, while McTaggart still requires major revaluation and recognition as a cultural entitlement in the education system. He will not be heard of in most schools in Scotland.

In the mass media of the later twentieth century, tartanry becomes an even more internationally familiar signifier of Scottishness. The single most dynamic critical intervention in this process was arguably *Scotch Reels*, the 1982 small anthology of essays edited by Colin McArthur.[11] In a groundbreaking act of self-conscious criticism and historical analysis, aspects of the representation of Scottish identity in literature, television and film were scrutinised and, generally, condemned. If the analysis was timely – indeed, urgently needed – the condemnation, as Ian Brown in his contributions to this volume and others in other chapters show, can now be seen to lack subtlety or broad-based insight. It is possible, rather than seeking total rejection, to read texts and history as yielding things that may be progressive, as we have noted above, and there are examples of the contributors to *Scotch Reels* subsequently doing that. McArthur himself later observed

> Undoubtedly the *Scotch Reels'* analysts tended to see the popular iconography of Scottishness as irretrievably tarnished by the ideological use to which they [sic] had been put. On the other hand, since its appearance in 1982 there have been persuasive arguments indicating that *Scotch Reels'* view may indeed have been too rigid and that this same iconography is more malleable than was supposed.[12]

However, one of the most effective visual demonstrations of the history of Tartanry Rampant in the book is Murray Grigor's 'From Scott-land to Disneyland'. This collects popular prints, photographs, tapestries, calendars, stills from films like *Annie Laurie* (1918), *The Young Lochinvar* (1923), Laurel and Hardy in *Bonnie Scotland* (1935), Shirley Temple in *Wee Willie Winkie* (1938), *Bonnie Prince Charlie* (1948), Disney's *Rob Roy – The Highland Rogue* (1953),

Brigadoon (1954) and, by contrast, Peter Watkins's bloody *Culloden* (1964).[13] Of the written essays, perhaps John Caughie sums up the problem we have been discussing most sharply in his provocatively-entitled 'Scottish television: what would it look like?'[14] Here, Caughie acknowledges that tartanry is 'central to debates about a Scottish national culture' and that, in terms of television, 'the memory of The White Heather Club lingers on' because it accorded with 'the recognisable discourses' of Scottish national identity 'so smoothly'. This is why such programmes seemed to Caughie then to have 'a particular regressive potency': 'they have a certain defining power, confirming and reinforcing the image of the "essentially Scottish"'. The problem for television, according to Caughie – and it is a problem that has its parallels in other media today – is 'the absence of a consistently alternative discourse'. While there are numerous representations of national character in TV programmes depicting England or America (in different genres, different geographical locations and so on), there are a smaller number representing Scotland, and the most familiar may be exaggerated out of proportion to their connection with anything actual.

Has this situation improved since 1982?

In 2010, with a devolved Parliament in Edinburgh and the Scottish National Party in government, control of television broadcasting remains with Westminster power in London. Television adaptations of great works of Scottish literature may be remembered from the 1970s and 1980s by a generation born in the 1950s or 1960s: *Sunset Song* (1971) and the rest of the *Scots Quair* trilogy, *Cloud Howe* (1982) and *Grey Granite* (1983), and Gibbon's short stories, *Clay, Smeddum and Greenden*, broadcast as a trilogy in a ninety-minute programme (1976), the adaptation of George Mackay Brown's short story *Andrina* (1981) directed by Bill Forsyth, serials based on Stevenson's *The Master of Ballantrae* (1975) and Scott's *Rob Roy* (1977), both closely following the narratives of each novel to wonderfully suspenseful effect, documentaries about the lives of Robert Louis Stevenson, Hugh MacDiarmid and William Soutar. Almost nothing of this sort has been forthcoming in the 1990s and early twenty-first century and, of the classics just named, none is available for purchase on DVD, as similar programmes based on work by Jane Austen, Charles Dickens, George Eliot and others are. Scotland's cultural and literary production is neglected, sidelined, made unavailable, not only through commercial priorities attached to the market value of English literature, but by the dominance of repressive myths that work – and are often made to work – to shut down diversity and preclude the general availability of 'a consistently alternative discourse'.[15]

But things change.

The signs for a positive or progressive conclusion are easily missed but there are a few.

In 1998, Alan Grant and Frank Quitely (whose real name is, quite frankly, Vince Deighan) respectively wrote and drew a work for DC Comics, *Batman: Scottish Connection*, on the cover of which Batman is seen in mortal combat with a kilted, masked, sword-wielding villain.[16] Behind them, a brilliant blue and white Saltire is rippling. The implication that the American hero is battling a nasty Scottish insurgent is deliberately misleading, as the story makes clear. The villain, Fergus Slith, is an American whose ancestors were Scottish, left Scotland because of the Highland Clearances, settled in America and passed on through the generations the thirst for vengeance on the Clan MacDubh, who evicted them. The villain has returned to Scotland to enact this vengeance, and to terrorise and kill as many innocent people as get in his way as well. Batman, or Bruce Wayne, is in Scotland on holiday, and to attend the Clan MacDubh family reunion in Edinburgh Castle, because, as he reveals, some of his own ancestors were Scots. This may allude to the suggestion that Bob Kane, the creator of Batman, named him Bruce Wayne commemorating stories of Robert the Bruce he had been told as a child. Effectively, Batman is fighting Fergus to let a new generation find its own way without the inheritance of bad belief and the murder of innocents. To return to the cover, then, the questions arise: who is fighting for the flag, the Saltire? Given the mythic history of Batman in America and internationally, and given that this officially approved Batman story is written and drawn by two Scots, what does that flag stand for?[17] Icons of Scotland, the Saltire, like the tartan, have become richer, more complex, more problematic than before.

After his internationally commercially successful series of crime genre novels featuring John Rebus, Ian Rankin wrote a graphic novel entitled *Dark Entries* (2009), whose main character, John Constantine, had established his own devoted following in the comic book series *Hellblazer*. The Scottish crime fiction novelist Denise Mina had already written a story in the series before Rankin. Constantine seems to be based on crime-genre film noir conventions, a lone investigator in a world where most of the population is increasingly under threat by a growing number of zombies, whose mission is universal conversion. It sounds like a familiar metaphorical scenario. In *Dark*

Entries, Constantine seems to be tricked into taking part in a reality TV show but he gradually discovers that the entire show is taking place in Hell, before an audience of the damned. In what could only be a disappointing denouement, he manages to escape through a television screen back into his own living room, but the mystery is sustained effectively enough for the most part. In one moment of seeming digression, Constantine recounts a guilty secret that relates to the story of Sawney Bean, the legendary cannibal who is said to have lived with his family in a cave near Girvan, in Ayrshire, eating the locals and passers-by. Constantine explains that the figure is 'a legend, conjured up as a commentary on the Highland Clearances' but that a woman he knew, Helen, had been the girlfriend of a man who had become so obsessed by this legend that the spirit of Sawney Bean had possessed him and he had begun to eat raw meat and had murdered Helen. Constantine confronted him and killed him, and now, in the main story of the novel, has been seeing him in and out of his own dreams. Sawney Bean appears in two panels: grim-faced, in unmistakable tartan plaid and kilt. Where the rest of the novel might have cosmopolitan provenance, this episode is indisputably Scottish.[18]

Is this merely a frisson of local colour Rankin inserts? In Denise Mina's contribution, the plot takes in Glasgow's Kelvingrove Museum and Art Gallery and Glasgow University, as well as a macabre story from Iona. Similarly, are these merely novelties? Or are these tessellations indicative of further possibilities in the graphic novel or comic book format? The conservatism of form in popular and mass media signifies one thing beyond question: a lot more remains in potential than has ever been done up till now.

One final example. In the late 1990s, an advertisement appeared in certain glossy magazines for Elle Macpherson underwear. The supermodel was shown in a matching set of tartan bra and panties, half-turning her physique towards a couple of blurred male figures seen from behind in the foreground. She had a defiant, self-determined look on her face. The caption read: 'It's Macpherson clan tartan! Who wants to know?'

The image, one might argue, offers the suggestion that there is a valuable overlap between the progressive aspects and purposes of self-determined feminism and those of nationalism. Yet it would have to be acknowledged that the entire statement is made within the discourse of capitalism, the conventions of advertising and the concurrent exploitation of constrictive myths of both femininity and Scottishness, so evocatively depicted. But this I would take as emphasising the point I have been arguing for, more or less implicitly, throughout this essay: that even within ideologies that enforce our constriction, we may find the seeds of our liberation.

Notes

1 MacDiarmid, *Lucky Poet*, pp. 1–3.
2 The photograph is reproduced in Wright, *MacDiarmid: An Illustrated Biography*.
3 Ibid.
4 Purser, *The Music of Scotland*, p. 6.
5 Duncan, 'Scott, the history of the novel, and the history of fiction', p. 95.
6 Ibid., p. 95.
7 Okri, 'Diary', p. 16. Quoted in Riach, *Representing Scotland*, pp. xiv–xv.
8 I am grateful to Ian Brown for drawing my attention to this series as an example of English Kailyard.
9 Both poems are quoted from Meek, *The Wiles of the World*. See also Gifford and Riach, *Scotlands*, for a range of work that might be reconsidered in this way, especially from the nineteenth and twentieth centuries, including popular songs such as 'Scotland the Brave' and 'Flower of Scotland'.
10 See Calder, 'Meditation on memorials', pp. 3–28, especially pp. 17–19, which gives a descriptive list of many of these monuments; see also pp. 8–9, where Calder quotes the relevant lines from the speech delivered by the minister in memory of the characters who were killed in the First World War in Lewis Grassic Gibbon's *Sunset Song*: 'They died for a world that is past, these men, but they did not die for this that we seem to inherit.'
11 McArthur, *Scotch Reels*.
12 McArthur, *Brigadoon*, p. 135.
13 McArthur, *Scotch Reels*, pp. 17–39.
14 Ibid., pp. 112–22.
15 Ibid., p.120.
16 Grant and Quitely, *Batman: Scottish Connection*.
17 See Riach, *Representing Scotland*, pp. 219–22. The cover of *Batman: Scottish Connection* is published as a frontispiece to this book.
18 Rankin and Dell'Edera, *Dark Entries*, pp. 78–9.

8

'WHA'S LIKE US?': ETHNIC REPRESENTATION IN MUSIC HALL AND POPULAR THEATRE AND THE REMAKING OF URBAN SCOTTISH SOCIETY

Paul Maloney

൭

The Scotch comic – so often reduced to the single and divisive figure of Harry Lauder – is cast as an inferiorist, Kitsch embodiment of Kailyard and tartanry. He is 'kailyard consciousness in tartan exterior', in Cairns Craig's phrase, and part of a 'cultural sub-nationalism' in Tom Nairn's.[1] However, more recently writers have taken a more understanding view of the Scotch comic, with Alasdair Cameron and Adrienne Scullion seeing the figure's representation of national identity in developmental terms, 'not as a betrayal of the nation [. . .] but as a very necessary link in an evolving chain of national consciousness which can only now be appreciated'. In this context, they write, 'the totemic images of the Scotch comic – the cocksure Highland laddie, the interfering husband-seeking spinster and the gossiping village worthies or (their urban equivalents) the window-hangers – were approved and even celebrated as symbols of a nationality which, under normal circumstances, audiences were never allowed to express.'[2]

In further exploring the figure, this chapter has been inspired by two other recent critical developments. The first is a new appreciation of the cultural economics of modern Scotland, of how the development of popular forms needs to be understood in relation to expanding economic markets and, specifically, how popular culture outputs and representations circulated in Scotland at the turn of the nineteenth and twentieth centuries. This awareness of markets was led by William Donaldson's key work on Scottish popular literature, which showed how technological advances led to the creation of a new mass market for affordable popular fiction and periodicals, of which Kailyard fiction was just one part.[3] If Donaldson's work suggests that Kailyard literature was not an inward-looking development, but a product at least partly aimed at wider markets, then, as others have observed, popular theatre genres like music hall and stage representations such as the tartan Scotch comic similarly need to be assessed as responses to the wider commercial environment and market pressures which produced them.

The second development, following on from this consideration of a wider range of social and economic factors, involves a new openness to the social complexity and potential heterogeneity of Scottish society in the late nineteenth and early twentieth centuries and the cosmopolitan influences acting upon it. David McCrone foreshadowed this approach by broadening the terms of the debate, attacking the narrowness of the discourses surrounding Kailyard and tartanry, and questioning, in the light of Scotland's complex relations with wider British culture and society, whether a separate 'national' Scottish culture was possible.[4] While McCrone's argument for a broader cultural pluralism was based on a late-twentieth-century perspective, David Goldie, in his work on early-twentieth-century Scotland, has also drawn on contemporary critical theory by suggesting that ideas on the hybridity of Scottish society could usefully be explored in earlier contexts:

> Cultural criticism has been eager to embrace this heterogeneity as it pertains in contemporary Scotland [. . .] But it is still arguably reluctant to project these ideas back a hundred years – to allow that Scotland at the beginning of the twentieth century was similarly, if not quite as complexly, hybrid as it was at the century's end.[5]

In this spirit this chapter examines the Scotch comic and its projection of Scottish identity alongside other 'national' stage representations popular in Scottish music halls at the time, which would also have contributed to creating 'an inclusive model of the national culture as the sum of all current cultural activity'.[6]

In the first part the tension between music hall as popular culture and commercial entertainment genre is explored. It considers the proposition that there was much more to the Scotch comic than Lauder's iconic tartanised version; that the figure was originally a product of urban industrial society, adapted to meet the demands of a market-driven commercial format – music hall – but that, post-

Lauder, it reconnected with earlier strands of this working-class performing tradition in ways which make it clear that the figure remained, at least in part, an expression of Scottish urban working-class culture. As an example of this reversion, and of the role tartan played as a signifier of national identity, this section explores the career of Tommy Lorne, the pre-eminent interwar Scottish comedian whose very cultural specificity affirmed the Scotch comic's enduring appeal.

The chapter's second part will move beyond modern tendencies to view the Scotch comic in isolation, comparing its projection of Scottish identity to other reductive 'national' or ethnic representations with which it competed on Scottish music hall stages. In exploring how these stage representations might have contributed to the sometimes-fractured community relations in Scottish cities, it will examine the very different impact of the Scotch comic tradition on a second performer, the Glasgow Jewish comedian Ike Freedman.

HISTORY

The Scotch comic predated Lauder by at least a generation in the music hall, and considerably longer in popular theatre. It represented a far more diverse performing tradition than his tartan embodiment suggests. Moreover, the figure continued to flourish, demonstrating a range of different contexts and emphases, well into the interwar years, in ways that make clear that tartan and its applications were by no means the preserve of Lauder's creation. At some level they were connected with wider issues concerning the search for a common Scottish identity. Part of the Scotch comic's complexity concerns too the extent to which it could be regarded as an expression of working-class popular culture, or a commercial entertainment format's manufactured product.

The Scottish music hall that emerged in the 1850s, developed and promoted by publicans in response to popular demand for affordable entertainment, arose from Scottish society's industrialisation, bringing large-scale population movement from rural areas to expanding towns and cities. The early halls' development, and the capital investment they represented, brought a rapid demand for performers. Initially the product of the convivial, participatory environment of the free-and-easy, these performers soon developed into professional music hall artists, while retaining the close ties to the audience that marked early music hall. Although as commercial entertainment music hall employed a cosmopolitan range of performers, stars from London and northern England frequently providing the leading attractions, music hall in Scotland as elsewhere was essentially localised, defined by its identification with local audiences. Scottish performers speaking in Scottish accents and performing Scottish songs, sketches and patter were enormously popular. The first generation had a variety of backgrounds reflecting Scottish entertainment culture's diffuse nature: singers at free-and-easies; actors specialising in comic roles from the National Drama, translating songs and character sketches onto the music hall stage; and concert singers, like James Houston, who had performed comic songs, readings and recitations across the country. Styles and modes of performances overlapped, as did material, reflecting the diversity of sources. The works of Burns, Jacobite songs and traditional songs and music combined with recitations, vernacular renditions of current music hall hits and topical songs commenting on local news and events.

Although it has been suggested that Scotch Comics emerged as a performing genre in the 1880s, the term was used in popular theatre billing in the 1860s. While its use may have been straightforwardly descriptive, performances like P. G. 'Packy' Fairley's 1867 appearance as 'The Celebrated Scotch Comedian, who will give, in character, Song and Dance, "The Newhaven Fishwife," "The Scotch Washerwoman," [and] "Have ye seen my Jamie"', suggest performance substance closely related to what was to come.[7] J. Wilson McLaren later recalled that by the 1870s 'no evening's programme was considered complete without a Scots comic'.[8] These comedians of the 1860s and 1870s – like R. S. Pillans, James Lumsden, Willie Cummings, James Willison, W. H. Lannigan, James Houston, N. C. Bostock, R. C. McGill and Harry Linn – were products of a new entertainment culture centred on the expanding music hall. With all its cosmopolitan influences, it also drew on other types of engagement culturally distinctive to the Scottish scene – soirees, conversaziones and Saturday concerts held by churches, temperance societies, trades associations and other improving organisations. It also embraced dramatic appearances in acting companies of legitimate theatres, where vernacular skills were in great demand for comic protagonists of pantomimes and in roles such as Bailie Nicol Jarvie and the Laird of Dumbiedykes.

The diversity of these different registers of professional activity, symptomatic of the smaller and more integrated Scottish market, required performers adept at switching constituencies – playing to raucous music hall audiences one performance, and the more constrained atmosphere of abstainers' Saturday night concerts or church conversaziones the next. Nonetheless, the common denominator for audiences was shared appreciation of Scottish language and culture, vested partly in language, dialect words and phrases, and partly in a familiar body of popular songs, poetry, readings and recitations, constantly renewed and extended by topical material: local news, events and personalities. While music hall performers elsewhere in Britain spoke in vernacular accents and incorporated topical material, in Scotland use of Scots words and speech, together with familiar performing material with Burns and Scott at its heart, expressed a popular performing culture not only local or regional, but genuinely national.

LAUDER

Most criticism of the Scotch comic, usually evoked in the capering, tartan-clad figure of Harry Lauder, centres on charges of cultural fraudulence. For Cairns Craig, the offensive aspect of Lauder's performance was its cultural aberrance, combining Lowland speech and manners with caricatured Highland dress, a juxtaposition that made a nonsense of Scottish history and culture. Hugh MacDiarmid went further, seeing the characterisation as malicious, enshrining

> those qualities of canniness, pawkiness and religiosity, which have been foisted upon the Scottish people by insidious English propaganda, as a means of destroying Scottish national pride, and of robbing Scots of their true attributes, which are the very opposite of these mentioned.[9]

In fact, as we have seen, the Scotch comic was not only indigenous, with longstanding Scottish popular theatre roots, but in its modern music hall manifestation a product of Scottish urban society.

Lauder, then, must be viewed in relation to this pre-existing tradition. His use of tartan aside, his performance shows marked continuities with the styles and practices of those preceding him. His repertoire comprised a range of individually characterised songs, with accompanying costume changes, patter and business in short sketches and vignettes. Characterisations consisted of established types – including drag impersonations – while his songs drew on types familiar from previous and still current performers. So 'The Saftest o' the Family', Lauder's affecting song with patter about a 'slow' boy, mirrored similarly pathetic numbers like J. C. Macdonald's 'Sandy Saft-Awee', and the Ayrshire comedian Bob Sloan's 'By Gings A'm Hungry', where he ate a slice of bread during his patter. Lauder's 'Risin' early in the Mornin', about having to leave a warm bed to start work before dawn, echoes Macdonald's 'Rise, Jock, Rise'.[10]

Even Lauder's anglicised delivery, subject of much debate, which he described as English sung with a Scottish accent, with the occasional Scots word or phrase thrown in, may have precedents in existing practice. Bill Findlay, discussing the Scotch comic and recitalist James Houston, suggests Scottish regional dialects were already in the process of being smoothed out in favour of a more standardised delivery better comprehended by audiences in large theatres and halls. Findlay suggests that one of the reasons Lauder's popularity in Scotland was apparently unaffected by his 'ersatz' language

> was because Lauder's 'stage Scots' was but an extension of an already existing convention – shaped by considerations of effective delivery – of Scotch comics using a diluted Scots: a convention which represented a continuity of earlier nineteenth century practice such as I suggest marked Houston's delivery of his Scots material.[11]

Notwithstanding his performing skill and charisma, Lauder's success can be seen as responding to developing market conditions. Music hall's 1890s rebranding as variety, the capitalisation and investment in new theatres and corresponding rush to contract leading artists offered considerable financial rewards to performers who could break through onto the lucrative national circuits. Lauder, having previously tried his hand as an Irish comedian, developed his homogenised Scottish persona. He took the sentimental aspect of the Scots comic repertoire, adapted the speech to standard English and used tartan to project Scottish identity in a way self-evidently unnecessary in Scotland, but a prerequisite for wider transferability. Thus, adapting pre-existing Scots comic motifs, he produced a transferable iconic character which achieved parity in the wider market with music hall's other national representations. Although the persona was popular in England, its international success – leading to twenty-two coast-to-coast United States tours – was due to the fact that it proved enormously resonant for expatriate Scots. For them its outsize, big-theatre projection of Scottish identity provided the self-affirming, resonant, vibrant statement needed by Scottish communities throughout the United States, Australasia and South Africa.

Many of the components of Lauder's success – the strategic planning of his American tours by William Morris, his exploitation of expatriate networks and use of new recording technology as a promotional tool – were essentially marketing innovations. His transforming innovation in performing terms, however, was making tartan the visual signature of his stage persona, to the extent that the two became inseparable in the public consciousness. In assessing the extravagant tartan costumes he popularised, it is important not to overstate their impact purely on the grounds of what seem – to modern audiences used to film and televisual close-up naturalism – their excessive exaggeration. Such outfits reflected the practical utility of stage costumes for large theatres, where the use of costume was part of performing technique. A photograph of one of Lauder's contemporaries, Jack (later Jock) Mills, shows him in costume featuring kilt, jacket with huge tartan check pattern, enormous buttons and glengarry with ribbons flying off at impossible tangents that, on inspection, can be seen to be wired into their wild trajectories. Mills' jaunty persona is completed with a walking stick with a carved head. The costume then is not simply caricature but rather all about scale and projection, presenting a version of Highland dress deliberately scaled up to be seen – and read – in theatres holding up to two thousand. Comedians had to make their impact and establish rapport with audiences very quickly and the quickest shorthand was visual presentation. The outfit tells us who Mills is, but is also witty and theatrical enough to make clear that it offers a stylised representation, of a sort music hall audiences were used to encountering on a weekly basis.

POST-LAUDER

Scottish comedians following Lauder, although inevitably defined in relation to his performance, offered a range of socio-economic, class and geographical types that often reconnected with strands of the pre-Lauder vernacular traditions. His initial success brought a first wave of imitators, contemporaries often bringing their own regional identity to their songs and comic delivery, but nevertheless riding his coat-tails in their eccentric profusion of tartan. Jack Lorimer ('The Hielan' Laddie' from Forres), Jock Mills, and Jock Whiteford all enjoyed varying degrees of success, with recording careers and international tours. Following these came a younger group of Scottish stars, clearly influenced by Lauder's performance style, whose emergence in the

Figure 8.1 Jack (better known as Jock) Mills: tartan as jaunty persona. Image courtesy of author's collection

1920s and 1930s overlapped his career's long Indian summer. This group, including Neil Kenyon, Will Fyffe, Harry Gordon and the younger Alec Finlay, all regularly wore the kilt on stage and performed character-based songs and sketches with a broadly Kailyard outlook. Albert Mackie termed them 'character' comedians but suggested they represented a more sophisticated presentation than Lauder. Kenyon's characters sometimes involved full-blown staged sketches with scenery and supporting cast, while Gordon used colleagues to animate his sketches of characters and situations in the fictional town of 'Inversnecky'. Although Fyffe became famous for 'I Belong to Glasgow', the heart of this style of material lay in the small-town settings of the character studies, populated by recognisable figures like posties and Italian ice cream sellers, leading Colm Brogan to term this school of performers 'pastoral'.[12]

A third group of Scottish comedians, however, offered a distinctly different performing style and profile. Emerging through pantomime and music hall, chiefly in Glasgow, the whiteface make-up and emphasis on physical clowning of some members of this group seemed more related to the European circus tradition than to the Lauder style. Mackie and others associated them with the French mimes of the Jean Gaspard Deburau and Italian clowning traditions.[13] If physical clowning was one feature, the other profound difference from the Lauder school was this group's more concentrated focus on day-to-day urban life and their working-class audiences. Although their material also largely consisted of character-based songs and sketches, it was less sentimentalised and inclined to couthiness than that of the Lauder-style comics. Part of this distinctively urban take relied on vernacular speech and dialect.

The leading protagonist and inspiration of this group was Tommy Lorne (1890–1935), probably the greatest interwar Scottish comedian, remaining an iconic figure after his early death. In almost every respect, Lorne was a refutation of the generic Lauder style in his performances' cultural specificity and rootedness. Born in Kirkintilloch, he grew up in the Garngad area of Glasgow, making his first stage appearances in talent competitions at the nearby Grand Theatre, Cowcaddens. After performing in local picture houses on a part-time basis while an apprentice chemist at Blochairn steel works, an industrial background shared by many other Glasgow comedians, he toured with a double act, Wallace and Lorne, before being called up for military service in the First World War. On his return Harry McKelvie recruited him for the famous Royal Princess's pantomimes, his debut being in *Peter Piper* in the 1920–1 season. An immediate success, he stayed for three productions before higher salaries seduced him to first the Pavilion and then the King's Theatre Edinburgh.

Lorne was a natural droll, as this style of sometimes mournful comic was termed, with a tall, gangling figure and long expressive hands that he accentuated with white gloves and make-up in the manner of a Victorian clown. With his high-pitched, squawky voice, and broad Glasgow delivery, and catchphrases like 'In the name of the wee man' and 'Ah'll get ye!', Lorne was in every sense an incontrovertible product of the city and urban environment in which he grew up. In this respect it was no accident that he made his breakthrough in pantomime: the productions at the Princess's Theatre in the Gorbals for which Lorne was engaged ran from December until April or even May the following year, and were a Glasgow institution. While Lauder may have introduced the Scotch comic to the wider British market using a diluted stage Scots, the Gorbals house had been the home of broad vernacular comedy for several generations. In 1911, a journalist wrote 'For 32 years the comic Scot has stalked through Princess's pantomime in different guises, but always his accent and humour have been of Glasgow.'[14]

Lorne emerged through a robust pantomime tradition where fantasy elements combined with scenes and sketches rooted in rituals of working-class life and the cast spoke the vernacular language of their Glasgow audiences. While Glasgow comedians became popular throughout Scotland, the vernacular aspect of the performance, its basis in the bond between working-class audiences and performers who spoke the same way, meant it also had a strong and distinctive socio-economic link to urban industrial society. For this reason Colm Brogan termed the Glasgow comics 'industrial' comedians – as opposed to 'pastoral' performers like Lauder and Fyffe, whom he thought 'all more or less divorced from reality' – and spoke of performers in terms of their social 'authenticity'. For Brogan, 'character' comedians like Lauder and Fyffe were

> in varying degrees the interpreters of an artificial dramatic convention. They may be counted as Scotch comedians, good in their kind, but the kind is not authentic. But the strictly Glasgow comedians are Glasgow from the toes up. Their humour and their type impersonations are immediately recognisable by a Glasgow audience from the depths of their own experience.[15]

Brogan's belief that Lorne was the greatest of the industrial comedians was based on his background as a genuine product of his urban working-class environment:

> Tommy's real name was Hugh Corcoran. He was bred in one of the most wretched slums in Europe and he knew Glasgow under the skin. The Clyde for him and his like was the stretch of water which separates the mortuary from the Gorbals. His best days as an artist were spent in the Gorbals. It is not a pretty neighbourhood, nor is it oppressively Scotch. Kosher meat is much in demand, and the pubs have names like Rooney. The local colour is Red.[16]

Brogan's reading locates both Lorne's genius as a performer and his Scottishness not in a backward-looking world of Kailyard fantasy, but the cosmopolitan urban melting pot of the south-side area around the Princess's. In other words, Lorne is a Scotch comic born of the people and the experience of modern urban living, and the people in question are also Jewish and Irish.

If these Glasgow comedians were then 'authentic', products of a vibrant urban working-class culture, what was their attitude to tartan and external trappings of national identity developed by Lauder? Was the kilt the preserve of the sentimentalised Scotch comic, or did it register on the consciousness of the urban comedian? And, if so, what did it signify?

Evidence of working-class attitudes to stage tartanry seems decidedly mixed. While David Goldie's suggestion that Scottish audiences, and particularly Glasgow ones, were a soft touch for kilted acts seems questionable, there is some evidence to support it. The Metropole in Stockwell Street, one of the city's leading working-class variety theatres, was famous between the 1930s and 1950s for its tartan 'winter' shows with titles like 'Scotland Forever' and 'Tartan Galore'. When interviewed, the theatre manager Alec Frutin explained the policy as a direct response to the popularity of Scottish music and performers with audiences, stating that 'The Metropole became very famous for Scottish shows [. . .] Because I used to run shows with the kilt and bagpipes and the bands [. . .] and made a lot of famous stars there.'[17] But elsewhere audience responses to such material could sometimes be unpredictable. The Glasgow comedian Fred Collins described how, around the First World War period, after working in England, he returned to play the Queen's and Tivoli Theatres in Glasgow, where 'rigged out in a most gorgeous kilt' and singing a song called 'Mackay and I in London' – about two Scots on the spree in the capital – he was shocked to get 'the bird' from the Tivoli audience. The next day, at a pub frequented by music hall professionals, he met the leader of a notorious Glasgow gang.

> He told me that it was his mob who had commenced the trouble, saying 'We don't want you to come from London swanking in an over-exaggerated kilt, and telling them all about Mackay and you as if we hadn't heard you were doing quite well away from the city. Give us your 'Sully Wullie' and numbers of that description and you'll always be sure of a good reception.[18]

If the anecdote shows working-class audiences as sensitive to any hint of condescension, it also suggests that at least in some contexts the kilt carried class connotations. Performers' stories are similarly shot through with allusions to the class-basis of stage costumes. One from the First World War period concerns the comedian Charlie Kemble failing badly before an audience at Kirkintilloch by trying 'to be a Scotch comic in evening dress', before taking the veteran J. B. Preston's advice 'to redden his nose, wear a daft wig, and put on baggy trousers and floppy shoes', after which he scored a great success. But if evening dress and broad comedy were not thought a suitable combination in this period, there was clearly also some degree of social progression in play: Alec Finlay subsequently developed his act as 'Scotland's Gentleman' out of necessity when, having forgotten his trousers, he combined his kilt with the top half of his evening dress, in a juxtaposition that inspired his song 'In my top hat, my white tie, my tail coat, and my kilt'.[19]

Perhaps mindful of class associations, the Glasgow comedians of the interwar years used tartan differently – usually more sparingly – in ways that were nevertheless careful to acknowledge the cultural charge carried by its signification of Scottish identity. Some, like Tommy Morgan and Dave Willis, the 'Scottish Charlie Chaplin', eschewed tartan completely, preferring to appear in lounge suits after the style of English variety comedians. Others also wore modern dress but retained vestigial traces of the tartan comic. Bert Bendon always sported his signature glengarry, adding tartan trews when playing his fey 'silly boy' role in pantomime. George West, known for his outlandish costumes, always reverted to the kilt and tammy for the final walkdown of his Princess's pantomimes, as did Will Fyffe, Alec Finlay and (when not playing dame) Harry Gordon at the Alhambra. Lorne himself cut a surreal figure, his stage costume of glengarry, a string tie worn over a detached collar, and mini-kilt, off-set by white-face make-up, offering a subversive parody of the Highland dress worn by Lauder and his followers. The shortness of the tartan pelmet was a calculated feature, so that 'when [he] bent to putt in a golfing scene, the brevity of his kilt led his feed to turn him round'. As Mackie comments,

> The Glasgow comic was not ashamed to convert the Highland dress into a comedy prop, or to play up to the English idea that there is something essentially funny, perhaps even suggestive, about the kilt – an idea not entirely foreign to the urban masses of Edinburgh and Glasgow, despite the popularity of the Glasgow Highlanders and the Dandy Ninth.[20]

Lorne's gawky, ugly duckling appearance in the mini-kilt, a feminised and vulnerable take in contrast to the swaggering Lauder, became the focus of great public affection. When Lorne did adopt the standard kilt, he subverted the effect by wearing sock-suspenders, or even – according to one account – by sporting a bunch of bananas in place of a sporran. The effect was comically subversive and irreverent, Highland dress being worn on Lorne's own terms, by a Scots comic who talked not about braes and glens but about New City Road and the wee pie shop in Lumphinnans.

In reframing Highland dress in jauntily absurdist vein, Lorne was not dismissing tartan or what it represented: he was rather ironically reclaiming it for urban working-class audiences for whom its roman-ticised rural associations meant little. Lorne's gentle satirising of the kilt provides a corrective, by resituating tartan and the kilt as one part – but not the defining feature – of a modern Scottish identity in which vernacular speech and references to working-class life and culture form the mainstay. On a personal level a journalist recalled that, although Lorne often wore 'the wee kilt [. . .] when he was doing the dafty behind the footlights [. . .] in real life he wore the kilt well', and recalled his 'Chieftain-like appearance in a braw kilt at the Cowal Games'.[21] By the time of his death Lorne had reached a professional parity with Lauder, and the two were subjects of a cartoon strip in the *Daily Record* – slogan 'wake each morn to Lauder and Lorne'. While Lauder was respected rather than loved, Lorne was referred to in folkloric terms.

Brogan's linking of Lorne and the Glasgow comedians with modern urban society and the multicultural landscape of the Gorbals, home to

Figure 8.2 Tommy Lorne and his comedy feed W. S. Percy: kilt, sock-suspenders and ironic drollery. Courtesy of Herald and Times Group

several different ethnic groups, including a large Jewish community and the Irish as well as numbers of immigrants from the Highlands, gives a hint of one of the possible roles of these Scotch comic performances. Pointing out that Lorne and Tommy Morgan were both of Irish extraction, he suggests:

It may be significant that that the two men who have broken most emphatically away from the Scotch comic's convention were not influenced by national ancestral memories of the pure Scot. They both might he said to belong to Glasgow more unconditionally than Will Fyffe ever could belong, even if he had been born and bred in the city.[22]

The implication is that old ('pure') essentialist notions of national identity, which modern writers might in any case now challenge, are being transcended by a new modern Scottish society, one born out of the experience of urban living in the new Glasgow, an industrial society which is by definition and experience moving towards multiculturalism. By the 1920s second- or third-generation Glaswegians of Irish extraction like Lorne and Morgan were part of the fabric of city life, despite the religious and tribal distinctions of surname and school that marked out west of Scotland sectarian prejudice. Brogan seems to see Lorne as symbolising acculturation, a process Lawrence Epstein describes as that by 'which two cultures borrow from each other so that what emerges is a new or blended culture'.[23] Brogan's mention of Lorne's Glasgow Irish background also raises the question of how other immigrant groups present in Scottish society might have been influenced by – or themselves influenced – the Scotch comic figure. If Lorne and Morgan were equipped to offer a sophisticated parsing of the tartanised conventions handed down by Lauder, members of more recently arrived immigrant groups had a different response to the Scotch comic.

Music hall had always featured representations of different national and ethnic groups, usually in reductive stereotypes emphasising what were portrayed as national characteristics or traits. Disparagingly, the Irish were depicted as boisterous, excitable, prone to alcoholism and violence, though also capable of charm and lyrical whimsy, and the Jews as venal, untrustworthy and unhygienic. The Irish were the largest of the immigrant groups who played a central role in professional music hall development in Scotland. In contrast, the Eastern European Jews who arrived in Glasgow from the 1880s presented different challenges in terms of assimilation and integration, speaking largely uncomprehended languages – usually Yiddish or Russian – and bringing distinctive dress and cultural and religious values that instantly marked them as alien. Moreover, the Jewish stage representation, the Hebrew comedian, introduced into British music hall from American vaudeville at the turn of the twentieth century, was for the most part highly derogatory. Its stock presentation of the Jew was as a shabby street trader, whose 'comic' material generally revolved around 'Jewish' traits like firesetting.

In theorising these performances and their possible impact, American writers' views of Jewish stage representations offer important insights into the wider function of such ethnic characterisations, and the ways that they might have contributed to social cohesion. In the process they also tell us something about the possible role and meanings of the Scotch comic representation. For example, on the question of the dubious cultural authenticity of such performances, Robert Snyder suggests that dialect acts like the Hebrew comic 'did not often present immigrant culture to their ethnically diverse audiences. Instead they expressed a synthetic ethnicity formed from elements of immigrant experiences, mass culture and the stereotypical national and racial characters of the America theatre.' These representations then were not meant to be balanced or realistic, but 'provided simple characteristics that roughly explained immigrants to native-born Americans and introduced immigrant Americans to each other. They were identifying markers on a bewildering landscape of races, nationalities and cultures.'[24] Lawrence Epstein echoes Snyder in suggesting, as already noted, that the function of such representations was acculturation, defined as 'a process by which two cultures borrow from each other so that what emerges is a new or blended culture'.[25]

The idea of acculturation – of these representations having a role in educating audiences about cultural difference, at a particular phase of social development when relations between different groups in society were often conflicted – is relevant to the Scottish context. The notion of the process involving blending or exchange also helps explain the emergence in the early twentieth century of hybrid versions of these music hall representations, acts featuring combinations of more than one ethnic identity, where comedy derived from the interplay of supposed national or ethnic characteristics.

In the context of such hybrid acts, the career of Ike Freedman (1895–1960), the leading Glasgow Jewish comedian between the 1920s and 1940s, demonstrates a very distinctive response to the Scotch comic legacy. Freedman was born Isaac Solomon in Wigan, of parents who were newly arrived in Britain from Grodna in Belarus. In 1900, the family moved to Glasgow, where Freedman grew up in the Gorbals. After appearing locally at the Paragon cinema, he made his professional debut at the Olympia, Bridgeton Cross in 1921, and was soon appearing in cinemas and music halls across Glasgow and the west of Scotland. By the late 1920s Freedman was working throughout Britain, mostly in the touring revues which were the stock in trade for variety performers. Increasingly well known in Scottish music hall, he was regarded on a localised level within Glasgow as a rising star. He went on to record for the Scottish Beltona and Regal labels, travelled to New York to play for six weeks of vaudeville for the Radio–Keith–Orpheum circuit and broadcast regularly on the BBC.

Freedman is particularly significant because his career reflected the Scottish immigrant experience. He began performing as a Hebrew comedian, representing Jewish culture in the form of the 'dialect' character, a gutturally accented street trader whose material, all about short-changing and sharp practice, perpetuated a negative image of Jews as sly and untrustworthy. However Freedman's song, 'Only a Jew', which became his signature and remained the culmination of his act throughout his career, was an emotive plea for compassion and understanding for the stateless, itinerant Jew, who roams the world, with 'Never a welcome where'er I may stray / And there's no land I can call my own'. Moreover, Freedman also sang songs about other ethnicities: Italian numbers like 'Romeo' and 'My Queen of Italy' were delivered in the exaggerated 'ice-a-cream' accent ascribed to the Italian immigrants who worked in Glasgow's cafés and fish shops. Other songs explored the comic incongruity of mixed relationships: in 'The Irish Italian Jew', the protagonist Antonio Ferraro, an Italian-Jewish ice cream seller, goes to Ireland and falls in love with 'Dainty Nancy Morgan', a 'pretty little Irisher colleen'. In 'My Yiddisher Irish Girl', Ike's character, Solomon Cohen, similarly falls for an Irish girl but, when the question arises of where they should settle down, chooses Ireland, the reason being:

For it's the last place the Devil would look to find a Hebrew
So I'm going to live in Erin's Isle.

Freedman also played with the Scotch comic figure, combining the reputation for meanness of the Hebrew comedian and the Lauder-style Scotch comic: in 'Ikey Granitestein from Aberdeen', sung in Freedman's recording in his best pawky Scots-Jewish, the eponymous character achieves notoriety by being both Jewish *and* Aberdonian, the jaunty, Scottish dance-band accompanied chorus combining one of Freedman's craftiest rhymes.

Ikey Granitestein from Aberdeen.
He's the meanest man that you have ever seen.
He would pinch your tie and collar,
Do you for a dollar.
Watch a baby cut its teeth and try and steal the molar.[26]

Derogatory and self-deprecating caricature in such routines becomes a means of intercultural mediation, accommodating the outsider to host communities.

Freedman's professional journey took him from 'Hebrew' comedian through an increasingly exotic range of hybrid combinations – overlapping Irish, Jewish, Italian and Scottish characterisations that juxtaposed the figures' supposed 'national' characteristics to increasingly ludicrous effect. Yet it finally resolved in its latter stages with his final incarnation as 'The Scottish Hebrew Gentleman'. Here Freedman confounded the conventions of the 'Hebrew' performance by appearing in immaculate evening dress with top hat, white spats and cigarette holder. A sophisticated, cosmopolitan figure, as remote from the shabby barrow trader associations of the dialect performance as possible, he nevertheless retained his distinctive Glasgow accent, called his audience 'customers' and retained Jewish words and idioms. Like Lorne, and before him Lauder, Freedman developed an inherited ethnic performance – in Freedman's case, one much more culturally constrictive and specifically 'other' – which he developed in a way that reflected his experience. What emerged clearly from his performance, however, was an uncompromising determination to be both Jewish *and* Scottish, in a way that allowed both equal validity. Freedman, who performed in touring revues with other leading Glasgow comedians of his generation like Tommy Morgan and Jack Anthony, regularly wore the kilt in the latter stages of his career.

Like Lorne, Freedman was an authentic product of the urban experience, whose evolving performance encompassed the growing cultural diversity of Scottish society, but which in its vernacular idioms and wordplay also drew heavily on the Scotch comic performance. While Lorne's travestying of the kilt was gently satirical – an urban working-class dig at the pictorial glens of Lauder's imaginary, and a reminder that the heart of Scotland was now in the towns and cities – for Freedman and other Jewish music hall performers the kilt signified assimilation and belonging. While Freedman chose to navigate his path out of the cul de sac of the dialect comic genre, making his performance into something transformative, other performers

Figure 8.3 Ike Freedman as 'The Scottish Hebrew Gentleman', a sophisticate in top hat with cigarette holder. Courtesy of collection of Sally Solomon

embraced the tartan representation at face value. So the Scotch comedian Jock Mackay, shown in photographs wearing the kilt and carrying bagpipes, was born Max Kuttner in Glasgow in 1879, one of five children of William Kuttner, a traveller in jewellery, and Clara Brach, who probably came from Witkowo in Prussia, now Poland.[27]

Freedman in the 1920s and 1930s represents the most sophisticated development of hybrid ethnic characterisations, the import of which was surely to confront audiences, once the laughter had settled, with the ridiculousness of seeing people purely in terms of supposed national or ethnic characteristics, rather than as individuals. However the Scotch comic figure not only provided a point of departure for such constructions, but had itself been used in the same way since the turn of the century, as a means of exploring cultural difference through hybrid characterisations.

While these hybridised performances threw up all sorts of ethnic conjunctions, often now with uncomfortable connotations, the net result was often to question the essentialist premise of the original Scottish representation. Such performances in the pre-First World War period included the Scottish blackface minstrel Will Candlish, who 'although a negro comedian, used to play all the latest choruses on the bagpipes', and the Scotch comic R. C. McGill's 'Heilan' Chinaman' song.[28] Jack Lorimer's 'Ching-a-ling' routine offered a Chinese Scotsman, dressed in a kilt and Chinese coolie wig, whose chorus ran:

> Ching-a-ling, ching ching a-ling'
> Hoch ay, hoch ay.
> It's a broad brecht moonlecht necht ternecht
> Comin' thru' the rye.
> I'm half Scotch and half Chinese
> As sure as eggs are eggs,
> And I dinny care a damn
> If ma auld pugtail
> Keeps ticklin' ma legs.[29]

And if middle-class Scots anyway blanched at Scotch comics' traducing their national culture, the *Jewish Chronicle*, which similarly despaired at the self-hating jokes of Hebrew comedians, was equally mortified by the 'Whitechapel Scotchmen' of a London cycling club, who 'bear[ing] testimony to the influence of the music hall upon impressionable youth', turned out for a charity race dressed as Kosher Scotsmen, 'bowler-hatted, kilted and bewhiskered', where 'in almost every case the dangling sporran [. . .] was a matzo'.[30]

Did the presence of a range of different ethnic groups, and their mirroring in stage representations, affect attitudes to the Scotch comics in the city? Jim Friel, who regularly went to variety during his boyhood in the 1940s, believed that 'pseudo tartanry was never all that popular in Glasgow, and [I] attribute this to the Irish and Jewish influences'.[31] However, the Metropole tartan shows were produced by the theatre owners, the Frutin family, first-generation Russian Jewish immigrants. And performers as resourceful and diverse as Lorne, one of a large number of Glasgow variety stars of Irish extraction, and Ike Freedman, who regularly wore the kilt in his latter years, were highly capable of using tartan and its range of associations very much on their own terms.

CONCLUSION

Given the value of the Scotch comic as a hybrid composite that allowed for the celebration and exploration of Scottish identity, Lauder's was not the only model. Other Scottish comedians used tartan differently, often more critically, sometimes satirically or ironically, but in ways which nevertheless usually formed part of a positive discourse around questions of Scottish identity and belonging. Tommy Lorne's sometimes irreverent, tongue-in-cheek approach to the kilt signalled an interrogation of older rural associations by more modern industrial notions of Scottish identity, while performers like Ike Freedman regarded the kilt and Highland dress as embodying the values and cultural identity of their adopted country. With hindsight the Scotch comic figure was not inflexible. It was fluid and porous, in the sense that it provided a template for versions of Scottish identity which allowed Scots, and particularly the urban working classes, newly enfranchised economically, to negotiate images of Scottish identity that connected the present with the historic past through celebration of a shared culture.

Notes

1 Craig, 'Myths against history', p. 13; Nairn, *The Break-Up of Britain*, p. 131.
2 Cameron and Scullion, 'W. F. Frame and the Scottish popular theatre tradition', pp. 45, 39.

3 Donaldson, *Popular Literature in Victorian Scotland.*
4 McCrone, *Understanding Scotland* (1992), pp. 174–96.
5 Goldie, 'The British invention of Scottish culture: World War I and before', p. 129.
6 Goldie, 'Hugh MacDiarmid, Harry Lauder and Scottish popular culture'.
7 *The Scotsman*, 9 December 1867, p. 1.
8 McLaren, *Edinburgh Memories and Some Worthies*, pp. 207–8
9 MacDiarmid, 'Scottish people and "Scotch comedians"', p. 114.
10 *Sunday Mail*, 24 November 1935.
11 Findlay, 'Scots language and popular entertainment', p. 33.
12 Brogan, 'The Glasgow comedians', p. 171.
13 Mackie, *The Scotch Comedians*, pp. 12–13.
14 *Glasgow Herald*, 15 December 1911, p. 12.
15 Brogan, *The Glasgow Story*, p. 152.
16 Brogan, 'The Glasgow comedians', p. 172.
17 Interview with Alex Frutin by Ben Braber, AUD OHP 0001, Glasgow Jewish Archive Centre.
18 *Weekly News*, 1 March 1930.
19 House, *Comics in Kilts*, pp. 25, 29.
20 Mackie, *The Scotch Comedians*, p. 52.
21 *Evening Times*, 18 April 1935, p. 4.
22 Brogan, *The Glasgow Story*, p. 153.
23 Epstein, *The Haunted Smile*, p. 105.
24 Snyder, *The Voice of the City*, p. 110.
25 Epstein, *The Haunted Smile*, p. 105.
26 Recorded by Beltona Records (M-14499-1).
27 I am grateful to Harvey Kaplan of the Scottish Jewish Archive Centre for this information.
28 For Candlish and McGill see Neil McFadyen, *Sunday Mail*, 24 November and 27 October 1935.
29 Wall, *The Fool on the Hill*, pp. 31–2. Max Wall was Lorimer's son.
30 *Jewish Chronicle*, 1 August 1913, p. 31.
31 Jim Friel, quoted in Devlin, *Kings, Queens and People's Palaces*, p. 185.

9

LITERARY TARTANRY AS TRANSLATION

Susanne Hagemann

ৎ

'Translation' is a word with various meanings. It is most commonly associated with a certain relationship between (written) texts in different languages, but can be used in wider senses as well. Thus, cultures and societies can be translated, and it has been argued that they constitute themselves in and through translation.

This chapter will explore a range of translation processes in Compton Mackenzie's Highland farce *The Monarch of the Glen* (1941) and, more generally, in what may be called literary tartanry. The term 'tartanry' will mostly be used here to refer to 'the assimilation of all things Scottish to a clannic (hence plaid-clad) origin, and linked by association of ideas to Northern scenery, Celtic speech and artefacts, the battle of Culloden [. . .] and a twilit Ossianic past',[1] but the narrower meaning of 'the cult of tartan as a symbol of identity'[2] will play a role as well. Literary tartanry is often traced back to Ossian and Sir Walter Scott. In later periods it surfaced for instance in Celtic-Twilight authors such as Fiona Macleod, occasionally in some exponents of the Scottish Renaissance (though Neil Gunn and Fionn Mac Colla, for example, would have denied the association)[3] and in popular writers from Lillian Beckwith to Allie Mackay. While attaching the label to a literary text (or, for that matter, to any other cultural product) has traditionally had negative connotations, the present chapter will attempt to shed new light on the complexities of this representational phenomenon by exploring its translational dimension.

The Monarch of the Glen is a good example of literary tartanry not least because it includes, in fact is positively awash with, all the ingredients listed above. It centres on the adventures of three North Americans, Carrie Royde née Macdonald, her husband Chester and his sister Myrtle, in the Scottish Highlands, where they visit chieftain Donald MacDonald of Ben Nevis in his castle, Glenbogle, and immerse themselves in (a version of) Scottish culture. In the course of the novel, Chester buys a shooting lodge from Ben Nevis's friend, Hugh Cameron of Kilwhillie, and Myrtle gets engaged to Scottish nationalist poet Alan Macmillan. An important strand of the plot is concerned with an invasion of Ben Nevis's territory by English hikers, at the end successfully repulsed by the chieftain with the help of his family, his guests and a group of nationalists from Glasgow.

Focusing on translation processes in this novel does not narrow down our perspective on literary tartanry as much as might be thought at first glance. In fact, as Doris Bachmann-Medick has shown, recent research in the humanities points towards what she calls a 'translational turn', translation being on the way to becoming a central concept in a number of academic fields, from cultural studies to ethnography and history.[4] This development was enabled by the 1980s' cultural turn in translation studies, as a result of which

> the familiar categories of text-related translation, such as original, equivalence or faithfulness, were increasingly supplemented by new key categories of cultural translation such as cultural representation and transformation, alterity, displacement, discontinuity, cultural difference and power.[5]

As this list suggests, the process of translation is neither innocent nor smooth, and has little to do with the familiar metaphor of bridge-building: 'translation will not enrich intercultural dynamics until it grapples with differences, struggles for meaning, and resistances, instead of taking the notion of (harmonising) bridges of cultural understanding as its starting point'.[6]

It will become apparent in the course of this chapter that the categories of cultural translation listed by Bachmann-Medick are all present in *The Monarch of the Glen*. The discussion will start with how they affect linguistic translation.

The three language pairs which are translationally relevant in Mackenzie's novel are Gaelic and English, Scots and English, and the British and American varieties of English. Among these pairs, Gaelic/English is both the most prominent and most obviously connected with tartanry. Translation takes place in both directions, from Gaelic into English and from English into Gaelic. It usually involves isolated names and phrases rather than complete texts. Equivalence of some kind (presumably semantic equivalence at the level of words) is taken for granted both by the characters and by the narrator.

However, translation processes are less straightforward than the simplistic equation of Gaelic with English words might suggest. They highlight three interrelated aspects of the Gaelic language as it is used in the novel: its potential as a source of misunderstanding, its 'difficult' pronunciation and spelling and its role as a national symbol. The following dialogue illustrates the first two of these aspects:

> 'I'll tell you what you might do, Alan,' said [James Buchanan]. 'You might move up to that cave on Ben Cruet. They're not likely to find you there.'
> 'Uaimh na laoigh,' the bard muttered, paying such great attention to the correct pronunciation of the Gaelic that Myrtle thought he was groaning.
> 'Oh, you're in pain,' she exclaimed with quick sympathy.
> The bard looked at her in astonishment.
> 'No, I'm not.'
> 'But you groaned as if you were in pain.'
> 'I wasn't groaning,' said the bard indignantly. 'I was saying the name of the cave in Gaelic. Uaimh na laoigh. The Cave of the Calf.'[7]

Translation serves to clear up a misunderstanding, but also to emphasise the radical alterity of the Gaelic language. This is later reinforced when Myrtle comments on the same placename: 'Isn't that the most melancholy sound you ever heard, Carrie? It's like one of those sad noises you hear out at sea in a fog.' (p. 139) The fog in this case is presumably a Celtic mist, suffused with Celtic melancholy.

In other instances, where translation is not necessary for communication to function, the aspect of alterity becomes even more obvious. When Ben Nevis shows his guests an ancient judgement seat and explains: 'Cahavrayanishvickickyackan we call it in the Gaelic', Chester responds by saying that 'the more I hear of Gaelic the more it reminds me of the Carroway language. That sounds very like "pleased to meet you" in Carroway. It sounds a bit like ducks in a marsh too, but then so does "pleased to meet you" in Carroway.' (p. 227) Translation results in Chester conflating Gaelic with the language of a native American tribe, and linking it first with ducks and later with the sound of a machine gun (p. 228). Thus, translation becomes an agent of alterity. In rendering the dialogue in writing, the narrator reinforces this function by stringing together five Gaelic words to form a monstrous-looking single word with Anglicised spelling. This emphasis on alterity is a phenomenon that only occurs with Gaelic. In the case of the other two language pairs, Scots/English and British/American English, translation usually serves to promote understanding, for example when Ben Nevis explains the meaning of *muckle hart* to Chester (p. 126), or Carrie tells him that lifts are what he calls elevators (p. 218).

What is particularly noteworthy is that the characters who most frequently translate from or into Gaelic are not actually native or even fluent speakers. Ben Nevis learned Gaelic as a child from his nurse, but can no longer speak it (presumably as a result of being educated in Harrow and Cambridge). Alan Macmillan has made a serious attempt to learn it, but is still at the stage of working through *Gaelic Without Tears*. Carrie is an enthusiastic beginner. By contrast, native speakers such as Ben Nevis's keepers Duncan MacDonald and Neil Maclennan are described as using Gaelic, but rarely translate. This raises the question of whose interests are being served by Gaelic/English translation. It can be argued that the main function of linguistic translation for the individual non-native translators is symbolic: for Alan as a nationalist it is associated with the rebirth of Scotland; for Ben Nevis, with his territory and perhaps his claim to authority; for Carrie, with the land of her ancestors. The same applies to the translational activities of two disembodied voices: the fictitious romanticising guidebook *Summer Days Among the Heather*, which Carrie is reading at the beginning of the novel, includes translations of Gaelic names and phrases, as well as an English version of a sixteenth-century Gaelic poem; and the narrator of *The Monarch of the Glen* likewise quotes and translates some Gaelic phrases for the benefit of the narratee. These translations serve to enhance local colour, forming part of what the narrator calls 'Highland scenery and romance' (p. 11).

There are different forms of resistance to non-native translation. In one case, it seems to be the Gaelic language itself that resists appropriation. When Alan attempts to teach Myrtle how to pronounce a Gaelic placename, he chokes: 'In his endeavour to make the "laoigh" sufficiently guttural, the "gh" broke away from the preceding vowels and entered his windpipe.' (p. 100) In other cases, native speakers draw attention to the non-native translators' linguistic inadequacy. Thus, when Carrie uses a Gaelic phrase in conversation with Neil Maclennan, he does not understand her until she tells him in English what she has been trying to say: that is, he forces her to back-translate in order to make her original translation intelligible. The translators' social status links linguistic translation with forms of material or representational power, but the various forms of resistance show that power is not exclusively vested in translation.

Another form of translation is that between different discourses or social positions. This is a more recent, and less widely known, area of research and will therefore be explained in some detail. The framework used here has been developed by Martin Fuchs, and is based on the concept of nonequivalency:

> Considering translation as an interactional process of transfer of meanings, but a transfer which changes these very meanings, opens up a new field. Basically, the notion of nonequivalency in translation forces us to take into account the fact or possibility that people relate to others, and even interact with them, across and through differences, across boundaries – differences or boundaries, I mean, between discourses, between cultural contexts, between social positions, or between social fields (subsystems or institutions). People can understand each other, or new things, without the guarantee or even the possibility of a fully shared understanding of the meanings involved.[8]

Fuchs distinguishes between implicit and explicit translation: 'Translations occur implicitly in shared situations (to which both sides bring different registers), between these registers without the help of an explicit mediating term, whereas explicit translation refers to and relies on explicit bridging terms.'[9] Explicit translation, he argues, involves agency and a felt need for social change: 'One translates one's condition, or a critique of one's condition, and one's desires – in the last instance *oneself* – into a language which one hopes others will understand and take up.'[10] This translation into what Fuchs calls a 'third idiom' may succeed, or fail for a variety of reasons.

The Monarch of the Glen includes both implicit and explicit translation. A good example is the conflict between Ben Nevis and the hikers. Its immediate occasion is the hikers' disturbing the grouse and thus spoiling the Twelfth of August for Ben Nevis. More generally, the spread of hiking raises the issue of legitimate landscape use; and on a representational level, crowds of hikers with portable radios are at odds with traditional Scottish iconography: 'The capture, both materially and culturally, of Highland estates for sporting purposes in the nineteenth century has bequeathed an iconography of Scottish landscape which is largely bereft of people.'[11] In view of these different social contexts, it comes as no surprise that the parties involved deploy a variety of discourses to voice their grievances. When Ben Nevis, on hearing of the hikers' presence, proposes to lock them up in his castle, the first reaction of his friend Colonel Lindsay-Wolseley is to warn him against the possible legal consequences of such an action. When this fails, Lindsay-Wolseley tries to dissuade Ben Nevis by translating his objections into the language of politics: 'we landed proprietors cannot afford to stir up popular feeling in these democratic days'. (p. 28) Ben Nevis counters by a translation into the language of sport: 'I thought you might enjoy the kind of sport you must often have enjoyed at Peshawar.' (p. 28) These acts of translation ultimately fail because, despite the change of register, they do not involve a genuine transfer of meanings: Lindsay-Wolseley continues to invoke the twentieth-century political order; Ben Nevis, the historical power of a Highland chieftain.

Other registers used by the various participants in the hiking conflict include those of anti-Bolshevism, anti-Fascism, democracy, history and war. The last two are of particular interest. With the language of war, Ben Nevis and the hikers do have a common idiom that transcends their individual social positions and helps them to get their messages across; but the very nature of this universal idiom precludes its being used constructively to bring about the kind of change which according to Fuchs is the objective of explicit translation. When the register of historical warfare is used, war slides into history. Thus, Ben Nevis proposes using Lochaber axes and boiling water (as a substitute for boiling oil) against the hikers besieging his castle. The fact that he is subsequently persuaded to replace boiling by soapy water, and the need for axes is obviated by the arrival of reinforcements, draws attention to the symbolic, rather than material, value of these weapons. Defeat and victory are likewise translated into historical terms: the capture of Ben Nevis, Chester and Duncan MacDonald by the hikers is described by the narrator as 'the most humiliating defeat in all [the] long and bellicose history [of the MacDonalds of Ben Nevis]' (p. 246), and at the end of the novel Ben Nevis's chaplain celebrates victory by composing a martial poem strongly reminiscent in both content and style of the anonymous sixteenth-century one quoted in Carrie's guidebook (pp. 16 and 272). The narrator's involvement in this particular process of social translation suggests that the historical register is central to the novel; and in fact clan warfare forms part of the trappings of tartanry. Meanings are in this case negotiated not between characters but between the narrator and the narratee, tartanry constituting an idiom that makes violence acceptable by distancing it through time and, in the examples quoted, humour.

Another instance of social translation that attempts to make violence acceptable concerns the Highland Clearances. When Carrie tells Ben Nevis that one of her ancestors was forced from his croft by the Ben Nevis of the time, he replies that this is what comes of loyalty, and explains:

> 'Loyalty to the old Stuarts. We managed to keep the land, but it was only by raising regiments for the Government. And then of course once Highlanders had started settling in Canada the only sound economic policy was to settle as many more of them as possible. That was why my grandfather had to make a second clearance. He hated doing it of course, but it was for their own good [. . .]' (p. 13)

He subsequently expands on this, telling Carrie that if her ancestor had not been forced to emigrate to Canada, she would still be living on a croft, instead of being in a position to buy a shooting lodge (p. 86). As an explicit translation produced by Ben Nevis for Carrie, this move is designed to mediate between the perpetrators' and the victims' descendants. As an implicit translation offered by the narrator to the narratee, it has a connection with tartanry, albeit a different one from historical warfare: since the acts of violence committed during the Clearances are at odds with the discourse of tartanry, they are glossed over in a translation which focuses on the prosperity of the emigrants' descendants.

Generally speaking, social translation is often directly or indirectly linked with tartanry. Carrie at one point asks Neil Maclennan whether he would lay down his life for Ben Nevis. Her question is motivated by assumptions about clan loyalty (though she does not explain why a Maclennan should feel this sort of loyalty towards a MacDonald chieftain); but he translates it into a Calvinist register:

> 'I wouldn't want to die for anybody [. . .] Och, I don't take to the notion of dying at all. It's very difficult to know what is going to happen. I wouldn't mind death so much at all if I was sure his friend Satan wasn't waiting round the corner just behind him. It's a terrible business that, right enough. The minister was preaching about it last Sunday morning.' (p. 115)

This register is pertinent to Scotland and ideas of Scottishness but not, at first sight, to tartanry. Neil declares clan loyalty irrelevant to the contemporary world because, as he says, 'there's no clans left now' (p. 115). However, he does not dispute the historical relevance of Carrie's assumptions. On the level of the narrative, it can therefore be argued that Neil's translation is part of the same distancing process that affects clan warfare. Mackenzie's tartanry world comprises the past as well as the present, and heroic deaths belong to the former rather than the latter.

A third form of translation that occurs in *The Monarch of the Glen* is cultural translation. This is defined by Bachmann-Medick as 'translation of and between cultures', though she cautions that such translation processes do not involve cultures in their entirety, but only individual sections or key concepts.[12] Cultural translation involves making (representations of) aspects of one culture accessible to another. In *The Monarch of the Glen*, it is almost invariably associated with tartanry. One example is Carrie's guidebook, which translates a section of Scottish, or more precisely Highland, culture into a framework familiar to its target audience. While this audience is not explicitly defined, the book's style and the type of information provided (allusions to English literature, an expected desire to get away from 'the superficial luxury of our so-called civilization' [p. 12], etc.) point towards the urban British middle class. The main attractions of Ben Nevis's estate for this audience are initially described with the words: 'Apart from the wild magnificence of the natural scene Glenbogle literally teems with historic memories and romantic legends.' (p. 11) The following passages read like a catalogue of a certain definition of tartanry, including as they do mountains, a loch, heather and bog-myrtle, a castle, clan chiefs, clan warfare, a claymore, piping, poetry, Bonnie Prince Charlie, the Gaelic language, water-horses and a fairy woman (pp. 11–12, 15–16). This is a translation in so far as it involves two different cultural contexts, one of which is explained to members of the other in terms which make sense to them. Like all translations, whether cultural or otherwise, it does not provide access to the 'truth' about an immutable original, but constitutes one out of a range of possible target versions. Like many translations, it is influenced by assumptions about the target audience's expectations – in this case, by the assumption that the audience will be familiar with, and respond positively to, tartanry.

The tartanry translation of Highland culture offered by the guidebook is both reinforced and undermined by other translation processes. One of these, which involves the kilt and tartan, will be discussed later in a different context. Another example concerns naming conventions, which are something of a shibboleth in *The Monarch of the Glen*. They have a linguistic and a cultural dimension, the former being determined by the latter. Culture dictates that Highland landowners should be addressed by the names of their estates if and only if these are inherited. From a translational point of view, calling Ben Nevis 'Mr MacDonald', as some of the hikers do, is a case of insufficient cultural adaptation from English English to Highland English which he strongly resents. The relevant conventions are explained in some detail by Kilwhillie and the narrator in connection with Chester's question as to whether he would be addressed as Knocknacolly after buying the eponymous shooting lodge. The narrator comments that Kilwhillie 'did feel very strongly about these rich fellows who bought sporting estates in the Highlands and supposed that by doing so they could turn themselves into lairds of long lineage and ancient territorial privileges' (p. 90). Highland culture, in the version propagated by Kilwhillie, is based on the authenticity of descent. Translation in this case provides information which is self-evident to members of the source culture but not to those outside it: the naming conventions derived from this concept of authenticity will only make sense to Chester and to non-Scottish readers of the novel if they are made explicit.

Cultural translation meets with various forms of resistance. One of these is appropriation. At a meeting of English hikers, one of their leading members displaces Highland naming conventions by translating them into an English suburban context: 'MacDonald of Ben Nevis drove sixteen of you through Glenbogle with lorries and cars filled with his hirelings. Buckham of Primrose Hill with his volunteers will drive MacDonald of Ben Nevis from one end to the other of his own glen.' (p. 176) Displacement has a comic effect because the appropriated name form seems inappropriate in the target culture, and mocks the logic on which the corresponding source-culture form is based.

On a different level, the narrator creates a sense of discontinuity for instance by ironising Highland scenery:

> There are many tracts among the mountains of the North which cast a weariness and a disgust upon those who have to tramp across them. The view of the encircling bens may be sublime, but the sublime can become tiresome when exactly the same aspect of it is presented during an hour's plodding over featureless bog furrowed by burns every one of which takes the same dreary course and makes the same monotonous burbling. (p. 128)

The wild landscape of tartanry is transformed into an unpleasant experience for persons moving across it. This is just one example of how the narrator offers different target versions that alternately reinforce and undermine tartanry. The fact that these are indeed cultural translations becomes clear when they are compared with the locals' response to Highland scenery, which is practically oriented rather than aesthetic. Ben Nevis, for instance, rarely remarks on the landscape, and when he does, it is usually in connection with sport. The bog that prompts the narrator's above-quoted ironic description does not draw any comments from him, apart from telling Chester the placename and its meaning in English. And even when in another context he briefly exclaims, 'Splendid view, isn't it?' (p. 22), this is addressed to Chester and Myrtle and thus forms part of a translation process.

A dimension of cultural translation that needs to be distinguished from translation between two different cultures is that of culture as translation. As some theorists have argued, cultures are always already hybrid and therefore subject to translation; they constitute themselves through translation processes.[13] *The Monarch of the Glen* includes a number of examples. Gavin Wallace has drawn attention to the fact that Ben Nevis is profoundly anglicised: 'Everything his Scottish pretensions encounter is inscribed with his upper-class English accent and mannerisms.'[14] The character who most prominently embodies Highland identity thus at the same time exemplifies the difference invariably involved in identity constructions.

An even better example of how translation processes affect the constitution of culture is provided by the kilt and tartan. At an early stage in the novel, Chester consults Kilwhillie, an authority on Highland dress, about whether he as an American would be allowed to wear a kilt, explaining: 'when I was in Canada I was adopted into the Carroway tribe of Indians with the name of Butting Moose. That's Chester Royde Jr among the Carroways, and that's the way I want to feel in the Highlands [. . .] I aim to buy a place up here.' (p. 23) That is to say, Chester desires to become a (temporary) migrant. As Homi Bhabha reminds us, migrant culture highlights the fact that cultures are not homogeneous, clearly definable entities and that translation occurs inside them;[15] and the issue of Chester's kilt makes this very clear. Kilwhillie tells Chester that anybody may wear a kilt, but the tartan is a problem, since he has no 'right to a tartan' (p. 22), and wearing his wife's tartan would be against tradition. While 'subjects of King George' may wear the Stewart tartan (p. 22), Chester feels that this does not apply to him as a US citizen. As a solution Kilwhillie proposes a kilt of hodden grey, and when Chester, a lover of bright colours, objects, he mentions an eighteenth-century text referring to a purple kilt. Chester takes this up enthusiastically, and while Kilwhillie is obviously dismayed, he cannot help confirming that purple, or in fact any other plain colour, would be unusual but not contrary to the dress code. On the strength of this information, Chester decides to have two kilts made, one purple and one orange. The orange kilt occasions much comment and causes Kilwhillie acute suffering.

Since Chester has adhered to the rules explained to him by Kilwhillie, his orange kilt is not primarily a case of cultural translation into a new (American) context. What is at issue here is a largely unacknowledged hybridity within Highland culture, which enables persons not belonging to a Highland clan to wear a kilt. The translation process through which dress regulations have been adapted to non-Highlanders lies outside the novel; Chester merely makes it visible by transforming it through his choice of colour.[16] The result of this transformation process subsequently acquires a new status when a group of English hikers mistake Chester for Ben Nevis precisely on account of his orange kilt: the translation seems to them more authentic than the 'original'.

Ben Nevis himself, on first seeing the orange kilt from a distance, thinks that Chester is a Scottish nationalist. This paradoxically brackets Chester together with Alan Macmillan and James Buchanan, whom Ben Nevis's son Iain identifies as nationalists by the way they look: 'they were rigged up in reach-me-down kilts and had that awful earnest Highland look [. . .] Ghastly tartans too, neither of which ought to be allowed outside a music-hall. I'm sure they were Scottish Nationalists.' (p. 63) What Chester, Alan and James have in common is the brightness of their kilts and the fact that they come from outside the Highlands. Iain's comment on Alan and James's tartans – which through its music-hall reference associates the nationalists with Sir Harry Lauder – may seem unfair in so far as the colours are not freely chosen but go with their surnames. However, coincidental though they may be, the colours do have a translational significance. Alan and James are what Ian Maitland Hume calls 'new' kilt-wearers,[17] having taken a conscious decision as Glaswegians to wear the kilt as an expression of their Scottish identity. While they have, in Kilwhillie's words, the 'right to a tartan', the meanings they impose on it are not the conventional Highland ones. By an act of cross-cultural translation, they have appropriated the kilt and tartan for nationalist purposes; and it comes as no surprise that bright colours should be used for a political message. The form of Alan and James's translation is equivalent to that of the original; but its aims and contents are very different, and far removed from those associated with Chester's kilt.

Finally, Carrie Royde can be seen as exemplifying both cross-cultural translation and culture as translation, depending on how diasporic identity constructions are interpreted. A descendant of migrants, she identifies herself as a 'Canadian Scot' (p. 34), and the Celtic strand is dominant in her self-perception:

> As a girl Caroline Macdonald had suffered from the Lone Shieling complex. She had seen the fairies in a peach-orchard on the shores of Lake Ontario. She had repined at not having been christened Flora, but had derived a measure of consolation from the thought that Caroline was the feminine of Charles. (p. 12)

Carrie wears a tartan skirt, believes in second sight and extols Celtic mysticism. Some of these elements can be found in individual High-land characters as well: thus, Ben Nevis's daughters wear tartan skirts; Duncan MacDonald and Neil Maclennan seem to share Carrie's belief in the supernatural; and Kilwhillie possesses a collection of Jacobite relics, though he does not seem to show any Jacobite leanings. Other elements, in particular the romantic emotion with which Carrie invests all things Celtic, remain peculiar to herself.

If diasporic Celtitude is regarded as separate from the 'original', 'authentic' Celtitude of the Highlands, then Carrie's sense of self is based on cultural translation from a Scottish into a Canadian context, and its expression in Scotland constitutes an attempt at back-transla-tion. On the other hand, if, as Ian Brown has argued, diasporic identities should be treated as a valid 're-fashioning' rather than a secondary and negligible phenomenon,[18] then the act of translation which creates Carrie's Celtic identity occurs within a Celtic culture which is inevitably hybrid and open to Canadian as well as Highland interpretations. In the first case, the concept of tartanry which Carrie embodies is located outside Scotland, like the vision propagated by her guidebook; and her back-translation can be seen to fail because, taken as a whole, it has no equivalent in Highland culture and is therefore recognisably a foreign product. In the second case, Carrie's version of tartanry forms a legitimate part of Celtitude, and the fact that it does not closely correspond to any one local identity is a predictable result of cultural difference. In either case, translation produces a sense of discontinuity.

What, then, does a translational approach tell us about *The Monarch of the Glen* and about literary tartanry in general? From one point of view, translation in Mackenzie's novel is about linguistic and cultural understanding and, perhaps more importantly, about the negotiation of difference and the struggle for power over meaning. The connection between translation and tartanry plays a role in the complex process through which Highland culture is produced, represented and interpreted. From another point of view, translation can be seen as linked to the mock-heroic style that pervades the novel. Translation enables Mackenzie to deploy a number of voices simultaneously and to include tartanry without either explicitly endorsing or censuring it. Tartanry, associated with the heroic, is thus incorporated into the mock-heroic while retaining its own profile.

There is a close connection between translation and literary tartanry. Translation as a rule occurs in situations of linguistic, social and/or cultural contact, and is aimed at a target audience distinct from the source audience. Similarly, tartanry often includes a non-Highland or non-Scottish audience within and/or outside the text, that is, as literary characters or as the narratee or intended reader. This is not to say that tartanry will necessarily be addressed to an audience of outsiders but that cultural contact facilitates reflection on cultural identity, one facet of which is tartanry. In fact, this phenomenon is not restricted to the literary variety of tartanry but appears in other art forms as well – witness the prototypical example in film (and musical theatre), *Brigadoon* (1954). Tartanry is thus linked to situations that not only enable but enforce translation.

The use of translation processes and their relation to tartanry in *The Monarch of the Glen* have been shown to be quite sophisticated. On the one hand this supports Gavin Wallace's view that there is no conflict between Mackenzie's roles as an intellectual and an entertainer, and that his role as an entertainer should not lead to him being taken less seriously by literary critics.[19] On the other hand it could be asked how far the theoretical approach used determines the results obtained. Translation is one of the most complex of human activities, and looking at translation processes may well be a way of making any literary text that includes such processes appear sophisticated. If this is the case, then the present chapter, despite its focus on *The Monarch of the Glen*, says as much about translation and about literary tartanry as translation as about the individual novel used as an exemplar.

How does this chapter fit into the general project of revaluing tartanry, which is part of the larger project of revaluing Scottish popular culture? It has been argued that the concept of authenticity is not helpful in describing Scottish culture,[20] and this certainly applies to descriptions of the translation processes associated with literary tartanry. While the very notion of translation might seem to invoke the ideal of authenticity, in the shape of a (supposedly) sacred original, several branches of contemporary translation studies take the view that a translation is a text in its own right, rather than a derivative product which is inevitably inferior to the original. In *The Monarch of the Glen*, the sheer proliferation and discursive prominence of translations precludes their being treated as secondary phenomena.

More generally speaking, as far as the significance of tartanry for the representation of Scottishness is concerned, on one level the novel illustrates, through its nationalist characters, the translational transformation of Highland into Scottish identity constructions. On another level, the multiplicity of voices involved in the various translation processes suggests a viable way of interpreting tartanry, namely as one among a range of possible translations, which – like other translations or in fact like the hypothetical original – has no claim to universal validity, but does work in certain situations for certain audiences.

Notes

1 Tom Nairn, *After Britain*, pp. 250–1. For a very similar list, see Womack, *Improvement and Romance*, p. 1.

2 James Porter, 'The folklore of Northern Scotland', http://findarticles.com/p/articles/mi_m2386/is_v109/ai_21250626/, p. 2 (9 August 2009).

3 See, for example, Hagemann, *Die Schottische Renaissance*, pp. 190–1. See also Watson, 'Maps of desire', pp. 290–2, 295 for parallels between Hugh MacDiarmid's Gaelic Idea and the Celtic Twilight.

4 Bachmann-Medick, *Cultural Turns*, pp. 238–83 [in German]. For a shorter version in English, see Bachmann-Medick, 'Introduction', pp. 2–16.

5 Bachmann-Medick, 'Introduction', p. 5.

6 Bachmann-Medick, *Cultural Turns*, p. 268 (my translation).

7 Mackenzie, *The Monarch of the Glen*, pp. 97–8. All further references to *The Monarch of the Glen* will appear in parentheses in the text.

8 Fuchs, 'Reaching out', p. 26. Fuchs to some extent draws on Joachim Renn, *Übersetzungsverhältnisse*.

9 Fuchs, 'Reaching out', p. 28.

10 Ibid., pp. 31–2.

11 McCrone, Morris and Kiely, *Scotland – the Brand*, pp. 5–6.
12 Bachmann-Medick, *Cultural Turns*, pp. 239, 243, 261.
13 See Bachmann-Medick, *Cultural Turns*, pp. 246–8.
14 Wallace, 'Compton Mackenzie and the Scottish popular novel', p. 253.
15 Bhabha, *The Location of Culture*, p. 224.
16 See Hagemann, 'Performative parodies', pp. 131–2, for an interpretation of Chester's kilt in terms of parody.
17 Maitland Hume, 'Tartan and the wearing of the kilt', p. 62.
18 Brown, 'In exile from ourselves?', p. 140.
19 Wallace, 'Compton Mackenzie', pp. 254–5.
20 See, for example, McCrone, Morris and Kiely, *Scotland – the Brand*, p. 7, for heritage; Pittock, 'Material culture in modern Scotland', p. 65, for material culture; and Sassi, *Why Scottish Literature Matters*, p. 63, for literature.

10

LOOKING AT TARTAN IN FILM: HISTORY, IDENTITY AND SPECTACLE

Richard Butt

ॐ

In 1898, a film of four men in a variety of tartan costumes performing a Highland dance was projected onto the roof of a building in New York's Herald Square.[1] The film, *Dewar's It's Scotch* (1898), was produced by the Edison Manufacturing Company for the Scottish distillers who had opened their first office in New York three years earlier. While the depiction of 'natives' in traditional dress performing their national dance was common to travel films of the period, this film is significant not only as an innovative piece of advertising, but also in the ways in which it prefigures how tartan and tartanry will feature in cinema. The tartan kilts function as unambiguous signifiers of Scottishness, tartan is a global brand that Dewar's are looking to capitalise on in the development of their global market and the production of tartan images of Scotland by American film companies will preoccupy critics in later years. The utopian sensibility the scene conveys through the energy of the dancing and the men's laughter foreshadows films such as Ealing's *Whisky Galore* (1948) and *The Maggie* (1953), and Bill Forsyth's *Local Hero* (1983), where the céilidh functions as the symbolic resolution of the narrative conflict between the isolated Scottish community and the English/American interloper. Finally, the paradox of projecting historical costume onto a modern building will reappear in cinematic tartanry as a tension between the historical moment of a film's narrative and the contemporary moment in which that narrative was shot. This chapter examines the historical place of cinematic tartanry and the deployment of tartan in cinema more broadly, identifying both variety and continuity in the way in which tartan has functioned in film costume and narrative.

When tartan features as part of a film's iconography it is primarily as a component of a character's costume. It might be assumed, therefore, that its function is subservient to the film's narrative, as this is consistent with the way in which the work of costume designers is principally understood. Jane Gaines argues that in the period of silent cinema, for instance, screen costume 'had to have the kind of style and fabric combination which served the narrative by restating the emotions which the actress conveyed through gesture and emotion. Stepping into a costume *was* like stepping into a role.'[2] With the coming of sound, costume retained its primarily narrative function, but shifted from signifying emotion to signifying character; 'costumes are fitted to characters as a second skin, working in this capacity for the cause of the narrative by relaying information to the viewer about a "person".'[3] While this chapter is partly concerned with what tartan signifies about a character's personality, it argues that from tartan kilts in an historical epic to tartan skirts in Japanese horror, the meaning of tartan in film is not always exhausted by its narrative function.

In classic realist cinema the audience is supposed to look through the costumes to the personality of the characters underneath, because looking at the costumes in and for themselves would interrupt narrative progression and disturb narrative continuity. Stella Bruzzi, who introduced this distinction, argues however that particular scenes sometimes allow us to look both through and at the costumes. Such a scene, she suggests, 'gives the costumes a narrative purpose and allows them to exist independently of that dominant discourse'.[4] This is possible because 'clothing exists as a discourse not wholly dependent on the structures of narrative and character for signification'.[5] When tartan is deployed in film costume we are almost always obliged to look both through and at it, its cinematic deployment evoking the various discourses and practices in which tartan has been embedded, not all of which the film's narrative exploits.

On 26 May 1896, audiences in Glasgow watched their first moving pictures at the city's Skating Palace. Reviewing the event, *The Bailie* reported: 'Nothing could be finer than the representation of the Gordon Highlanders leaving Maryhill Barracks. The picture lasts several minutes, and was repeatedly applauded, as the swinging gait of the Highlanders stirred the patriotism of the audience.'[6] For Tom Nairn, the tartan uniforms of the Highland regiments were part of the 'sentimentalised savagery' of tartanry, evidence of both the Highland/ Lowland divide and the 'Anglophone appropriation of the debris of the destroyed Celtic culture'.[7] Critics identified such tartanry in film narratives set in Scotland's pre-industrial past, films whose iconography privileged tartan costumes in a Highland landscape. The original articulation of these arguments was in *Scotch Reels*, a collection of essays on the representation of Scotland published to coincide with the Scotch Reels event at the 1982 Edinburgh Film Festival. The collection's editor, Colin McArthur, argued that tartanry is one of just three discourses that have informed the cinematic image of Scotland. Drawing on work by Malcolm Chapman,[8] McArthur argued that tartanry's 'generative cause was that massive act of "symbolic appropriation" in the eighteenth century whereby rationalist, scientific Europe defined its own identity by fashioning the identity of the peoples on its periphery in terms of a set of binary oppositions to the qualities it most celebrated in itself'.[9] With its distinctive geography and turbulent history, and the publication of the work of MacPherson, Scott and Stevenson, McArthur argues that Scotland became a key romantic domain. *Bonnie Prince Charlie* (1948), *The Master of Ballantrae* (1953), *Rob Roy – The Highland Rogue* (1953), *Brigadoon* (1954) and *Kidnapped* (1960 and 1971) were the cinematic manifestation of this discourse. For John Caughie

> 'Tartanry' takes Culloden as its privileged moment: a moment recast as an epic of tragic loss and triumphal defeat, which is able to forget, with mythic amnesia, the actual historical tensions involved in the replacement of an absolutist, historically anachronistic and economically unproductive feudal system with a relatively productive free range agrarian system. If, economically, the epic transformation is tied to the industrial revolution, culturally, it is tied to the Romanticism which sought wildness in the now empty landscapes of one of the last 'wildernesses' of Europe, emptied by Cumberland and the Clearances, and filled, by Scott and MacPherson, with wild, charismatic men and fey elusive women.[10]

For Caughie and McArthur, the problem with this 'tartan monster' stalking Hollywood films is that it is 'almost entirely regressive', its appeal launched from a 'vanished' past.[11] *Scotch Reels* formed a critical intervention in discussions of Scottish cinema, setting the agenda for subsequent discussions which either appropriated that agenda or dismissed the films it critiqued as irrelevant to a serious national film culture. McArthur argues that tartanry was hegemonic in cinematic representation of Scotland. Yet, of all the feature films with identifiably Scottish narratives produced before his collection was published, relatively few concern the Jacobite rebellion and, while Scott and Stevenson are the most frequently adapted Scottish authors across cinema's history, the majority of those adaptations are not of their Scottish narratives, but of novels like *Ivanhoe*, *Treasure Island* and *Strange Case of Dr Jekyll and Mr Hyde*. Moreover, the proportion of historical narratives and literary adaptations in Scottish film is no different from other national cinemas – France's 'Tradition de la Qualité' or England's Merchant Ivory heritage films for instance – and they too have had their critics. It might be argued that what distinguishes tartanry from these traditions is that they did not have the representation of their country's past imposed on them by Hollywood. But the earliest example of substantial cinematic tartanry, *Rob Roy* (1911), was shot and produced in Scotland for United Films, a British production company. Similarly, it was British production companies that were responsible for the first wave of cinematic tartanry in the early 1920s, with productions of *Rob Roy* (1922), *Mary Queen of Scots* (1922) and *Bonnie Prince Charlie* (1923). While Hollywood studios produced 1950s cinematic tartanry, the wave began with a London Films production of *Bonnie Prince Charlie* (1948) and ended with a British adaptation of *Kidnapped* (1971).

While tartanry is not hegemonic in representations of Scotland on film, its cinematic form is nonetheless deserving of attention. Hollywood's hegemony in the production of cinematic tartanry in the 1950s, a dominance that was matched by the box office success of individual titles, was determined by a number of factors. Costume drama is expensive to produce, and in the 1950s, as Sue Harper has demonstrated, the British industry was 'riven by economic difficulties and a decline in overall confidence',[12] making it an unreceptive risk-averse climate for the genre. Since the mid-1940s, British film producers had been bound by the same title registration system as the Motion Picture Association of America, which meant that film production companies had exclusive legal rights to film any out-of-copyright titles they had registered an interest in. Consequently, Harper argues, 'costume film-makers in Britain no longer had first call on their own classic novelists. In effect, the most "cinematic" novels of Scott, Dickens and Robert Louis Stevenson were the property of MGM and Disney, and the British were prevented from making films of them.'[13] Finally, British film producers have generally avoided tartanry's politically charged 'privileged moment' of the Jacobite rebellion, but such domestic sensibilities did not trouble the Hollywood studios. They, according to Harper, 'deployed the romantic Scottish rebellion against British rationality as a sort of "prequel" to the American War of Independence, and were thus able to incorporate the rebellion into a debate about individualism versus legitimacy'.[14]

Narratives of individual struggle against a powerful enemy worked well within Hollywood's dominant storytelling mode, providing a narrative space for the seeker-hero whose physical actions drive the narrative forward along a cause-and-effect chain of movement, while maintaining tartan's discursive role as a signifier of allegiance and resistance. Indeed, a further part of the appeal of the Jacobite period to American producers was that 'the fights and kilts afforded endless opportunities for masculine display'.[15] Cinematic tartanry stages masculinity, with different star personas and screen performances ensuring variation in that display. The swashbuckling flamboyance of Errol Flynn in *The Master of Ballantrae* and rugged individualism of Richard Todd in *Rob Roy* offers different screen images of ideal masculinity to those of David Niven in *Bonnie Prince Charlie* (1948) and Michael Caine in *Kidnapped* (1971).

Many of these features are still observable in the narratives of *Rob Roy* (1995) and *Braveheart* (1995). The opening scenes of both films foreground their concern with constructing images of a powerful, omnipotent masculinity. When Rob Roy (Liam Neeson) confronts the tinkers who have rustled the cattle in his protection, killing one who tries to attack him, they discard their weapons, to the disgust of the old tinker woman who cries: 'Are you men, or what are you? He killed Tam, and you stand and let him, and him as much an outlaw as any of you. Not a man among you.' The tinkers' acknowledgement of Rob's authority over them is visually prefigured by his mastery of the Highland landscape in the previous scene, in which his tall kilted figure stands alone, up above his men on a rocky outcrop surveying the lochs and mountains that extend below him. Similarly, *Braveheart*'s narrative begins with the young Wallace disobeying his father's authority by following him to the gathering of the nobles, with the resulting trauma of witnessing the dead Highlanders and their young pages, hung by the English army from the roof of the hut. This traumatic revelation of men's treachery and brutality marks the end of Wallace's childhood innocence, but not his entry to mature masculinity. Forbidding him to join him against the English, his father says, 'I know you can fight, but it's our wits that make us men.' While Wallace (Mel Gibson) later displays his tactical wits in defeating an English enemy better equipped and of greater numbers, it is his muscular masculinity, manifest in the overt display of his bare biceps, that is central to the film's spectacle.

Both film's narratives provide a stage for the performance of fantasies of male power over women, the enemy and the landscape, but they are also a space in which the apparent omnipotence of that power is tested and qualified.[16] In his final duel with Archibald Cunningham (Tim Roth), Rob is wounded first on his torso and then his arm and shoulder, the bloodied marks showing through his slashed shirt. Myra MacDonald and Jane Sillars have argued of Rob's opponent that 'Archie's nationality, his sexuality, his class and his identity are in dispute and in disguise. When Archie strips off his clothes and his powdered wig to reveal the skinhead below, he displays his identity to be little more than a costume, a series of masquerades.'[17] Yet during the fight it is Rob who labours with his heavy sword while Archie's use of his foil is precise and economical. Rob drags his weapon along the flagstones, lurching drunkenly and panting heavily. When Archie slashes him across the stomach he falls to the floor, dropping his weapon. As Archie prepares to kill him, Rob seizes Archie's blade with one hand, grabs his own sword with the other and fatally slashes Archie across the heart in a victory that is neither inevitable nor masterful. Wallace's omnipotent masculinity is similarly tested when he is wounded at the battle of Falkirk and, in a visceral depiction of the physical destruction of the vulnerable male body, later tortured and executed. Despite the violent retribution that marks their narratives of personal revenge and national resistance to tyranny, it is difficult therefore to read these films as triumphalist individualism. As Yvonne Tasker has argued, 'the action scenario is not simply a narrative of empowerment, in which we identify with a heroic figure who triumphs over all obstacles, but is also a dramatisation of the social limits of power'.[18] Such limits are central to the narrative of *Tunes of Glory* (1960), James Kennaway's adaptation of his own novel, which centres on the tragic struggle for patriarchal authority between two senior officers in a Highland regiment.

In *Braveheart* tartan functions as more than simply a component of historical costume, compelling us to look at it, rather than just through it, by foregrounding the textile and its significance through the tartan strip Wallace cuts from his kilt to give to his wife, Murron (Catherine McCormack). The tartan strip both represents and betrays their relationship, leading to Murron's execution, and is retrieved from the ground by Wallace after he has enacted his revenge. At the end of the film, as the Highlanders face the English army at Bannockburn,

Wallace's lifelong friend hurls Wallace's sword into the sky. The camera follows it as it tumbles over itself in slow motion, landing in the ground between the two armies and, with a cry of 'Wallace, Wallace, Wallace', the Highlanders charge at the English troops. As they run towards the camera their roar fades to silence, replaced by Wallace's voice narrating the outcome of the battle. At the words 'they fought like Scotsmen, and won their freedom', the shot dissolves to the final image of the film, Wallace's sword protruding from the ground with Murron's strip of tartan tied to the pommel like a pennant.

This strip of tartan cloth is polysemic. When Wallace gives Murron the tartan strip it acts as a token of his love, and an index of his being. It has this significance not simply because Wallace is always seen wearing tartan, but because of the (assumed) historic relationship between a Highlander's tartan and their geographical origins and allegiance. Throughout the narrative, the tartan costume also acts as a visual signifier of Wallace and his followers' difference from and resistance to the tyranny of the English. The tartan strip thus ties the personal narrative of love and revenge to the national narrative of historical change and resistance. These meanings are not entirely reliant on the narrative: for the contemporary audience they are already part of the discourses that tartan as a textile is embedded within. Central to the formation of these meanings was the proscription of tartan as part of the 1746 Disarming Act's proscriptions. As Jonathan Faiers argues, in identifying the textile as 'a sign of rebellion and an expression of anti-government sympathies',[19] the Act had the paradoxical effect of ensuring that that is precisely what it would come to signify. While the Act takes place some centuries after the period in which *Braveheart* is set, it nonetheless informs our modern reading of tartan's significance.

Cinematic tartanry is pejoratively described in the academic discourse as 'regressive', politically disabling in its reduction of history to 'the domain of myth'.[20] But *Braveheart*'s closing images suggest this is too restrictive a reading of these historical narratives. Alongside the tartan costumes, set battle scenes and fight sequences, the other component of their spectacular mise-en-scène is landscape. Drawing on the work of Siegfried Kracauer, Rosalind Galt argues that in the historical film 'the indexical landscape image undercuts the historicity of the narrative, breaking the spectator's belief in the diegetic world'.[21] There is a tension then, in tartanry's mise-en-scène, between the time of its narrative and the time of its filming. *Braveheart* narrates events that took place over seven hundred years ago, yet the landscapes in which the film was shot are from the pro-filmic present. *Braveheart*'s opening images call attention to this temporal conflict. The film's first shot is of mist, which clears to reveal the film's title. For Colin MacArthur, the mist references 'the analogous openings of *Brigadoon*, *Scotch Myths* and *Local Hero*' and locates the film in ' "the mists of time", the margins of recorded history, the domain of myth'.[22] But this image is followed by a succession of fast-moving helicopter shots of mountain peaks, ridges and lochs. The technical quality of these images draws attention to their contemporariness and thus the film's moment of production. As the shots move down from above the mountains to their lower slopes, the captions 'Scotland' '1280 AD' appear, anchoring the historical and geographical location of the narrative, but not that of the filmic image. This tension is reinforced by the words spoken by the narrator, 'Let me tell you the story of William Wallace', the voice speaking from a moment in time after the narrative events they accompany. While *Braveheart* might be unusual in foregrounding this tension, it is tension common to all historical films, particularly those set in the more remote historical past. Following Galt and Kracauer we can argue that the Highlanders of the narrative and the landscape they move in occupy two different realities. The costumed Highlanders belong to a fictional universe bounded by the film, a historical masquerade, whereas Glencoe, Glen Nevis and Eilean Donan Castle, whose repeated employment as film locations gives them a recognisable familiarity, are part of an ongoing authentic reality.

Galt notes that for Walter Benjamin, 'the privileged signifier of an affective relationship to the past is imagined as a long shot, a distanced view of a natural landscape',[23] arguing that the 'irruption' of contemporary landscape into historical film narratives produces a similar auratic effect. This effect is the result of our projection onto those landscapes of a sense of loss, an emotional response to the historical events those landscapes witnessed; in the case of tartanry the defeat of the Jacobites at Culloden, the Glencoe massacre, the Highland Clearances and mass emigration. Anchoring this cinematic invocation of loss are scenes of characters in mourning within that landscape; in *Braveheart* the young Wallace and other mourners at the burial of his father and brother, and Robert the Bruce walking amongst the grieving wives and mothers after the battle of Falkirk for instance. The audience's emotional response to these scenes is cued by cinematic tartanry's predominantly elegiac soundtrack, a component of the elegiac discourse that commentators argue predominates the representation of the Celtic periphery more generally.[24] *Braveheart*'s final shot of the tartan ribbon tied to Wallace's sword is thus a contemporary memorial of a historical event.

Cinematic tartanry is by no means the exclusive domain of Highland dress in film iconography. Highland costume had always been a distinctive feature of adaptations of Scottish literary classics, historical costume dramas and original screenplays set in Scotland. Harry Lauder, in his various screen appearances – *Harry Lauder in a Hurry* (1908), *Auld Lang Syne* (1929) and *The End of the Road* (1936) – always appeared in a variation of the tartan costume of his stage persona. In an adaptation of John Buchan's *Huntingtower* (1927), for instance, he wore a tartan suit and his trademark tam o'shanter as retired grocer Dickson McCunn, aided by Gorbal Die-Hards in makeshift tartan kilts. In British melodrama *The Brothers* (1947), set on the Isle of Skye, the women wear tartan shawls and the men tartan scarves; and Orson Welles and his retinue wore tartan for his version of *Macbeth* (1948). While these films are narratively and generically different from each other and those just under discussion, the associations of resistance and melancholy discussed above resonate in these images too, a consequence of the social history of tartan as a textile. Even Vincente Minnelli's vibrant musical fantasy *Brigadoon* (1954) features a narrative of individual rebellion and historical loss. Jonathan Faiers argues that Irene Sharaff's costume design for the film pulls narrative and spectacle together, observing that many of the costumes of the mythical village's inhabitants 'are of "supernatural" tartan, their setts shot through with stripes of silver, adding an ethereal shimmer to their wearers' that accentuates the 'supernatural and literally timeless qualities' of the village.[25]

The kilted Scotsman has a long history as a comic figure, and this is exploited in cinema as early as 1903 in *The Effects of Too Much Scotch*, a Gaumont trick film in which a drunken Scot's clothes come to life after he undresses. This comic stereotype is also appropriated in the Three Stooges short *Pardon My Scotch* (1935), in which the trio is persuaded to pose as Scotsmen in an attempt to pass off an intoxicating potion they have concocted in a chemist as Scotch whisky. In comic fantasy *The Ghost Goes West* (1935), Robert Donat plays an eighteenth-century Scottish ghost condemned to haunt his family's castle until he can prove his valour. In a reversal of what was to become the standard narrative of Scottish culture-clash comedies, it is Donat's ghost and his castle that are moved, brick by brick, to Florida, after the castle is purchased by the daughter of an American millionaire. Directed by René Clair, the film was the top UK box office draw of the year, indicative of the resonance this kind of representation of Scotland and the Scots had with the popular imagination and the financial capital it could generate at the cinema.

Inevitably, the kilt also lent itself to a more carnivalesque cinematic deployment. Prior to its prohibition in the 1746 Act, the kilt was caricatured as 'barbaric' and symptomatic of its wearer's licentious potential. This cultural legacy provided comic opportunities for the image of the kilted Scotsman in films such as Laurel and Hardy's *Bonnie Scotland* (1935), *Battle of the Sexes* (1959), starring Peter Sellars, and *Austin Powers: The Spy Who Shagged Me* (1999), in which Dr Evil's oversexed Scottish henchman Fat Bastard first appears in Highland regimental dress playing the bagpipes. The apotheosis of this trope is probably *Carry on . . . up the Khyber* (1968), where the Third Foot and Mouth Highlanders find their colonial authority threatened by the revelation that these 'devils in skirts' apparently wear underpants under their kilts. As the British outpost guarding the Khyber Pass is on the verge of being overthrown by the Khasi of Kalabar (Kenneth Williams) and his followers, Sir Sidney Ruff-Diamond (Sid James) orders his men to line up and raise their kilts at the advancing natives. The natives flee in terror of what is revealed underneath, the scene effectively repeated at the commencement of the Battle of Stirling in Gibson's *Braveheart*, both films reproducing the association of the tartan kilt with masculine virility and resistance.

When women are costumed in tartan it is primarily as part of cinema's construction of the image of woman as 'feminine'.[26] Tartan was a valuable and versatile textile for early costume designers, working well within the aesthetics of black and white film, which required 'screen costume to exhibit a sufficient contrast of light and dark and a strong line in order to make an interesting photographic composition'.[27] Lilian Gish wore a tartan cape for MGM's production of *Annie Laurie* (1927), as did Katharine Hepburn in John Ford's production of *Mary of Scotland* (1936) for RKO. Both stars were surrounded by extras in traditional Highland dress. The internationalisation of the textile within the field of fashion ensured that tartan costume was not restricted to films with an ostensibly Scottish subject. Gloria Swanson wore a black and white tartan ensemble for Fox Studios' screen version of Hammerstein and Kern's musical romantic comedy *Music in the Air* (1934), despite the action being set in Bavaria. Distinctive tartan setts provide the line and contrast Gaines describes, working well with screen icons such as Gish, Hepburn and

Swanson, whose distinctive faces are set off by their tartan capes and collars. Such star and studio endorsement of the textile both reflected and informed its place in the fashion industry. This is in turn reflected in its presence in later films where it features as part of the fashionable ensemble of young actresses like Anna Karina, whose Odile wears a tartan skirt with black sweater in the Madison dance sequence in Jean-Luc Godard's *Bande à Part* (1964), Ali McGraw, whose Radcliffe College music student Jennifer Cavalleri wears a variety of tartan scarves and skirts in *Love Story* (1970), and Barbra Streisand, who wears a range of setts from a soft pink and grey tartan coat to a more vibrant Stewart-style skirt with braces and tam o'shanter as the time-shifting Daisy Gamble in another Minnelli musical, *On a Clear Day You Can See Forever* (1970).

Since the 1980s, tartan, or plaid, has been a recurrent component of the American high school movie's wardrobe, a genre which, following writer John Hughes' form setting *Pretty in Pink* (1986), has fore-grounded the role of clothing in maintaining the social distinction of the films' characters. In Hughes' film, it functions to denote the working-class credentials of Andie's (Molly Ringwald) fellow scholar-ship student Duckie (Jon Cryer), who often wears a plaid shirt under his more idiosyncratic jackets and waistcoats. In *Clueless* (1993), director Amy Heckerling's transposition of Jane Austen's *Emma* to an exclusive Beverly Hills high school, costume designer Mona May dressed many of the male characters in what she describes as 'very grunge orientated fashion, you could call it Seattle style, you know, Nirvana look with the plaid shirts'.[28] The haute couture potential of tartan is reserved for the film's central character, Cher (Alicia Silverstone). The film begins with Cher's browsing through her options for that day's clothing on her computer programme, the majority of which feature a combination of vibrant tartan outfits, before settling on a mustard, black and white tartan jacket with matching short skirt, white knee socks and white court shoes. Dressed in this outfit she picks up her best friend Dion, who is similarly clad in black and white tartan accessorised with a Dr Seuss hat. The textile dominates Cher's fifty-six costume changes, comprising what Heckerling refers to as the 'hyper style' of her character. Indeed, one could argue that the film's different social groups are effectively distinguished by their preference for either hard (mass-produced) preppy tartan, like Cher and Dion, or the soft (cottage industry) grunge tartan of new girl Tai, whose style Cher attempts to transform, and Cher's stepbrother Josh, whose dress sense she bemoans but with whom she eventually realises she is in love.

Tartan is also part of the logic of the field of fashion in Terry Zwigoff's *Ghost World* (2001), although Enid's (Thora Birch) green and black tartan skirt is used to signify her individuality and thus her distinction from the high school 'clans'. Her tartan skirt was later replicated in British fashion designer Luella Bartley's 2007 autumn collection.

If the plaid shirts of Duckie, Tai and Josh are historically derived from their place in American manual labour workwear, Cher, Dion and Enid's short tartan skirts are partly informed by the uniforms of American schoolgirls. The pleated tartan skirt has been a component of girls' school uniforms since the early twentieth century in the UK – *The Prime of Miss Jean Brodie* (1969) costumed some of the charismatic teacher's pupils in the tartan skirts that are typical of Edinburgh's private schools – and the practice spread into Europe, America and Japan. The fetishised image of the uniformed schoolgirl is a significant feature of certain genres of Japanese cinema, particularly in recent gore films such as *Yo Yo Girl Cop* (2006), *Attack Girls' Swim Team Versus The Undead* (2007) and *The Machine Girl* (2008). Quentin Tarantino's *Kill Bill: Volume 1* (2003) pays homage to this figure through the character of sadistic tartan-skirted schoolgirl assassin Gogo Yubari (Chiaki Kuriyama). This image is both invoked and temporarily destabilised in Alejandro González Iñárritu's network narrative *Babel* (2006). One of the narrative strands concerns Chieko (Rinko Kikuchi), a deaf and mute Tokyo schoolgirl whose father's rifle fires the shot that connects the different international strands of the film's narrative together. In a series of encounters with figures of patriarchal authority Chieko is misunderstood, ignored, humiliated and rejected, while her body, costumed in her school uniform of short tartan skirt, black jumper and white socks, is subjected to the voyeuristic gaze of the men she encounters. In one scene, a young man approaches Chieko in a café after he and his friends have been furtively looking at her and her fellow schoolgirls. When she struggles to make herself understood, he turns his back on her and returns to his smirking friends. In the toilet, Chieko complains to her friend that 'They look at us like we're monsters.' Removing her knickers, she declares that 'now they're going to meet the real hairy monster'. On returning to her seat, she reveals herself to the boys at the other table. The incredulous reactions of the boys, and the hilarity of Chieko and her friends, suggest that she is momentarily empowered, and that this empowerment comes from her disruption of the male voyeuristic gaze through the unveiling of the reality that the school uniform fetish serves to disavow.

Atom Egoyan's *Exotica* (1994) provides another interrogation of the tartan-skirted schoolgirl fetish. The film is centred around the 'Exotica', an upmarket, tropical-themed striptease and table dancing club in Toronto. Each night, Christina (Mia Kirshner) performs on stage in schoolgirl uniform to Leonard Cohen's 'Everybody Knows', before dancing at the table of Francis Brown (Bruce Greenwood), under the apparently jealous gaze of Eric (Elias Koteas), the club's emcee. As the director notes, the film's narrative is structured 'like a striptease, gradually revealing an emotionally loaded history'.[29] The history that is unveiled is that Francis's daughter, Lisa, was murdered, Christina was Lisa's babysitter and was herself abused as a younger child, and was with Eric in the search party that found Lisa's body, dressed in the same uniform that Christina now wears in her performance for Francis. Eric, who prevents Christina seeing Lisa's body by covering her eyes, longs to return to the relationship he once had with Christina prior to her employment as a sex-worker. In gazing on Christina in her schoolgirl uniform, both men desire not Christina, whose fetishised body is forbidden to their touch, but the lost innocent subject that this fetish substitutes.

Since the 1990s, most Scottish film-makers have looked outwards to international art house cinema rather than backwards to the nation's past for their aesthetic style and narrative subjects. The consequence is that tartan is largely absent in the iconography of recent Scottish films; the only tartan in *Trainspotting* (1996) is a scarf worn by an American tourist the lads mug in a pub toilet during the Edinburgh Festival. One exception to this is the romantic comedy *Nina's Heavenly Delights* (2006). Set in the Scottish Asian community of contemporary Glasgow, the film plays with some of the cinematic tropes of tartan and tartanry discussed in this chapter. While the narrative is primarily concerned with the eponymous heroine's forbidden love for her girlfriend Lisa, Nina's fourteen-year-old sister Priya (Zoe Henretty) also has a secret. In a reworking of the proscription of tartan under the 1746 Act and subsequent acts of Highland rebellion, Priya has continued to practise Scottish Highland dancing despite having been forbidden to do so by her parents, keeping her tartan dance costume hidden in her room. Priya reveals her act of resistance to her mother shortly before Nina and Lisa come out on public television, the film ending in a hybrid *Brigadoon*–Bollywood dance sequence in what looks like a touristic Highland landscape but is finally revealed to be a studio back projection. As with many of the films discussed in this chapter, these scenes require us to look at, rather than through, the tartan components of the film's costume. Tartan's varied cinematic deployment evokes its equally varied history, a history that film itself both reproduces and refashions.

Notes

 1 Buxton, *The Enduring Legacy of Dewars*, p. 24.
 2 Gaines, 'Costume and narrative', p. 184 (emphasis in original).
 3 Ibid., p. 181.
 4 Bruzzi, *Undressing Cinema*, p. 1.
 5 Ibid., p. 2.
 6 *The Bailie*, May 27 1896, Scottish Film Archive, Glasgow.
 7 Nairn, *The Break-Up of Britain*, pp. 167–8.
 8 Chapman, *The Gaelic Vision in Scottish Culture*.
 9 McArthur, 'Scotland and cinema: the iniquity of the fathers', p. 41.
10 Caughie, 'Representing Scotland', p. 15.
11 Ibid., p. 15.
12 Harper, 'Bonnie Prince Charlie revisited', p. 276.
13 Ibid., p. 277.
14 Ibid., p. 282.
15 Ibid., p. 282.
16 See Neale, 'Masculinity as spectacle', p. 6.
17 MacDonald and Sillars, 'Gender, spaces, changes', p. 186.
18 Tasker, *Spectacular Bodies*, p. 117.
19 Faiers, *Tartan*, p. 22.
20 MacArthur, *Brigadoon*, p. 141.
21 Galt, *New European Cinema*, p. 63.
22 MacArthur, *Brigadoon*, p. 141.
23 Galt, *New European Cinema*, p. 66.
24 See Spring, 'Lost land of dreams: representing St Kilda', p. 2.
25 Faiers, *Tartan*, p. 246.
26 Gaines, 'Costume and narrative'.
27 Ibid., p. 184.
28 May, 'Fashion 101'.
29 Egoyan, DVD Sleeve Notes, *Exotica*.

11

TARTAN COMICS AND COMIC TARTANRY

Margaret Munro

❧

The use of tartan in performance, often in the form of the kilt, can be represented as perpetuating an unrealistic, stereotypical Scottish identity. However, as Paul Maloney has made clear, Scottish performers have seen its use as vital in providing an instantly recognisable signifier of identity. From W. F. Frame and Harry Lauder through to Jimmy Logan, Andy Stewart and Craig Hill, this symbol marks comic entertainers as Scottish, allowing audiences to identify with them, and creates, whether consciously or unconsciously, an expectation of the mode of performance. This chapter considers ways in which this motif has been used in the last fifty years by performers and recognised by audiences both nationally and internationally as a Scottish emblem.

The various ways in which identity may be created often focus on the difference between national and collective identity.[1] Philip Schlesinger argues that 'national identity is best understood as a specific form of collective identity',[2] but that relevant work has mostly 'failed to conceptualize *national* identity as opposed to the identities of emergent collectivities within established nation-states'.[3] He suggests 'collective identity requires the constant action of an agent within a determinate set of social relations. It also requires us to take account of space and time.'[4] He further suggests, 'national identity is constructed within a definite social space' and that 'within the social space, cultural space is where the elaboration of various cultural identities takes place'.[5] This 'cultural space' clearly includes performance spaces where the performers encourage the reinforcement of their, or their audience's, cultural identity by the use of cultural signifiers.

Schlesinger also regards time as important in the process of creating identity. He suggests that the relationship between the past and present 'should be understood, at least in part, as an imaginary one, mediated by the continual, selective reconstitution of "traditions" and of "social memory"'.[6] The collective identity associated with shared history, experiences and memories may lead to the creation of a national 'imagined community',[7] a term used by Benedict Anderson. Performers, therefore, undertake this mediation and use shared cultural signifiers, particularly in the cases under discussion, those of tartan and tartanry, to create or reinforce specific cultural identities. Stuart Hall argues that national culture is 'one of the principal sources of cultural identity'[8] and that 'in fact, national identities are not things we are born with, but are formed and transformed within and in relation to *representations*'.[9] The focus of this chapter's discussion, then, is representations by Scottish comic performers of tartanry, including kilt-wearing.

That Scottish identity has largely been constructed on myth was a central argument of Scottish critics, particularly in the 1970s and early 1980s. Yet this is hardly new information: the foundation myths of, say, Rome were integral to the manufacture of Roman identity. It seems improbable that Scottish identity uniquely in the world would not, at least in part, be founded on its national myths. Yet, critics of the period made much of the mythic tartan underpinning of Scottish cultural identity. Julie Davidson seems surprised that 'the fact is that for most Scots the myths have taken on reality. We share an inherited nostalgia for a land that never was.'[10] Murray Grigor believes that 'myths have their beginnings in the reality of a country's past. In Scotland, history and mythology come so closely interwoven, that it's often hard to see the real country and its people',[11] whilst Steve Bruce makes a suggestion of 'competing visions', comprising 'the "Balmorality" of the Scottish Tourist Board, the small town sentimentality of the "kailyard" school of Scottish literature, the revolutionary fervour of "Red Clydeside" and the violence of the Glasgow hard man'.[12] Andrew Marr believes that there are many myths in Scotland and that 'Scotland is bound by them and littered with them – strong, wiry myths, often contradictory, complex and fankled [. . .] But Scottishness continues to be defined as much by culture and history as by anything else.'[13] In fact it is an error to attack mythic underpinning in itself. According to Raphael Samuel, 'if we turn to almost any historical field, this persistent blindness to myth undeniably robs us of much of our power to understand and interpret the past'. He further argues, 'the mythical elements in memory, in short, need to be seen both as evidence of the past, and as a continuing historical force in the present'.[14] Elizabeth Tonkin suggests 'myth is a representation of the past which historians recognize but generally as an alternative to proper history'.[15] As Ian Brown, drawing on the work of Lévi-

Strauss and Barthes, argues in his chapter, myths must be analysed and not just dismissed. In his study of mythologies, Barthes argues that myth 'is a message' and 'a mode of signification' and that 'mythology can only have an historical foundation', the message not only spoken, but represented by images; for example 'photography, cinema, reporting, sport, shows, publicity'.[16] All of these, of course, are used in representations of Scotland. He further argues that 'what the world supplies to myth is an historical reality, defined, even if this goes back quite a while, by the way in which men have produced or used it; and what myth gives in return is a *natural* image of this reality'.[17]

Murray Pittock discusses the continuing promotion of tartan as a signifier of 'Scottishness' during the nineteenth century elsewhere in this volume. Suffice it to say that for the Scottish diaspora tartan was, and is, recognised as a Scottish signifier. Scots comics used it to create an instantly recognisable image and identity. Offstage, W. F. Frame wore 'a shepherd tartan suit of a dambrod [draughtboard] check that was calculated to catch the eye at a distance'.[18] Elspeth King is damning of the identity originated by Frame, later copied by others, describing him thus:

> the escapist stereotype developed in urban Glasgow by Frame, the boot and soor milk boy and apprentice engineer, was the 'Bonnie Hieland Laddie', resplendent in kilt and toorie, accompanied by pipes and dispensing incomprehensible pawky patter and springs [sic] of heather indiscriminately. This gross caricature was further developed and refined by a visit to the USA, where he took the Carnegie Hall by storm in 1898, and was subsequently copied by Lauder and others.[19]

This stereotype provided the diaspora with their link to home. It was a symbol of the identity they had left behind in their 'unchanging homeland'. But the caricature represented on stage is an identity criticised by those such as King as being both mythical and unrealistic. Michael Newton's chapter, however, offers an alternative reading of this phenomenon, drawing attention to the importance of iconic significations for diasporic populations seeking to sustain a sense of cultural identity in alien surroundings, however much these significations may from time to time be exploited and trivialised. It is surely as a result of this need that Frame's use of tartan proved lucrative, providing the style of entertainment desired and demanded by his audience, who would inevitably, like any emigrant community, remember their 'homeland' in frozen significations.

It is Lauder, however, who is recognised as taking the imagery to international success, or notoriety, in the 1900s. He is much denigrated today for the image he portrayed,[20] but Lauder knew exactly what he was doing in creating what verged on self-conscious parody of himself. Tartan was iconic for Scots performers, particularly if they were performing for the diaspora. Lauder, a Lowland comic wearing Highland costume, perfected the use of tartan to create his own personal brand, embedding it into his identity, thus ensuring that audiences remembered him. Ian Gale, in 1997, describes the portrait of Lauder painted by H. M. Bateman in 1915 thus:

> not merely a caricature of an entertainer, but a caricature of a caricature. For here is the cant Scotsman, with his kilt, bonnet, plaid and lush's red nose. Here is the image of Scotland as she is still sold worldwide – the image we must destroy.[21]

In the 2009 National Library of Scotland exhibition,[22] a Gaumont-British Picture Corporation clip showed Lauder performing clad in tartan from head to toe with a backdrop of mountains, heather, croft and loch, cramming every symbol of 'Scottishness' into one small stage. In this clip, Lauder is shown performing 'My Ain Dear Nell', jigging about on stage to rousing applause and cheering. His popularity here is undeniable. Further Gaumont footage shows Lauder's triumphant journey from London to Liverpool, dressed more sombrely, but still wearing his tartan kilt. He is piped, in a clearly successful publicity stunt, aboard the *Lusitania* by a pipe band in full regalia. By constantly using tartan, Lauder ensures that a connection is made to and with him, guaranteeing instant recognition. There are indications that he does not take himself too seriously in his self-caricaturing: for example, on the cover of *Tomlyn's Gem Collection of Scottish Songs*, on display in the exhibition, he had, in cartoon mode, sketched himself smoking a pipe. Here is a performer prepared to satirise himself in order to create his personal, unmistakeable identity. That this was successful cannot be denied, particularly in the days before mass media instantly disseminated images worldwide. The fact he still engenders much disputatious discussion further highlights the success of his ploy, ensuring his place in comic performance. It could be argued that this success was achieved at the cost of creating a stereotypical identity of and for the Scottish population.

However, this ignores the fact that Lauder did present other stage personae,[23] with detractors preferring to focus solely on his tartanised identity.

Lauder's tartan imagery, however, was not intended to reflect contemporary Scottish society, but to provide him with an identity that was visually instantly recognisable and identified him as a Scottish artist. When beginning their careers, music hall performers would possibly only be on stage for five minutes. It was crucial to create a persona that would be instantly recognised, and Lauder, with his tartan regalia and twisted walking sticks, succeeded in doing this. Billy Crockett, a retired performer who worked in Scotland and abroad from the late 1930s on, reinforced in interview the use of tartanry as immediate signifier of identity in comic performance. An advertising poster for one of his shows presents him resplendent in an eye-catching, garish yellow and black tartan outfit. He believed that the further away from home one performed, the more 'patriotic' the audience. He performed in Las Vegas in the *Dynamite Revue*, a show with dancing girls, but still did 'the Scotch Act' with the dancers wearing tartan. Crockett, with his very visual image, believed that you had to sell yourself to the audience within a few minutes and used the wearing of the kilt to do so.[24]

Performers' use of tartan on stage helped create almost self-fulfilling stereotypes, where both performer and audience knew what was expected and provided. Tartan represents shared history. To criticise and disparage both performers and their use of tartan as a signifier of identity is to fail to understand the significance and importance it held for the audience. As Cairns Craig cautions,

> it assumes that the past is definable in terms of a single dominant (Tartan/Kailyard) and that the implications of that dominant can be reversed simply by an act of the will. It is founded, therefore, precisely on the ability to negate the past, to deny that – however fraudulent it may have been – it remains part of *our* past, and a real part of our past because the community of which we are a part has lived through those images and symbols, lived with them and given them a meanings and a significances [*sic*] that may be very different from their origins. If all culture is to be defined in terms of authenticity of origin, not much is going to survive.[25]

Craig's statement, written in 1996, appears to contradict his earlier denigration of the use of tartanry and Kailyard[26] and surely reflects a reassessment of the use of these cultural icons. Here he suggests that there is a risk that in destroying the myth, the culture may also be destroyed. Yet, the perpetuation of this myth was illustrated and criticised in the exhibition *Scotch Myths – An Exploration of Scotchness* at the 1981 Edinburgh Festival. Here postcards exemplified caricature. Music hall artistes, for example W. F. Frame and Harry Lauder, were very popular on postcards, where 'the postcard artist amplified and sanctified the music hall image of Scotland', with the twentieth-century Scot described as 'mean, pawky, canny, fighting, sentimental and dressed to kilt [*sic*] in tartan and feathered bonnet [. . .] Captured forever on a picture postcard the iconography of Scotchness. The lost tribe roaming in the gloaming.'[27] Myth and caricature were exploited and profited from. The 'Heederum-Hoderum' of 'Scottish Kitsch' was used to provide a symbol of Scottishness, where 'Scots themselves were conspiring in the manufacture of the caricature and profiting by it'.[28] Certainly, commercial enterprise was benefiting from the tartan identity that Frame and Lauder had also successfully exploited, but for those experiencing the changes wrought by urbanisation and industrialisation – or emigration – tartan provided a connection with their, often mythical, rural idyll. As Richard Finlay argues,

> Tartanry, Highlandism and the rural representation of Scotland in the Kailyard novels, were all indicative of the manufacture of a Scottish identity which had little to do with the reality of a rapidly urbanising and industrialising society, but everything to do with the appropriation of symbolic representations of Scotland which were located in a mythical past.[29]

Finlay also suggests that

> it was during this period of rapid industrialisation and urbanisation that the Scots started to reinvent themselves. It was the era of Highlandism and tartanry, the romanticisation of the Scottish past, the sentimentalisation of rural life, and, the contribution of imperial Scotland to the British Empire.[30]

Andy Stewart was a comic performer who more recently employed and subverted the kilt, frequently deprecating himself and the tartan image he embedded in his persona during his performances. His popularity continues. His performance of 'A Scottish Soldier', awarded a Silver Disc for its sales in 1961, receives multiple YouTube hits, where the imagery used perpetuates the popular tartan-military myth discussed elsewhere in this volume. His 'Donald Where's Yir Troosers' uses the persona of the kilted Highlander forced to move to the industrialised south to find employment. A hit in 1961 and again in 1989, this song has achieved cult status, also with multiple hits for its audio recording on YouTube where the image is of Stewart accompanied by a woman in a tartan cloak. On his video *Andy Stewart's Scotland*,[31] Stewart performs it in a cocky, self-confident style, with a glint in his eye and a swing of his kilt reminiscent of Lauder. The song represents the kilt-wearer as in some sense alien, representing in Glasgow an alternative 'Highland' reality. According to his spoken introduction, the 'lassies shout' what he identifies as a general street cry to a kilted man: 'Donald where's yir troosers?' The sense of being alien in the kilt is developed in the third verse, which takes Donald to a more exotic location:

> Now I went down to London town
> And I had some fun on the underground
> The ladies turned their heads around saying
> 'Donald where are your trousers?'

Here the question is written in English and performed in cod-Received Pronunciation (RP). The transgressed boundaries are not only geographical, but those of class. Again the emphasis is on the disruption of anticipated sartorial convention that wearing the kilt, here on the London Underground, can represent. Stewart here plays the outsider in RP-speaking élite society, where his difference makes him novel and an object of interest, the song underscoring the thrill experienced by the ladies at his exotic, foreign appearance. It continues in its fifth verse subversively to hint at and celebrate the long-running question of what is, or is not, worn underneath the kilt, while Stewart draws on a saying about Highlanders to suggest that sophistication lies with the 'alien' kilt-wearer rather than the observer:

> The lasses want me every wan
> Well let them catch me if they can
> Ye cannae take the breeks off a Heiland man
> And I don't wear the troosers

Perhaps the most outlandish and ironic part of Stewart's performance is in verses six and seven where he impersonates Elvis Presley, rather well. As if to mark the potential for alternative readings of the kilt, Stewart enters a surrealist world where the kilt-wearer can embody any unlikely international cult figure he wishes:

> Oh man of all the rock and roll
> I'm a moving and grooving to save my soul
> Grab your kilt and GO GO GO
> Hey Donald whereyirtroosaz

The juxtaposition of a kilted performer, wearing this traditional symbol of Scottishness, with the modernity, at the time, of an impersonation of a rock'n'roll singer, created a cultural anachronism and was strategically intended as a comedic device. Stewart here deliberately undermined everything that tartanry stood for, subverting the traditional visual image he presented with oral contradiction in the modernity and varieties of style in which he was singing. He has confidence in his own performance: his gifts of mimicry and self-deprecation are apparent. The core of his humour is self-aware subversiveness.

Ian Pattison, creator of Rab C. Nesbitt, believes that the Scots comedy he grew up with, such as that of Stewart, was bizarre. He recollects 'Andy Stewart in a kilt doing Louis Armstrong impressions and you say to yourself, you know, is that an ironic statement or what?'[32] Such a strategy's success is demonstrated by the fact Pattison still remembers it years later and that Stewart's performances are still being viewed on the web by succeeding generations. The strategies employed by Stewart depend on audience knowledge of the myths referred to. Hall suggests that identity is increasingly critical when it is perceived to be changing and that as social contexts change so do our identities.[33] He describes the sociological conception of identity where 'the subject still has an inner core or essence that is "the real me", but this is formed and modified in a continuous dialogue with the cultural worlds "outside" and the identities which they offer'.[34] Those affected by industrialisation in Scotland clung to their images of their past, mythic and real, lives, whilst struggling to adapt to the reality of their situation. The sometimes surreal humour created by Stewart helps express and release the tensions associated with these conditions.

It can be argued that the stereotypical Scottish identities created on stage are negative and pejorative and Joshua Fishman, in his exam-

ination of stereotypes, suggests that the term 'stereotype' is indeed seen
as pejorative, negative and distorted.[35] William Vinache agrees that
stereotypes are seen as 'bad' not 'good' and that everyone learns
stereotypes, but that degrees of prejudice vary[36] whilst Richard Dyer
opens his discussion of stereotypes by saying 'the word "stereotypes"
is today almost always a term of abuse'.[37] Martin Barker further
questions, 'What is a stereotype? It is a shorthand image which fills
gaps in our knowledge. Where we do not know the reality, a stereotype gives us apparent knowledge. Their danger lies in just that.'[38]
Isobel Lindsay explores the relationship between stereotypes and
identity and considers stereotypes are essential in constructing identity, observing 'the conclusion is that since rapid social change has
made identity more fluid so it produces greater potential for the self-
selection or the manipulation of identity to achieve particular ends'.[39]
Certainly, tartan has been manipulated to represent a particular
stereotypical identity. The longevity of the particular stereotype of
tartanry may seem surprising, considering its alleged negative connotations. However, Tessa Perkins suggests that

> the strength of a stereotype results from a combination of three
> factors: its 'simplicity', its immediate recognisability (which makes
> its communicative role very important), and its implicit reference to
> an assumed consensus about some attribute or complex social
> relationships. Stereotypes are in this respect proto-types of 'shared
> cultural meanings'.[40]

The tartan stereotype fulfils all these criteria. Perkins further suggests
that 'cartoonists or comedians often appeal to the most stark (and
exaggerated) versions of a stereotype',[41] and that the media help to
form or create stereotypes and spread them.[42] Therefore the stereotypes perpetuated, and sometimes caricatured, by Scots comics have
already been accepted and recognised by society. Perhaps Barker best
sums up the complex ideology behind the creation and perpetuation of
stereotypes:

> The power of the visual metaphor is to suggest staticness, trapping
> us in the past. This is the reason for the obsessive use of words like
> 'traditional', 'age-old' and 'outdated' in such work [. . .] The
> implication clearly is that 'stereotypes' have no relevance to the
> present, and might well have declined but for their continued media
> representation. But also it is implied that stereotypes draw their
> power from ideas and images of the past; they are not creations in

the present, fought for and made convincing to use, but residues of already existing powers which dull and stultify us, trapping us back into those power relations. I want to suggest that this is yet another component of the peculiar issue of 'time' in theories of ideology. Once again, ideology is seen as a force from the past, barring our access to a future.[43]

If implied disapproval is seen as a key element in discussions of stereotypes, many performers, conversely, see these stereotypes, particularly the tartan image, positively, and deliberately employ them to gain instant recognition, both locally and internationally. Jimmy Logan makes several observations on this in his autobiography. He describes the denigration of the kilted tartan identity thus:

> the problem was born out of Scotland's desire to be a thriving modern nation, but somewhere along the line some-one decided the best way to do that was to ditch our heritage. As a result wonderful parts of our culture like the kilt, tartan, heather and so on took an absolute hammering from just about every quarter.[44]

He continues, 'whether people liked it or not – that was what symbolised Scotland abroad – and we were loved for it. It had, and deserved, its place within a culture that was respected and envied on the international playing field.'[45] Logan's is the performer's opinion of tartan's significance. His many years' experience as a comedian reinforces the beliefs of previous comics, like Frame and Lauder, illustrating the pragmatic artist's viewpoint. He admits that there were critics of this symbolic representation and caricatures them thus: 'these critics were convinced that all of Scotland's ills were caused by people who wore this awful kilt, kept saying "Hoots Mon" and told terrible Scottish jokes'.[46] Logan suggests that in the 1960s and 1970s the tartan image was ridiculed and criticised, but insists that 'going abroad with the kilt representing Scotland is like possessing a passport inscribed in gold. Attempts to kill that culture should always be opposed.'[47] He further suggests that outside Scotland the symbols of tartanry and the kilt were loved and it was only domestic Scots who criticised them.[48] He therefore sees the symbolism of tartanry as positive representation of Scotland to be worn with pride, as a welcome symbol of Scottish culture.

Logan consciously modelled himself on Lauder, whom he believed was a music hall and international superstar. He wrote his one-man show *Lauder* because he wanted to ensure that Lauder was given the respect he deserved. He asserts that Lauder's American contract insisted that he must always wear the kilt and never be seen wearing trousers.[49] Logan himself made good use of the kilt in his comic performances. An archive clip shows a young, kilted Logan telling the audience, 'The object of the exercise tonight is very simple. You're going to find out what a Scotsman wears under his kilt'.[50] With exaggerated drum rolls for dramatic effect, interrupted by several jokes which build the tension, he finally pulls off his kilt to reveal a mini-kilt four inches above the knees underneath. Although Logan respected the kilt as an icon of Scottish identity, he was not above employing it ironically as the key factor in his comic performance. He also plays on the sexual innuendo related to the question of what a Scotsman wears under his kilt, with the audience anticipating a revelation, although knowing full well nothing salacious is likely to happen.

Such comedy could frequently be derived from toying with the kilt as icon. A 1968 clip of Stanley Baxter shows him performing 'A Scottish Soldier' clad in a knee-length kilt in a typical parody of Andy Stewart.[51] As the song progresses, the kilt lengthens whilst Baxter's voice simultaneously pitches higher. By the end of the song, Baxter is wearing a floor-length kilt and singing soprano, bearing an uncanny resemblance to Moira Anderson, a popular Scottish female singer of the period. These performances depend on the audience's knowledge so that the joke is understood and the performances' irony appreciated. They mock not only the kilt, but the popularity of the genre, and present self-parodic images. These are post-modern responses to the comic cult represented by Frame and Lauder. Since nationally and internationally the kilt is recognised as a symbol of Scotland and Scottishness, comics are primed to use and subvert its iconography, confident that audiences will be complicit with the performance's irony and self-deprecation. Scottish comics continue to use this as part of their performance. Craig Hill, in his version of this male stereotype, questions it by presenting its antithesis in his performance. Although kilted, Hill is a camp performer, implying gender ambiguity. His kilts are self-coloured, not tartan, and made of PVC or leather, but reference the stereotypical Scottish comic performer. That Hill does class himself as a Scottish performer is beyond doubt. In performance he frequently relates his upbringing in Glasgow and then qualifies it by stating that actually it was East Kilbride.[52] The title of his 2007 tour, *Craig Hill's Kilty Pleasures*, with its hidden pun on 'guilty', again subverts the kilt and its associated stereotypes, continuing to build on a tradition stretching back over one hundred years.

Faiers recognises the potential in tartan clothes beyond the kilt for both the traditional and the subversive. He observes

> tartan's subversive signification is arrived at out of a complex mixture of its historical rebellious associations and its unique ability to function as a vestimentary indicator of sartorial exhibitionism, as well as its specific theatrical antecedence via the figure of Harlequin. A tartan suit allows a performer to be a satirist, be risqué or act the fool; to break with convention and yet still engender popular appeal and recognition
> [. . .]
> As has been suggested, tartan can be conceived of as a textile of excess, and it is this excessive tendency that is most often capitalized upon when donned by the entertainer. This excess can be of a sexual, comedic, or transgressive order, the tartan suit often a sign of those who are outside conventional societal norms, its ostentation and vulgarity an indication of an inherent decadence or weakness.[53]

While the tartan kilt in comedy is predominantly Scottish male apparel, tartan clothes extend the range of potential comic subversion. A non-Scots figure like George Melly in his flamboyant tartan suits extended the potential for subversive tartan while Fran and Anna's performances exemplified the use of tartan to excess, while fracturing the male domination of the genre. These female singers of indeterminate age wore mini mini-kilts and tartan bunnets. They had few musical talents, often endlessly repeating the chorus of the song they were performing, but their tongue-in-cheek performances were loved by audiences for what they were: caricatures of a version of Scottishness. Their talent, or apparent lack of it, was frequently discussed, but gave them notoriety and ensured they were talked about. And they in turn could be parodied and satirised. Andy Cameron relates a pantomime performance where

> Ray Jeffries and I came doon as Fran and Anna, that was 1979, we'd them aw roarin and wi tears and the roar that went up, the roar was unbelievable and this night we came doon and we did, aw we did was 'blaw, blaw, ma kilt's awa', we repeated that line about fifteen times and then we took a bow. The place was in an uproar. And then one night a roar went up the back and here's the two of

them dressed exactly the same as us and they're bowin and they're wavin. That's absolutely true.[54]

The subversive performances of Fran and Anna were further subverted by the caricature of them during a pantomime performance, and on this occasion their subversion of the subversion of their subversive performance. The audience understood and acknowledged what was being represented and the performers themselves further acknowledged this.

The irony in the use of tartan in many Scots comics' performances appears to escape some critics. These represent the kilt and tartan as perpetuating an unrealistic, stereotypical Scottish identity. Perhaps they focus too closely on surface appearance and fail to see the underlying transgressive and satiric performative factors that make such comedy popular and successful. Scots comics' use of tartanry as a motif of their performance has evolved in meaning over the last century. As Pittock suggests, 'Kilts can now be as much for looking up, having fall off, suggest cross-dressing or celebrating gender ambiguity as they are symbols of Scottish manhood at play in the older sense'.[55] Their use and that of tartan have continued to be successful and popular in performance. That success and popularity reinforces the point that audiences understand the uses of tartan and are knowingly complicit in them.

Notes

1 For example, Schlesinger, *Media, State and Nation*.
2 Ibid., p. 153.
3 Ibid., p. 173.
4 Ibid., p. 173.
5 Ibid., p. 173.
6 Ibid., p. 174.
7 Anderson, *Imagined Communities*, pp. 6–7.
8 Hall, Held and McGrew, *Modernity and Its Futures*, p. 291.
9 Ibid., p. 292.
10 Davidson, 'Heederum-Hoderum', pp. 30–50.
11 Grigor, *Scotch Myths*, n.p.
12 Bruce, 'A failure of the imagination', pp. 1–16.
13 Marr, *The Battle for Scotland*, p. 49.
14 Samuel and Thompson, *The Myths We Live By*, pp. 4–5, 20.
15 Tonkin, 'History and the myth of realism', pp. 25–35.
16 Barthes, *Mythologies*, pp. 109–10.

17 Ibid., p. 142.
18 Moffat, *Join Me in Remembering*, p. 26.
19 King, 'Popular culture in Glasgow' p. 169.
20 Craig, 'Myths against history' pp. 7–15; McCrone, Morris and Kiely, *Scotland – the Brand*, p. 50; Bold, *Modern Scottish Literature*, p. 9; Grigor, *Scotch Myths*.
21 Gale, I., 'People's keeper. Edinburgh's Victorian pile, the National Portrait Gallery, is in line for a shake-up', *Scotland on Sunday*, 26 October 1997, Spectrum, pp. 20–1.
22 *Scots Music Abroad*, National Library of Scotland, George IV Bridge, Edinburgh, 6 March–23 May 2009.
23 Illustrations interspersed throughout Lauder, *Harry Lauder at Home and on Tour*, show him as an Irish character in 'Calligan, Call Again', p. 51, a schoolboy in 'I'm the Saftest o' the Family', p. 63 and as a drunk in 'Fou the Noo, Absolutely Fou', p. 75.
24 Conversation with Billy Crockett, 18 December 1997.
25 Craig, *Out of History*, p. 111.
26 See note 20.
27 Grigor, *Scotch Myths*, n.p.
28 Davidson, 'Heederum-Hoderum', p. 46.
29 Finlay, 'Controlling the past', pp. 127–42.
30 Finlay, 'Heroes, myths and anniversaries in modern Scotland', pp. 108–25.
31 *Andy Stewart's Scotland*, VITV 563, Scotdisc, BGS Productions Ltd, Kilsyth.
32 Interview with Ian Pattison, scriptwriter, 12 March 1998.
33 Hall, Held and McGrew, *Modernity and Its Futures*, p. 277.
34 Ibid., p. 276.
35 Fishman, 'An examination of the process and function of social stereotyping', pp. 27–64.
36 Vinache, 'Stereotypes as social concepts', pp. 229–43.
37 Dyer, 'The role of stereotypes', pp. 15–21.
38 Barker, *Comics: Ideology, Power and the Critics*, p. 196.
39 Lindsay, 'The uses and abuses of national stereotypes', pp. 133–48.
40 Perkins, 'Rethinking stereotypes', pp. 135–59.
41 Ibid., p. 146.
42 Ibid., p. 149.
43 Barker, 'The lost world of stereotypes', pp. 86–91.
44 Logan, *It's a Funny Life*, p. 242.
45 Ibid., p. 242.
46 Ibid., p. 255.
47 Ibid., p. 256.
48 Ibid., p. 265.
49 Ibid., pp. 255–8.

50 *Ronnie Corbett Tickles Your Fancy*, STV, 8–9 p.m., 31 December 1999.
51 *Hoots*, BBC1, 10.30–11 p.m., 10 February 2000.
52 Craig Hill, 21 February 2009, Brunton Theatre, Musselburgh.
53 Faiers, *Tartan*, p. 170.
54 Interview with Andy Cameron, comic, 20 August 1998.
55 Pittock, 'Material culture in modern Scotland' pp. 64–8.

12

ROCK, POP AND TARTAN

J. Mark Percival

ᐁ

INTRODUCTION

Tartan in post-1940s Anglo-US popular music culture is a site where notions of Scottishness and national identity meet discourses of commerce, creativity and authenticity. The focus of this chapter is on issues of tartan and meaning in rock and pop in an international context, and on the contrasting meanings constructed around the use of tartan by artists perceived as either Scottish or non-Scottish. The historical context and development of the multivalent, often contradictory significations of tartan are particularly visible in popular music, and are addressed in a number of key examples from the 1950s through to the early twenty-first century. Outside the UK, and predominantly in North America, the term 'plaid' is used as synonym of tartan, so when discussing US artists this convention will be followed.

The chapter divides its discussion of tartan and popular music culture into two broad eras:

1. Rock and roll to glam: tradition and showing out, 1954–75;
2. Punk and its legacy: irony, subversion and new authenticities, 1976–2010.

This is fifty-six years of western popular music history and it is of course impossible to address more than a handful of examples in the context of a single book chapter. The musicians, performers and genres included here have been chosen to illustrate best the shifting semiotics of tartan in UK and North American popular music. In the process it is hoped not only to draw together existing work, but also to shed new light on some of the best-known of these cases, and to establish potentially new relationships between them.

CONTEXT

Sharon MacDonald, in her analysis of the relationship between Scottish and Highland identities, discusses the attraction of the mythological, historical unity of Highland culture as shorthand for representing Scotland as a whole:

> Tartan, bag-pipes and whisky have all, at various times, been banned by Lowland authorities. However, the same cultural conspicuousness which could lead to their outlawing, was also a potent marker of difference which, once domesticated, could be appropriated as a symbol of Scottish distinctiveness.[1]

Here, 'domestication' of tartan and other powerful cultural symbols is part of a process in which those symbols become no longer threatening to the Scottish and English cultural and political institutions, yet remain distinctively Scottish. Yet it is also true, as Jonathan Faiers argues, that the sense of tartan as potentially disruptive remains in place alongside more mainstream, establishment uses of tartan by the tourism industry, the military and the aristocracy.[2] Faiers also explicitly addresses the point implicit in MacDonald – that the semiotics of tartan change over time, at times very rapidly.

Central then to most of the points made in this chapter is the notion that the semiotics of tartan is both flexible and frequently contradictory. Equally important is the argument that cultural context is crucial to interpretations of tartan. Meaning is thus negotiated according to time, place and, in the case of popular music, the prevailing discourses of pop, rock and authenticity in a given era. The last of these, the socially constructed notion of authenticity, permeates popular music discourse at all levels, from fans to the academy. Richard Peterson acknowledges the complexity of the notion of 'authenticity' in popular music, but suggests that the term is frequently associated with an array of positive values including honesty, integrity, truth and passion.[3] It is tartan's power to be flexibly authentic that makes it such a fascinating part of popular music culture.

Tartan's semiotic palette is complex and heterogeneous but its dominant signification, as MacDonald suggests, is that of Scotland. This of course can extend into lengthy arguments around what it means to be 'Scottish', but, as the present author has argued elsewhere, discourse in popular music frequently associates essentialist attributes such as honesty and integrity with the 'Scottishness' of musicians from north of the border.[4] Tartan in popular music signifies Scotland, and thus for some artists, critics and fans it may therefore also signify a glowingly positive authenticity in music. Yet tartan can also represent a peculiarly kitsch mainstream aesthetic, antithetical to indie or alternative music cultures. These significations become more interesting again if one considers that in the former case, the unironic authenticity represented by tartan may be understood as a good thing (honest, true, patriotic) or as a bad thing (naive, unreflective, conformist). Similarly, the kitsch, mainstream aesthetic associations of tartan may be seen as bad (stereotypical, unrepresentative, embarrassing) or good (an opportunity to be knowingly ironic or playful).

The table overleaf gathers some of the shifting meanings together and maps them against three key variables: place (within or outside Scotland), whether artists are Scottish or otherwise, and time.

ROCK AND ROLL TO GLAM: TRADITION AND SHOWING OUT, 1954–75

One of the earliest notable appearances of plaid in rock was in the form of the matching plaid suits worn in many of the live and TV appearances of Bill Haley and His Comets during the mid-1950s. Faiers argues that this was a continuation of a historical line stretching back to the first stirrings of jazz in the 1920s, a line which was far more concerned with, 'a sense of sartorial awareness [. . .] amongst [. . .] performers who like to "show out"'.[5] Bill Haley, in other words, was not interested in communicating consciously or otherwise rebellion or working-class solidarity. Plaid tuxedos drew attention to the wearer by virtue of their very difference from standard, sober mainstream suit patterns. Put more directly, tartan allowed artists the opportunity to emphasise the gulf between performer and audience.

The use of tartan as an attention-grabbing device recurs in popular music cultural history in the years following the 1950s, but it remained a largely kitsch expression of showbusiness performance or eccentricity until the arrival of punk in the mid-1970s. However, before the shock of the punk/new, Scottish rock bands of the 1960s for the most part avoided any association with tartan: it would not have been visually apparent to rock fans of the late 1960s and early 1970s that artists like Alex Harvey, Stone The Crows or Frankie Miller were from Scotland. The 1960s and the emergence of 'rock', along with a redrafting of the consensus on what might constitute 'authenticity',

Shifting semiotics of tartan in pop and rock

	Within Scotland	Outside Scotland
Scottish Artists	1960s–1970s: Tartan is perceived by rock culture as being mainstream, commercial, exploitative and shallow. Avoided by 'serious' artists such as Stone The Crows, Alex Harvey, Skids (also later known as The Skids).	1960s–1970s: Tartan is seen as unambiguous shorthand for 'Scotland'. It is unironic, though at times playful (Bay City Rollers).
	1980s: Tartan is ironic and kitsch, but used by a Scottish indie label (Postcard). Reappropriated as unironic, authentic, warmly patriotic (Big Country) or as knowing but affectionate kitsch (Jesse Rae).	1980s: Tartan seen as ambiguous shorthand for 'Scotland', unironic, overly serious (Big Country).
	1990s: Tartan deployed as critical patriotism (Arab Strap).	1990s: Tartan deployed as critical patriotism, but also as knowingly parodic stereotyping (Arab Strap).
Non-Scottish Artists		1960s–1970s: Tartan as unambiguous shorthand for Scotland (Rod Stewart); attention-grabbing showbusiness stage wear, unrelated to mainstream connotations of Scottishness (Slade, Jimi Hendrix); subversion of dominant codes, visible resistance (punk).
		1980s: Extension of 1970s tartan-as-costume (Spandau Ballet, Visage).
		1990s: Tartan as symbol of working-class integrity/ simultaneous rejection of conservative values associated with plaid in the form of the work shirt (Nirvana).

meant that serious bands were conscious of the need to clearly demonstrate their integrity and musicianship in ways analogous to earlier folk music narratives.[6] This was a time when displays of tartan by Scottish performers were associated with kitsch representations of Scottish traditional culture, such as nationally televised celebrations of New Year, or the BBC's *White Heather Club*:

> [The show] ran from 1958 to 1968. Andy Stewart presented and sang in the Scottish country dance music show, which, at its peak, drew in an audience of 10 million people and turned Stewart into an international star. This very Scottish image, awash with kilts and fiddles, is one which the rest of the network took to be a true representation of Scotland.[7]

Rock artists would have seen the *White Heather Club* vision of Scotland as unrepresentative (particularly of the Scottish urban experience) and entirely fabricated for the amusement of an ill-informed national UK mainstream audience. Tartan for these bands represented an inauthentic, nostalgic notion of Scotland quite at odds with their desire to be seen as serious artists in the UK as a whole and on the international stage. Bands prioritising commercial success, however, apparently had few qualms about the use of tartan.

GLAM ROCK, POP AND THE ROLLERS

In the very early 1970s glam rock emerged as a movement instigated by (and later transcended by) art rockers David Bowie and Roxy Music. Glam's sartorial approach was about extremes of colour and cut, and tartan was a perfect fit; it is, as Faiers puts it, 'a textile of excess'.[8] The foremost exponent of tartan in the service of stage presence was Noddy Holder of West Midlands four-piece Slade. Faiers sees Holder's look in a historical context:

> Holder [. . .] in his immaculately tailored tartan suits [. . .] suggested a direct sartorial link from the late nineteenth-century gent to 1970s glam rock [. . .] With his guttural voice, platform boots [. . .] and above all his extensive wardrobe of tartan, Holder carved a particular niche in the decadent and at times manufactured world of 1970s British pop.[9]

Holder's connection to tartan remains with him, according to a 2007 *Daily Mail* interview in which he describes answering his front door to his postman in his tartan pyjamas. There is a rather intriguing shift from public to private deployment of the plaid crosshatch here but it is in keeping with the nostalgic power of tartan.

Despite the enormous commercial success of Slade in the period from 1971 to 1976 they were still regarded as a rock band, with the associated aura of authenticity, rather than a pop band, with con- notations of insubstantiality and hyped success.[10] This was, and to an extent still is, a somewhat artificial distinction, concealing the many complexities of socially constructed authenticity.[11] The pop/rock credibility schism does, however, go some way to explaining the otherwise oddly contradictory lack of criticism of Holder (as opposed to the Bay City Rollers), an iconically English Midlands working- class man, associating himself with a quintessentially Scottish textile pattern.

It is worth noting the profile of one of the best-known 'wannabe' Scotsmen, Rod Stewart (born in London to a Scottish father and an English mother). Although Stewart first achieved success in the 1960s, it was in the 1970s that he increasingly deployed tartan to signify not only his connection to Scotland, but also his support for the Scottish national football team. In their empirical study of identity claims in Scotland, Richard Kiely, Frank Bechhofer and David McCrone argue Scots themselves are rarely flexible in under- standing claims to be Scottish from those who were not actually born in the country.[12] Scots strongly connect their notions of Scottishness to place of birth, and significantly less to any sense of cultural belonging.[13] Thus the deployment of tartan by popular musicians not born in Scotland would be perceived by Scots as an inauthentic claim on Scottish national identity, despite the power of tartan to signify Scottishness. Outside Scotland, however, it is perhaps not surprising that many casual fans of pop and rock assumed that Rod Stewart was Scottish.[14]

In a marked contrast with Noddy Holder and Rod Stewart, a Scottish group that achieved comparable levels of success in the same era was seen by many rock and mainstream critics as being very much in the tradition of kitsch, shallow, manufactured pop, not least in their use of tartan. For rock critics and fans, it was acceptable for the English Holder to wear tartan precisely because it was not about a representation of Scotland. In contrast, it was problematic for the same rock critics and fans that a successful Scottish pop group should wear a symbol of their nationality on their collective and literal sleeves. 'Serious' critics and musicians understood tartan-wearing Scots entertainers of the pre-punk era as largely cosy, mainstream, folksy, even kitsch. The Bay City Rollers' use of tartan would have appeared to fit this strand of tartan semiology. A representative *New Musical Express* feature from 1974 notes:

> The Rollers play exactly the same set every night and receive exactly the same uncritical response from a houseful of teenage girls decked out in tartan scarves and, more often than not, wearing the identikit shortened trousers.[15]

There are, then, additional nuances in the attribution of authenticity to rock and pop artists, not least amongst them the gendering of rock as male and pop as female.[16] The Bay City Rollers' audience was dominated by young women and girls, and despite the textual similarities between the sounds on Rollers records and those of their glam peers, they were clearly framed as pop rather than rock.[17] Tartan as deployed by the Bay City Rollers, despite a 'legitimacy' derived from their Scottish origin, was not about signifying allegiance to country or culture. Rather it became part of a glam-pop image that was readily adopted (and adapted) as a symbol of belonging by fans of the band. For fans of the band, tartan meant 'Bay City Rollers' and not in any direct sense 'Scotland'. As Faiers argues:

> Amongst many tartan-clad entertainers, perhaps none has capitalised quite so effectively on the power that tartan can demonstrate as a visual sign of collective adoration as the Bay City Rollers in the 1970s.[18]

This use of tartan as an outward sign of inner conviction has long historical roots in the evolution of tartan in Scotland and elsewhere, but there are three elements of Bay City Rollers fandom that foreshadow punk.[19] First, there is the use of tartan itself: Highland clan associations are irrelevant, but brighter tartans seemed to have been favoured. Second, tartan is used to demonstrate allegiance to a musical cause: a clear message partly to like-minded fans and partly to uncomprehending outsiders, of belonging. Third, Bay City Rollers fans were actively involved in the low-cost, do-it-yourself creation of tartan-based clothing. Contemporary sources suggest that the band themselves instigated the tartan modification of their own clothes before their first major TV appearance:

> When the Rollers appeared on *Top Of The Pops* they were still too broke to afford any flashy new outfits. Instead, before they drove to London, they sat up all night at Eric's digs chopping off their trousers bottoms and sewing bits of tartan to their cheap army surplus shirts.[20]

Whether this was press spin to a receptive journalist or approximately true, the DIY element meant that fans of the band were able to modify existing baggy trousers and shirts with cheap tartan strips from local fabric shops and adopt widely available tartan scarves to signify their pop allegiance.[21]

PUNK AND ITS LEGACY: IRONY, SUBVERSION AND NEW AUTHENTICITIES, 1976–2010

Jon Savage and Roger Sabin have documented the origins of punk well.[22] It is often the case, however, that less well researched or critical work than theirs tends to reproduce mythological aspects of punk. Not least of these is the notion that punk in 1976 represented a year zero, a point in popular music cultural history at which all reference points were reset and everything was abruptly new. To some of those who hit their teens in the mid- to late 1970s, this may well have appeared to be what was happening. In retrospect, however, it is clear that there were antecedents to punk in terms of both sound and fan activity. With punk, in the UK at least, there was an added high culture (even *haute couture*) ingredient missing from the resolutely mass cultural impact of the Bay City Rollers. As Faiers puts it, 'It is with Vivienne Westwood and Malcolm McLaren's launch of [their shop] Seditionaries [. . .] in late 1976, that tartan becomes indelibly associated with punk'.[23] He points out that Westwood's couture was both too exclusive and too expensive for most punks, but second-hand tartan fabric was readily available and customisable into 'bum-flaps' and aprons. It is also true that cheap Westwood imitations rapidly became available in the months following punk's emergence as part of national UK popular music culture. The other contemporary cauldron of punk was in Lower Manhattan, but early US punks tended to favour jeans, leather jackets and ripped t-shirts, rather than reappropriated tartan or plaid.[24]

It is unlikely that contemporary punks would have appreciated the suggestion that there was a similarity between their do-it-yourself approach to sartorial identity with that of Bay City Rollers fans only a few years earlier. Despite the wildly divergent ideologies underpinning the music and attitude of the Sex Pistols and the Bay City Rollers, as far as punk and glam pop fan behaviour was concerned, manipulation and display of tartan was a symbol of subcultural belonging. For punk in particular, however, there was multilayered meaning in tartan. Faiers suggests that Westwood was more than peripherally aware of the cultural history of tartan in her early designs:

> The history of tartan as a fabric expressive of revolt and opposition, its remarkable status as a cloth outlawed by the English and its associations with royalty made it the perfect textile for a range of clothing that aimed to make anarchy, alienation and indeed sedition wearable.[25]

It may have been unlikely that many tartan-wearing punks would have been familiar with the arguments around the politics of anarchy and sedition, but this re-imagining of tartan would in later years imbue the design with further layers of meaning with the complex, often contradictory values of punk.[26]

NEW ROMANTICS, INDIE POP AND BIG COUNTRY

In the aftermath of punk, the New Romantic movement moved in 1980 from its birthplace in London's Blitz club to the national stage. The New Romantics were, for the most part, apolitical and the level of subversion involved little more than men wearing make-up, Boy George not withstanding. Dressing up, often in Hollywood-inspired costume, was central to early New Romantic bands like Spandau Ballet, Duran Duran and Visage. Tartan showed up again, albeit briefly, but it was here merely part of a palette of styles and textures that were part of the Bowie-influenced 'look'.[27] Few fans of the accessible electropop and funk that characterised the first months of the movement dressed up to the level of key scene members and bands. Tartan when it appeared on stage or the street did not have the sense of subversion associated with punks, nor did it signify an unambiguous commitment to a band (as with the Bay City Rollers) or an ideology (punk). As Dave Rimmer suggested in an earlier book, it was like punk never happened.[28]

At around the same time as the New Romantic movement was developing in London and was dressing up in kilts as a form of attention-seeking fancy dress, a young Scottish music fan was setting up a Glasgow-based independent label, Postcard Records.[29] The label would over the course of two years (1980–1) release thirteen singles and invent indie pop (a 1960s-influenced sound characterised by jangling or chiming guitars and fey vocals). In marked contrast to the resistance of 'serious' Scottish musicians, Postcard Records' founder, Alan Horne, was happy to use tartan in his record artwork to signify the label's Scottish home. The sense of Scottishness was reinforced by the label's slogan, 'The Sound of Young Scotland', derived, perhaps optimistically, from US black pop label Motown's 1960s branding as 'The Sound of Young America'. Not all of the 7-inch singles on Postcard used tartan in the artwork, but two records by Aztec Camera ('Mattress of Wire' and 'Just Like Gold'), one by Josef K ('Chance Meeting') and one by Orange Juice ('Poor Old Soul') displayed tartan on the printed label in camel, blue, green and red respectively. The picture sleeves for 'Just Like Gold', 'Chance Meeting' and 'Poor Old Soul' were identical designs, with a circular central disc cutout allowing the record's label to be read. The front of the picture sleeves featured thirteen separate drawings in 1960s British comic-style of kilted Scots (male and female) pursuing a number of stereo-typically Highland activities. These activities included hill walking, shooting, fishing, drinking beer and curling. The back of the sleeve contained only one image carried over from the front: a dancing Highland boy.

The use of tartan by Postcard Records can be read as a continuation of the subversive reappropriation of tartan instigated by Vivienne Westwood's couture but it was in fact something much more than that. It was in part a statement that the seriousness of the bands and movements before Postcard had been supplanted by an affectionately ironic Scottish understanding of tartan. It signified a lightness of touch that situated the bands on Postcard as modern pop rather than the rock of the previous decade. It was also an unironic signifier of national identity for the first genuinely innovative and successful independent label in Scotland – a label that would work to establish a new perception of music in Scotland for an industry largely focused in London. It was, in other words, more important that the English music industry, media and indeed potential customers understood that Postcard was Scottish, than that they understood the complex and multilayered semiology of tartan for most Scots. It was Scottish fans who would be able to decode (consciously or otherwise) the message that this tartan display was as much about reclaiming tartan not only from the English, but also from a conservative Scottish mainstream culture that positioned tartan as a symbol of officially sanctioned events such as Scottish country dancing, fiddlers rallies or the BBC's *White Heather Club* version of Scotland. If the Postcard record label was reinventing Scottish pop and reappropriating tartan for a post-punk generation, what then was happening to Scottish rock?

One of the small handful of Scottish bands to emerge from the punk era was Dunfermline four-piece The Skids. Their UK breakthrough came with the Top 20 single *Into The Valley* (1979) and they went on to release four studio albums before breaking up in 1981. The Skids, though, did not, following many of their Scottish pre-punk rock predecessors, wear tartan, despite the tartan/punk association established by Vivienne Westwood. The band did, however, have a guitarist and co-songwriter, Stuart Adamson, who formed a new, more accessibly mainstream band, Big Country, following his departure from The Skids. Big Country made much more explicit aural and, at times, visual reference to Scottish musical and cultural traditions. Adamson's guitar used several modulation effects to achieve a sound often described by contemporary reviewers as close to that of bagpipes, though Adamson himself claimed at the time that had not been his intention.[30] The guitar and vocal melodies on *The Crossing* (1983), the band's first studio album, are clearly influenced by traditional Celtic music and many of the lyrics indicate a preoccupation with the romance and landscape of the Highlands.

The music's Scottish themes were reflected in the tartan shirts frequently worn on stage in their breakthrough year of 1983 by Adamson, second guitarist Bruce Watson and bass player Tony Butler. Live shows supporting the release of *The Crossing* used a painted backdrop of Highland lochs and mountains. Both of these visual codes are clearly visible in the video release of their 1983/1984 New Year's Eve concert at the Glasgow Barrowland Ballroom (reissued on DVD in 2009). Tartan and ongoing restatements of Scottishness litter this live performance on an occasion, Hogmanay, largely perceived as being a particularly Scottish party. Midway through the show, Big Country stop their show to announce the New Year, and the full Dundonald and Dysart Pipe Band takes the stage to perform three traditional tunes to the apparent delight of the young, predominantly male crowd. Big Country return for the second half of their set and finish the evening by leading the crowd in an *a cappella* version of the traditional Scots New Year song, 'Auld Lang Syne'. The whole show is an unambiguous celebration of Scottish traditional and contemporary culture in a context that would have been almost unthinkable for early generations of Scots rock performers. Tartan is deployed as a symbol of mainstream Scottish culture of the people, not of the aristocracy or subcultural punk. Again, the flexible polysemy of tartan here allowed a modern, post-punk Scottish rock band to adapt tartan to its own ends and, in this performance at least, tap into its audience's sentiment and apolitical patriotism on a most Scottish occasion.

Big Country was arguably the first successful Scottish rock band, rather than a traditional music or folk-rock group, to foreground tartan as part of their image as part of an aesthetic that referenced tradition in a modern rock context. Some members of the audience at live shows on 1983's *The Crossing* tour also sported tartan shirts but despite the short six years between the year punk broke and Big Country's debut album, tartan for Adamson and his band was about Scotland and Scottishness, and not about subversion. Could this have been at least part of the reason that the band faced a startlingly quick critical backlash? Did mainstream (English) rock critics interpret these nods to traditional representations of Scotland ('bagpipe' guitars, romantic patriotism, non-ironic displays of tartan) as kitsch and essentially, in a post-punk world, un-rock? Later albums, from 1984's *Steeltown* onwards, gradually moved Big Country away from the early trademark guitars and towards a more mainstream rock sound, but Adamson would still appear on stage from time to time in a tartan shirt or suit. Whether this was a response to some of Big Country's more negative critics, or an attempt to follow U2 to anthemic Celtic global fame is not clear. The band, however, did not recapture the level of sales of their first two albums and a year after completing a successful farewell tour in 2000, Adamson took his own life.[31] This was a tragic end to a career characterised, in its early years at least, by innovation, risk taking and often-spectacular statements of national identity.

GRUNGE AND PLAID – BLUE-COLLAR AMERICA

In the late 1980s, grunge began to attract attention as a definable popular music sub-genre in the Pacific Northwest of the US, largely (but not exclusively) under the aegis of indie label Sub Pop. Tartan (as 'plaid' in North America) had already become a signifier of blue-collar, working-class origins and related notions of integrity and honesty. Tartan was shorthand for a particular strand of socially constructed authenticity, most closely related to the 'real', the 'not-pretence' in Peterson's discussion of the fabrication of authenticity. As Faiers puts it: 'the tartan shirt is almost as ubiquitous as jeans or overalls and has come to symbolise a basic, unpretentious sensibility'.[32] The biggest band to break out of the Seattle indie scene into the rock mainstream was Nirvana, with their second studio album, *Nevermind* (1991). Alongside their alternative rock sounds, they brought with them Kurt Cobain's plaid shirt, not only an echo of the singer-guitarist's working-class origins in Aberdeen, Washington, but also symbolic of his band's commitment to notions of authenticity and truth derived from the punk and hardcore movements of the late 1970s and early 1980s. Plaid here weaves together multiple, often contradictory, semiotic layers. Cobain's plaid shirt was both 'natural' (manual workers in his hometown wore them) but arguably also ironic. In interviews and song lyrics, Cobain rejected the conservative attitudes of small-town America, most notably in lyrics of the song 'In Bloom' from *Nevermind* in which he describes a music fan who sings along with lyrics he doesn't understand. By wearing the plaid shirt, Cobain celebrated his origins whilst knowing that large numbers of Americans who dressed similarly would not share his values.

The alternative rock movement of which Nirvana was part was often represented as drawing together several strands of earlier subcultures, in particular the militant independence of post-punk and hard core, alongside the sounds of classic rock and accessible melodies, as journalist Stevie Chick put it, 'the Sex Pistols and Led Zeppelin and Beatles [. . .] that, pre-Nirvana, seemed at odds with one another'.[33] Grunge was also framed as a reaction to the Los Angeles Metal scene of the mid- to late 1980s, out of which Guns N' Roses emerged to global success in 1987 with the album *Appetite For Destruction*. Although frequently positioned by critics as opposites, Nirvana and Guns N' Roses were connected by similar sonic influences, with GN'R as 'heirs to the delinquent lineage of the Rolling Stones and the Sex Pistols'.[34] Nirvana were even offered the opportunity to open shows for the Guns N' Roses 1992 world tour, but turned it down, sparking the beginnings of a feud between Axl Rose and Cobain, lead singers in each band.[35]

Yet the legacy of punk ideology and iconography connected the two bands in ways that neither would have recognised at the time. Cobain's plaid shirt signified the working-class integrity of (mythological) punk, but Rose's use of tartan kilts on stage alluded not only to his Scottish heritage but more clearly to the visual code of Vivienne Westwood's punk rebellion. In both cases however, tartan (plaid) is deployed to communicate particular authenticities. For Cobain it was an authenticity built around a commitment to principles of independence from a corporate music industry. For Rose it was partly a typically American nostalgia for distant cultural and ethnic roots, but also an opportunity to provoke and to reinforce the outsider myths of rock ideology. The specific referent of tartan is different in each case, yet both examples illustrate tartan's power to signify both belonging and counter-cultural resistance.

PASTICHE AND UBIQUITY

Grunge probably marked the last explicitly ideological deployment of tartan in popular music. It would, however, continue to appear in the costume of popular music performers like André Benjamin of Outkast, whose affection for tartan is evident on the sleeve of the group's 2003 album, *Speakerboxxx / The Love Below*. Faiers characterises Benjamin as being part of a line of earlier 'loud gents' in popular music performance, including Jimi Hendrix and Noddy Holder.[36] There may be, as Faiers argues, an element of nostalgia or post-punk irony in the wearing of a tartan suit, but once more the semiotic rules appear to be different for non-Scottish musicians. A deeply intelligent independent Scottish band like Arab Strap, audibly defiantly Scottish, has used traditional Scottish formal kilt outfits in press photographs taken in the Highlands in the early 2000s. They did not, however, perform in kilts and the use of stereotypical image of the Scottish musician is both ironic and in some ways affectionate. The band is from small-town, central-belt Scotland, not from the Highlands, nor are their lyrics thematically traditional. Part of the message of these images (sun-drenched loch-side, backdrop of mountains) is that the band and their fans both know that there is an affectionate swipe being directed at earlier generations of artists, some discussed by Margaret Munro, who exploited tartanry in pursuit of commercial success, both domestically and internationally. This deployment of tartan and traditional Highland imagery captures the essence of something peculiarly Scottish, which might be described as critical patriotism.

Elsewhere something very interesting was happening to the distinctive Burberry Nova check, a traditionally differentiated term for a pattern that is, in any substantive sense, a tartan. The pattern – described by Faiers as the English tartan – had spent most of the twentieth century associated with aristocracy and the aspirational upper middle classes, but by the early 2000s it was simultaneously being worn by fans of polo and of football. Faiers argues that the Nova check exhibited the same power as other tartans to signify both tradition and change, conformity and resistance, and above all, a tribal sense of belonging.[37] The comedy Welsh hip hop group Goldie Lookin Chain (GLC) utilised the Nova check on a customised Vauxhall Cavalier in a promotional video. In this case the use of the check is not satirising the check itself; it was rather part of the group's ongoing parody of so called 'chav' (British underclass) culture and the excesses of hip hop.

SUMMARY AND CONCLUSION

Despite punk rock's apparent transformation of the values associated with tartan, cultural context remains central to the semiotics of tartan in popular music. This chapter has argued that the connotations of the deployment of tartan as identity coding in popular music are complex, polysemic and often contradictory, not least in Scotland itself. Tartan is, Faiers suggests, 'above all, a textile of *contradiction*' (original emphasis) whilst being 'simultaneously [. . .] quintessentially traditional and rebellious'.[38]

The decoding of tartan in pop is dependent on several key variables: place, time and pop cultural context, primarily the prevailing contemporary discourses of authenticity in popular music. First, place matters in at least two ways: whether artists are identified as Scottish (that is, are they actually from Scotland, usually having been born there or moved there at very young age) or non-Scottish; and whether discourse around those artists is happening within Scotland or outside Scotland. This sets up at least four possible strands of argument around the use of tartan in pop: the discourse around 'Scottish' artists within or outside Scotland; the discourse around non-Scottish artists within or outside Scotland. To further complicate matters, there may be substantial overlap in these discourses: the tendency to valorise positive essentialist attributes of Scottish artists is visible in both Scottish and English popular critical and journalistic writing.[39]

Second, time matters. The meanings of tartan in pop change over time because the meaning of tartan changes over time. Clearly the two issues are related, especially when changes in the meaning of tartan are driven by shifts in popular music culture, most notably Vivienne Westwood's appropriation of tartan into displays of, amongst other things, rebellion, resistance and belonging in punk. More often, modified or new meanings of tartan are initiated or constrained elsewhere in the cultural or political spheres, as notions of Scottishness and Scottish national identity are renegotiated nationally and internationally.

Third, cultural context matters. This is dependent on both place and time but it is more importantly about discourses of authenticity in popular music. Prevailing rock orthodox authenticity in the 1960s and early 1970s privileged (apparent) innovation, counter-cultural, alternative lifestyles and a rejection of mainstream values and institutions. Tartan, for many Scots rockers in this period, would have been seen as representative of a kitsch, creatively irrelevant mainstream entertainment culture. It was not until the post-punk period that evidence of a shift in the coding of tartan became apparent in the form of the ironic, yet affectionate and effective use of tartan in the visual design of pioneering Glasgow-based indie label Postcard Records from 1980 to 1981. Irony was not visible in Big Country's unashamed reappropriation of tartan as explicit signifier of a romantic, patriotic Scottishness. While this appeared to work well within Scotland, it rapidly became a problem in terms of perception of the band by the London-based music press, which tended to see this use of tartan as sentimental, rather than Romantic, and kitsch rather than evocative.

In North America, tartan (or plaid) in a non-musical context signified several, typically conflicting, authenticities for bands in the late 1980s grunge scene, notably Nirvana. Plaid in US popular culture, as Ian Brown traces in his Introduction, represented solid, working-class integrity, but for Nirvana's Kurt Cobain it simultaneously represented an ironic rejection of reactionary values associated with small-town America.

The ubiquity of tartan at the end of the first decade of the twenty-first century has brought with it Robbie Williams in a kilt and a temporary consolidation of meaning around 'Celtic' musics, within Scotland and elsewhere. For alternative or independent pop and rock artists from Scotland, tartan again would appear to suggest mainstream entertainment or association with any number of hybrid genres derived from traditional or folk musics. Tartan, then, retains its polysemic power in popular music: it is simultaneously 'authentic' and 'inauthentic'; ironic and straight; conformist and rebellious. Tartan in pop continues to be all of these things and therefore also continues to signify not just Scotland, but many Scotlands.

Notes

1 MacDonald, *Reimagining Culture*, p. 5.
2 Faiers, *Tartan, passim.*
3 Peterson, *Creating Country Music.*
4 Percival, 'Britpop or Eng-pop?'
5 Faiers, *Tartan*, p. 175.
6 Keightley, 'Reconsidering rock'.
7 BBC Online, 'BBC Scotland: from the wireless to the web'.
8 Faiers, *Tartan*, p. 170.
9 Ibid., p. 170.
10 Roberts, *British Hit Singles and Albums.*
11 Frith, *Performing Rites*; Peterson, *Creating Country Music.*
12 Kiely, Bechhofer and McCrone, 'Birth, blood and belonging'.
13 Ibid., p.166.
14 Mäkelä, 'Tartan boys'.
15 Charlesworth, 'The Bay City Rollers: kings of pop!'.
16 Frith, *Sound Effects.*
17 Sullivan, *Bye Bye Baby.*
18 Faiers, *Tartan*, pp. 126–8.
19 Cheape, *Tartan. The Highland Habit*; Martin, 'From clan to punk'; Faiers, *Tartan.*
20 Coon, 'Inside the Bay City Rollers' camp'.
21 Mäkelä, 'Tartan boys'.
22 Savage, *England's Dreaming*; Sabin, *Punk Rock: So What?*
23 Faiers, *Tartan*, p. 98.
24 Heylin, *From the Velvets to the Voidoids.*
25 Faiers, *Tartan*, p. 98.
26 Laing, *One Chord Wonders.*
27 Rimmer, *New Romantics.*
28 Rimmer, *Like Punk Never Happened.*
29 Hogg, *All That Ever Mattered.*
30 Sweeting, 'Obituary: Stuart Adamson'.
31 Mclean, 'Big Country, but not big enough'; Sweeting, 'Obituary: Stuart Adamson'.
32 Faiers, *Tartan*, p. 124; Peterson, *Creating Country Music.*
33 Chick, 'Nirvana: with the lights out'.
34 Reynolds, 'Guns N' Roses'.
35 Wall, *W. Axl Rose.*
36 Faiers, *Tartan*, p. 175.
37 Ibid., p. 227.
38 Ibid., p. 1.
39 Percival, 'Britpop or Eng-pop?'

13

CLASS WARRIORS OR GENEROUS MEN IN SKIRTS? THE TARTAN ARMY IN THE SCOTTISH AND FOREIGN PRESS

Hugh O'Donnell

൜

In the meantime the old town becomes the headquarters of the inhabitants of what was once Caledonia. Foccacia and orechiette drown, literally, in rivers of beer. They all join in, enthusiastically, under the amused gaze of the locals, old and young. A woman dressed in black exclaims: 'Mother of God, and that is what they do with a skirt?' (*La Repubblica*, 28 March 2007)

INTRODUCTION

The arrival of Scottish football fans in a foreign city is excellent news for local journalists. Many – though by no means all – dress in an often-incongruous variation on Highland dress. They combine kilts, white socks, Timberland boots (affectionately known as 'Timbies'), T-shirts and a wide variety of headgear ranging from tammies (tam o'shanters), glengarries (military-style hats with a tartan band) often with a feather, or indeed some kind of accoutrement – for example, helmets with horns – borrowed from the opposing fans. Underwear is deemed superfluous by many, and shots of fans 'mooning' appear regularly in foreign newspapers and television reports.[1] Although a visit by Scottish fans is by no means everyone's cup of tea – their arrival is often accompanied by large-scale litter pollution, much of it in the shape of depleted 'cairry-oots', raucous singing and occasionally less seemly incidents such as urinating in bushes or local fountains – the coverage is unswervingly positive, stressing their friendly nature and their valuable contribution to the local economy, in particular the pubs and bars.

These descriptions of visiting Scottish football fans share some elements with how the fans are dealt with in the Scottish media, but are not identical. They contain elements that are not present – or are at best peripheral – in Scottish descriptions and omit others which are central to the complex relationship between Scottish journalists and their readers. This chapter focuses primarily on press coverage of Scottish fans both in Scotland and in the four countries against whom Scotland played in the recent qualifying round for the 2010 World Cup: Iceland, Macedonia, the Netherlands and Norway. However, it also ranges more widely in both time and space, in an effort to pin down what (if anything) the 'Tartan Army' might actually be, and whether there might, in fact, be more than one of them.

THE TARTAN ARMY: A BRIEF HISTORY

The Tartan Army, like tartan itself perhaps, appears (wrongly in both cases) to have always been with us, but the link between Scottish football fans and tartan is in fact a relatively recent phenomenon. Photographs of Scottish fans taken in London in the mid-1950s show not primarily tartan – it is in fact present in only relatively moderate proportions – but a predominantly working-class form of attire. In the 1970s tartan was clearly more visible, but seldom (almost never) in the form of kilts: it overwhelmingly took the form of tartan scarves and occasionally tartan trews, worn by what BBC journalist Julian Taylor described as 'high-spirited Rod Stewart clones, resplendent in 70s chic'.[2] Anyone who cares to view footage of the (in)famous Wembley invasion in 1977 – widely available on YouTube – will see scarves in abundance but no kilts.[3] In fact, the kilt did not emerge as a standard (although never universal) mode of attire until the early 1980s, with the consensus among fans whose memory goes back far enough being that the 1982 World Cup held in Spain was the moment when this particular mode of dress 'took off'. An article in *The Observer* (3 June 2001), quoting Hamish Husband, president of the Association of Tartan Army Clubs, put it like this:

> Hamish Husband, a Scotland home-and-away fan for 25 years, says it all took off at the 1982 World Cup in Spain when about 20,000 travelled. Many were families and they took a holiday to coincide with the tournament.

Figure 13.1 Scottish football fans in Piccadilly Circus in 1953. © The Scotsman Publications Ltd; licensor www.scran.ac.uk

Figure 13.2 The 1977 Wembley invasion: 'Rod Stewart chic' but still no kilts. © The Scotsman Publications Ltd; licensor www.scran.ac.uk

By the 1990 World Cup in France, the 'uniform' was firmly established, with widespread media coverage of kilted Scots and their boisterous but friendly behaviour. The travelling fans were also by then routinely referred to as the Tartan Army.

The term 'Tartan Army' itself has, to say the least, a colourful history. It first entered the public domain in the mid-1970s not in relation to football fans, but as a media nickname for the self-styled Army for the Provisional Government of Scotland, a tiny group of Scottish nationalists (with a small 'n') who carried out low-level 'terrorist' attacks in the early 1970s. Despite a high-profile trial of those involved in 1975–6, this origin of the name, in a striking example of the selective nature of collective memory, is now almost completely forgotten. How the name came to be transferred to Scottish football fans is to a large extent a matter of conjecture – a website detailing the activities of the Army for the Provisional Government of Scotland attributes the shift to a journalist from the *Daily Record*.[4] It seems reasonable, nonetheless, to think that Andy Cameron's 1978 song 'We're on the march wi' Ally's Army', written on the occasion of the 1978 World Cup held in Argentina, might have provided a link between the two. Whatever the particular mix that led to the conflation of football fans, tartan and the notion of an army, the term is now astonishingly successful (though foreign journalists' attempts at translating it into other languages often produce such curiosities as 'army of the kilts' or even 'army of the skirts'!).

A (VERY) BRIEF NOTE ON METHODOLOGY

The analysis offered below is based on the concepts of discourse and discursive formation developed by French theorist Michel Foucault, particularly in his book *The Architecture of Knowledge*.[5] Very broadly, what was interesting for Foucault was not what was to be found about a particular issue in a specific book, a specific article and so on, but the way in which particular topics were represented. Discourses concerning such topics interested him, appearing in a vast array of outlets, definitely finite in number and materially present (there is absolutely nothing metaphysical about his understanding of discourse) but simply too numerous for any individual or group of individuals ever to be able to gather them all together. These modes of representation could be linguistic, but could just as easily take any other expressive form: graphic, audiovisual, architectural, musical, choreographic and so on. To the extent that these discourses follow certain rules regarding what can and cannot be said, they constitute a discursive formation. These formations are, in Foucault's words, 'systems of dispersion' – 'dispersion' because they are spread over an uncountable number of sites, and 'systems' because they are not simply spaces of unrestrained creativity: there are limits to what can be said while remaining within the formation in question.[6]

What this chapter offers, then, is not a sociological analysis of what Scottish football fans get up to when following the team (particularly abroad). Much valuable ethnographic work has been done here.[7] It is rather a study of the Tartan Army quite specifically as a discursive formation, in other words how the concept of the 'Tartan Army' emerges from the coverage it receives in a range of different countries. As we will see, such an approach produces not one Tartan Army, but two, in each of which tartan plays a quite different role.

Approaching the Tartan Army in this way also highlights two other features that for Foucault characterise any discursive formation. The first of these is what he termed 'rarity'. By this he meant the easily ascertainable fact that, in relation to any issue, the number of things actually said in fact represents the tiniest proportion of the number of things that could potentially be said. The Tartan Army is a striking example of this phenomenon: media coverage – and this chapter focuses on press coverage (though discourses of the Tartan Army also emerge, of course, on television, in the internet and so on) – circles endlessly round a very small number of constantly repeated ideas. The second is Foucault's assertion that any discourse, once it is firmly established, will tend to become what he calls an 'object of desire': in other words, competition will arise between different parties for control over what it actually means. As he puts it, discourse 'allows or prevents the realization of a desire, serves or resists various interests, participates in challenge and struggle, and becomes a theme of appropriation or rivalry'.[8] Again, the Tartan Army provides a striking example of this phenomenon.

THE TARTAN ARMY SEEN FROM HOME

This section starts with the obvious point – but one still very much worth making – that in Scotland the term 'Tartan Army' refers only to fans of the national football team. In particular it has no connection with sports such as tennis or rugby. In fact suggestions that it might are a cause of occasional humour in the relationship between Scottish journalists and fans. A particularly illustrative example can be found in an article by sports journalist James Traynor in the *Daily Record* on 24 September 2007. A few days earlier it had emerged that the Scottish Football Association (SFA) had spent part of a committee meeting discussing what kind of toilet paper to buy for the association's toilets. Traynor's mirthful article on this subject contained the following:

> After all, it's well known the favoured sheet of the Tartan Army remains that old jaggy stuff you used to get in the school bogs back in the 70s. Can't remember what it was called, but the Tartan Army like it because it's a bit like them.[9]
> It's rough, tough and takes sh*t off no man.
> Still, the Tartan Army could have had it worse. They could have been rugby fans

The idea that the Tartan Army might become involved in tennis provokes similar mirth. A long article also published in the *Daily Record*, in this case on 25 June 2009, speculates colourfully on the imagined scenario of the fans arriving in London to support Scottish tennis player Andy Murray. It contains the following:

The chinless wonders of the All England Tennis and Croquet Club have been crying into their Pimms after a jolly awful opening day at the Championships when six Brits were turfed out. Monday equalled Britain's worst opening-day effort in the modern era and stiff upper lips were beginning to tremble.

Just imagine the pristine surroundings of Wimbledon, the leafy avenues of the well-heeled as kilted aliens descend to clipped cries of: 'Quick chaps, get the women and Bentleys indoors.'

The ladies and gentlemen of prim and proper England took a while to generate a real atmosphere as Murray beat Robert Kendrick in four sets on Tuesday and we can't risk another low-key support. It's time to roll.

The Range Rovers and people carriers will trundle out of Dunblane but this is a job for the Tartan Army.

[Murray Mound] was once named something else in honour of Timmy [Tim Henman], who fitted Middle England's identikit perfectly.[10] Polite, brave little man slugging it out against Johnny Foreigner and all the odds. And of course, gallant loser.

But the Tartan Army would still remember Henman in song, I'm sure. 'We hate Timmy's Hill, he's a . . .'[11] Feel free to add on but remember the civil liberties police will be listening.

This could be Murray's moment but it could also be the Tartan Army's finest hour. This time they could be cheering a Scottish win. He and they deserve nothing less.

And you know what, crisp, ever-so-proper and dapper Wimbledon also deserve them. Just for a dose of reality. As well as a laugh.

It should be immediately clear from these two articles that the exclusive association between the Tartan Army and football is not in any sense a question of sport, but a question of class. Traynor's article not only immediately excludes anyone who went to a private school – whose 'bogs' presumably did not stock Izal[12] – it also constructs the Tartan Army as rough and tough and as a place where you can say 'shit' (and worse), even if you have to doctor it slightly for publication purposes. The second article continues in much the same vein, contrasting the merry-making and irreverence of the Scottish fans with stiff upper lips both north and south (though mostly south) of the border, and likewise presenting it as an environment where non-PC terms such as 'poof' can still be used with impunity. In fact, with the explicit references to the 1970s and the implicit references to the 1980s, these articles construct the Tartan Army as a site of nostalgic working-class masculinity. There, an irreverent and to some extent defiant masculinity can still be displayed so long as you identify yourself as working class (or at the very least have working-class origins).

In postmodern times class may be increasingly difficult to define as the old established differentiators of dress and other cultural markers increasingly lose their traction. Sociological studies of the fans, in particular the away fans, strongly suggest internal divisions along occupational and income lines. Yet, even so, at the level of discourse the Tartan Army emerges in Scottish press coverage as a site of continuing, even celebratory, working-class identity, cocking a mirthful snook at the chinless Pimm's-drinking wonders of Wimbledon and beyond who have no idea how to get enjoyment out of life.

Around this central core of nostalgic working-class male identity (and this despite the fact that the fan body contains a small, but nonetheless perfectly visible, percentage of women) circle a number of other complementary features of the Tartan Army as constructed by the Scottish press. These can be listed as follows:

Friendliness and humour, even in defeat. At the level of discourse, the Scottish fans are not 'gallant losers' like Tim Henman; they don't care whether the team wins or loses, and will have a party one way or the other. In the non-discursive world it goes without saying that the fans actually do care about the team performance, as anyone who has attended a Scotland international match will know. However, the rules of this particular discursive formation exclude statements to that effect. In addition, denizens of other countries do not count as 'Johnny Foreigner' for the Tartan Army – they are fellow football supporters to be fraternised with or, if they are female, to be chatted up.

Great ambassadors for the country. The phrase 'the best fans in the world' recurs endlessly. When the Macedonian police refused to allow the Scottish fans to enter the Macedonian end of the stadium in Skopje in September 2008 the *Daily Record* (8 September 2008) opined:

> The Tartan Army are the all-singing, all-dancing arm of the Scotland football experience. Yes, fans can be loud, raucous even, colourful and brash.
>
> Experienced members of the Tartan Army make sure that they police themselves.
>
> And the track record over decades shows that the Tartan Army do not do violence.

It is a shame no one seems to have told the Macedonian football beaks or their police.

Maybe they should take a lesson from the Tartan Army on how to be true ambassadors for their country.

Here (at last) is a place where the Scottish working class can represent its country on its own irreverent terms, and with pride, despite the narrow-mindedness of foreign bureaucracies.

Ingenuity and resourcefulness. Stories abound of how the travelling fans get round alcohol bans in foreign cities, limitations on the number of tickets available, prohibitive prices for foodstuffs and so on. These are not limited to the back pages of the newspapers. When Scotland played Macedonia in Skopje *The Sun* ran a front-page article with the headline 'Tartan Army' which had the 'tan' element of the word 'Tartan' coloured not black (like the rest of the headline) but . . . tan! The subheading ran 'Fans use fake bake to beat home-end ticket ban'. A longer article on page 5 recounted how fans were using fake tans in order to pass themselves off as Macedonians and thereby gain entry to the 'home' end of the stadium, from which they had been banned. When Scotland played Norway in August 2009, *The Sun* (12 August 2009) explained in detail how the fans were preparing for the exorbitant Scandinavian prices:

> Canny Scotland fans have prepared for tonight's crucial World Cup qualifier against Norway by cramming cases full of boil-up snacks.
>
> And our thirsty supporters are having to shell out an eye-watering £8 A PINT, while a burger will set them back £15 and a pizza a wallet-busting £30!
>
> Retired chef Stewart Coutts, 61, from Errol, Tayside, said he was considering BUTCHERING pal Bruce Elder, from Dundee, rather than stump-up Norwegian prices.

The article was accompanied by a photograph of Scottish fans – all with a beer glass in their hand and one of them wearing a horned Viking helmet – with a case full of Pot Noodles and the like. The link with less-than-elastic working-class purse strings was obvious.

Copious drinking – which does not, however, unlike in the case of the fans of certain other countries, lead to aggressiveness. When Strathclyde police decided to confiscate alcohol from the Scottish fans before the Scotland–Norway game at Hampden in October 2008, the Scottish version of the *News of the World* (12 October 2008) rushed to the fans' defence as follows:

> The Tartan Army are the pride of Scotland and have travelled the globe as great ambassadors for our nation [. . .] But despite their love of a party, the Tartan Army are known as the best-behaved fans in the world.
>
> Which is why yesterday's heavy-handed police action – confiscating carry-outs from supporters' buses and trains – is all the more baffling.
>
> We're all behind the cops when they tackle anti-social behaviour in our communities, but they went a step too far before the Norway game.
>
> It is not, alas, only foreign bureaucracies which can be narrow-minded.

Boisterousness, colourfulness and fun. The Tartan Army brings colour to even the drabbest of occasions, offsetting where necessary the misery of a defeat on the park. When the team went down 1–0 to Macedonia in Skopje, the *Sunday Herald* had this to say (7 September 2008):

> It was an impressive display by Scotland in Skopje yesterday. I'm talking about the variety of headgear sported by our fans in the Gradski stadium. We'll get to the football later, sadly.
>
> There were the usual tammies and toories and hats of a Scottish military nature which must have been hot and sweaty in the 100-degree heat. But nothing compared to one supporter's Russian army-style furry bunnet except maybe the leather Viking helmet, complete with horns, favoured by another.

References to fans 'livening up' foreign capitals are legion.

THE TARTAN ARMY SEEN FROM ABROAD

Foreign journalists' understanding of what constitutes the Tartan Army is a more eclectic one than that of their Scottish counterparts. Beyond national football team supporters, they will at times apply it not only to visiting fans of particular clubs, but also on occasions to fans of the Scottish rugby team (not entirely surprisingly, since some of the latter also often wear kilts). This confusion, however, is not in any sense an incidental detail, since what is most often missing in the 'Continental' version of the Tartan Army is the idea that it might have anything to do with the concept of class. Their sense of the historicity of the Tartan Army is also much diluted. A good example of this can be found in a lengthy article which appeared in the Dutch newspaper *De Telegraaf* on 13 November 1999, which used the term 'Tartan Army' also to include the national team itself. In the article the journalist muses about his meeting with a Scottish fan named (no doubt to the journalist's great delight) William Wallace and their conversation about the first game between Scotland and England in 1872 and a later famous match in Hampden:

> William Wallace [the fan] hadn't been born yet [in 1872]. Perhaps he saw the light of day in 1937 when the Tartan Army laughingly brushed the English aside before 149,547 spectators.

Again, there is nothing trivial about this lack of historical precision. The absence of class in foreign journalists' construction of the Tartan Army – and for that matter of the notion of ingenuity and inventiveness that accompanies it in Scottish descriptions – is more than made up for by the Scottish fans' absorption into a metaphysical realm of timeless ideals, here that of model fandom and the quintessence of sport. In this version, the Scottish fans are not ambassadors for Scotland – the idea never emerges – but universal ambassadors for certain sporting ideals. As a result, while descriptions of the Tartan Army abroad share a number of the features of the Scottish version, it should be clear that we are nonetheless dealing with a quite different discursive formation, with quite different rules regarding what can and cannot be said, and thereby producing a quite different object.

The following provides a small selection of articles (from a very large and ever-increasing store available) – given here in chronological order and often contrasting the Scottish fans with their English counterparts – presenting those elements which both the Scottish and the European discursive formation have in common. These relate overwhelmingly to the good nature and friendly behaviour of the fans.

> [The Scots are] the other fans from the island [. . .] Many of them soon got really drunk, but they remained peaceful. No trace of violence. (*Frankfurter Rundschau*, Germany, 20 June 1992)

They sang and laughed, clapped their opponents, and cheered their own players like heroes even when they lost [. . .] They drank and had fun, but they quarrelled with no-one, and were incredibly popular in their base in Norrköping. Just think that neighbours and football supporters can be as different as the Scots and the English! (*Aftenposten*, Sweden, 29 June 1992)

Scotland has the most cheerful group of fans in Europe, the Tartan Army [. . .] Nowadays the Tartan Army is an army without ranks, made up of football supporters who follow Scotland to all the corners of the earth, but with the peculiarity that they just don't fight. They're no longer about war, but about drinking and singing. Anyone who has any puff left after that plays the bagpipes. (*De Volkskrant*, Netherlands, 14 November 2003)

While their team is ranked 86th in the world, the kilted Scots laugh and assert that they are the best supporters in the world [. . .] they sing when they win and when they lose. Yesterday these colourful gentlemen put on a wonderful show on Karl Johan [. . . they are] about a football-fellowship and an intensity which exceeds what most other nations have to offer. (*Aftenposten*, Norway, 7 September 2005).

At the John Paul II airport [. . .] glamour is tartan like the kilts worn by the indestructible Tartan Army, the name given to the highly sporting fans of McLeish's team. They're drinking beer by the litre, since they won't be able to do so tomorrow. They're knocking it back. That's the way they do things. But you can be sure they won't be breaking any heads. Their sporting culture doesn't allow that. (*Gazzetta dello Sport*, Italy, 3 March 2007)

The Scottish fans drink copiously, but all stick firmly to the agreement to remain friendly even in the deepest inebriation. While we normally avoid drunken football fans due to the risk of aggression you can spend a pleasant evening with the Scottish fans even if they have a few litres of beer of a start. (*Der Spiegel*, Germany, 7 October 2007)

There are also many references to the various strategies used by the Scottish fans to 'romance' the locals, ranging from wearing a tee-shirt announcing their love of the host country, through wearing the opposing team's colours to other forms of more up-close-and-personal fraternising:

Most [of the Scottish fans] are wearing tartan kilts. As a kind of fraternal gesture some are wearing an orange cap or have put on an orange kilt. (*De Volkskrant*, Netherlands, 19 November 2003)

William Baxter, captain of the Tartan Army supporters team which is taking on a 'group of friends' from Bari in a friendly being put on in Green Park in via Fanelli, is getting ready for the match by downing beer in Biancofarina, a pub in Vittorio Emanuele avenue. He's put on a tee-shirt saying 'Congratulations Italy, World Champions. The Tartan Army salutes you'. (*La Repubblica*, Italy, 28 March 2007)

At away fixtures the visiting Scottish fans regularly contact the 'opposing fans' and organise friendly matches with them before the national teams take the stage. (*news.at*, Austria, 30 May 2007)

The Scottish fans have livened up Skopje. For three days now they've been strolling around town wearing T-shirts which say in English 'I love Macedonia', and they have been showing their friendship through their actions. They put their arms round and get their photograph taken with anyone who stops for a moment when they see them. In some places they've organised mini-concerts in the evenings. Gathered in groups, wearing their kilts, they play their bagpipes, and talk to anyone who is interested about their culture and traditions. They relax along with the locals. (*Vest*, Macedonia, 9 September 2008)

Coverage of the Tartan Army in Europe in the early 2000s was to all intents and purposes a continuation of what had happened in the 1990s. Footage shown by Sweden's public service broadcaster SVT during the 1992 European Championships showed Scottish and Dutch fans fraternising in very much the same way as described by *De Volkskrant* above. The only noticeable difference was the slow spread of the discourse to ever more countries following the vagaries of group allocation in international competitions. A very recent development, however, relates to increasingly frequent references to charitable donations made by the Tartan Army (the question of in what way, if any, these donations can reasonably be described as coming from the, unitary, 'Tartan Army' must remain, for now, open). The earliest example I have been able to find is in *La Repubblica*, in the article referring to William Baxter already mentioned:

His [William Baxter's] heart is beating fast: "We gave a donation of

1500 euros to the childrens hospital". Passion and solidarity. (*La Repubblica*, Italy, 28 March 2007).

After this, donations become a standard part of reporting any visit by the travelling Scottish fans:

Representatives of the 'Tartan Army', or the Kilted Army, as the Scottish fans are called, yesterday made a donation of 5000 euros to the Children's Day Centre in Shutka and 10000 euros to the 'Topaansko Pole' Centre for the Rehabilitation of Children. (*Vest*, Macedonia, 9 September 2008)

Generous and good-natured men in skirts have brightened up the town in different ways.
    The atmosphere among the fans of the Scottish team was the pick of the bunch yesterday evening even though they took three points from a sprightly Icelandic team.
    However the Scots didn't just come here to take points as a gift after the football game. The Tartan Army Sunshine fan charity didn't come empty handed and made a handsome donation to the Hringurinn Women's Association. (*Morgunblaðið*, Iceland, 11 September 2008)

[The Tartan Army] haven't come empty handed to Oslo. Before coming to every country they visit with the national team they collect money for a good cause. Previously the Tartan Army has given money to the paediatric ward in both the Rikshospital and the Radiumhospital. Yesterday they presented a cheque to the Benjamin Hermansen's memorial fund.
    It was highly emotional when Neil MacDonald from the supporters' Sunshine Appeal gave a speech before he handed over a cheque for 1000 pounds, a good 10,000 kroner, to Benjamin Hermansen's mother Marit (*Dagsavisen*, Norway, 11 August 2009).

On the few occasions where the press do not pick this up, the websites of receiving institutions fill the gap. The following report on the website of the Ronald McDonald Only Friends Centre in the Netherlands was accompanied by a photograph of fans in full Highland gear:

The Tartan Army Sunshine Appeal, as they call themselves, follow every game of the national football team faithfully. In every country they visit they choose a specific organization and collect money for that good cause. On this occasion it was the Ronald McDonald Only Friends Centre. To the accompaniment of the impressive sounds of the bagpipes the Scots handed over a cheque for no less than 1000 Scottish pounds.[13]

All of this takes place in a framing discourse of the quintessence of sport and ideal fandom, concepts that have been visible in some of the quotations above. This section finishes with a small selection of quotations where these ideas are very much to the fore. The first example relates to the fact that, during their visit to Oslo in August 2009, a group of Scottish fans – as they often do – chose a very unglamorous local team to go and support. In this case it was the small local team Skeid (whose name is pronounced 'shide' in Norwegian, thereby giving the fans the opportunity to tweak one of their traditional songs and sing 'We're Skeid and we know we are' during the match).[14] Coverage of the match in the newspaper *Dagsavisven* (11 August 2009), whose title was quite precisely 'We're Skeid and we know we are', contained the following quotes from fans, reproduced with obvious approval:

> 'Our motivation is that we love football, but we mean football's soul, not the Champions League or commercialism. Football doesn't have to be us versus them. The idea of football is socialising, and everything round about that.'
> 'Having a good time together like this, that's the basic idea of football.'

And finally a view from Italy's most read newspaper, the daily *Gazzetta dello Sport*:

> Above all it's the tremendous spectacle of the Scottish fans, so passionate and colourful but entirely sporting. The risk of trouble is absolutely zero, what we have here is the quintessence of football. (*Gazzetta dello Sport*, 11 November 2008)

THE TARTAN ARMY AS AN OBJECT OF DESIRE

As exemplars of ideal fandom and the quintessence of football, it is perhaps unsurprising that the Tartan Army – or more correctly the discourse of the Tartan Army – has become a sustained object of desire, the index of a better future. Expressions to this effect recur persistently, with more urgency in countries where fan behaviour is viewed as a problem, but also in less pressing ways elsewhere where the fan experience is seen as somehow just not colourful or enjoyable enough, as somehow sub-optimal.

The most pressing views come from England. Thus, in an article entitled 'English football fans urged to behave more like Tartan Army', *The Independent* (17 March 2001) had this to say:

> The official England football supporters' club was scrapped yesterday in a drive to halt the racism and xenophobia which accompanies the national team on its travels.
>
> One of the recommendations urges the media to promote a more positive image of the English football fan and sight [*sic*] the Scottish media's portrayal of a 'Tartan Army'.
>
> The report reads: 'The Scottish experience would seem to provide a starting point. The Tartan Army concept is based on traditional images of Scottish culture and national pride at being distinct from the English in appearance and behaviour'.

An article in *The Observer* a few months later (3 June 2001), this time entitled 'Why aren't England fans like the Tartan Army?', returned to the same topic:

> The FA want rid of the violent image attached to the national team's supporters - and see Scotland as the role model to bring decent fans in. Are they right?
>
> The Tartan Army are pleased to meet those from elsewhere. It's like an election campaign when you go abroad with Scotland, with people insisting on shaking hands with everyone they meet in the street, kissing babies and having their picture taken.

Examples of articles offering less dramatic but in some sense 'envious' contrasts follow below from a variety of different countries:

> 'We are coming . . .' resounds from the all-encompassing Scottish section, in the midst of which you can make out the old familiar: 'Iceland! Clap-clap-clap . . .'
>
> Why don't we have friendly songs like theirs? And what is it with this endless [. . .] clapping of ours? (*Morgunblaðið*, Iceland, 31 March 2003)

> [The Scotland supporter] is [. . .] wearing the Scottish football

supporter's national dress: heavy shoes, thick socks, bare legs and thighs, a kilt with nothing underneath, a sealskin purse [sporran] and a bonnet with a feather in it. Say what you like, but it's something different from a Norwegian Viking helmet made of plastic.

Scottish football fans have style. (*Aftenposten*, Norway, 7 September 2005)

The Tartan Army is considered the best-behaved group of national football supporters around the world [. . .] True to their reputation of being friendly and contrary to the Icelanders, the Scottish seem to have fun when they drink and do not see it as their immediate goal to beat up the next unfortunate soul to cross their path. So the Scots drank, shouted and sang all through the game while the Icelanders cursed at their team when nothing went their way. (*The Reykjavík Grapevine*, 12 September 2008)

Amazingly (to this author at least), even the Portuguese Secret Service has got in on the act. Their official website offers the following in a section on fan violence:

In Scotland the Tartan Army also behaves in an orderly fashion. Consequently, if the media were to focus extensively and positively on the attitude of these groups they would be carrying out an extremely valuable pedagogical task, encouraging the pride of well-behaved fans and presenting them as the example to be followed by young people.[15]

The (perhaps inevitable) culmination of the appropriation of the Tartan Army – or more exactly the Tartan Army discourse – by official bureaucracies (and we should bear in mind that the Scottish version of the Tartan Army is constructed as the opponent, or even the subverter, of official bureaucracies) has been the various awards made by official bodies. These include the 1992 UEFA Fair Play Award for the European Championship of that year, being voted best supporters by journalists at the 1998 World Cup, thereby winning the Per Ludos Fraternitas trophy, presented by the International Association for Non-Violence in Sport, and the award of the Fair Play prize by the Belgian Olympic Committee in 2001, all the subject of regular comment in the press of European countries.

CONCLUSION: TARTAN IN THE DOMESTIC AND INTERNATIONAL
ARENA

Whatever the differences in the two discourses of the Tartan Army
outlined above, a point they share is the centrality of tartan, in
particular the kilt, as the most visible manifestation of fans, and
the one which exerts the greatest fascination above all on journalists
from continental Europe. But just as the meaning of words derives not
from the words themselves, but from the discourses in which they are
inserted, so too the meaning of tartan varies considerably depending
on whether the Tartan Army is being constructed as a reality from
within or outwith Scotland. Perhaps the most striking feature of tartan
apparel as it is deployed by Scottish football fans is the ways in which
it fails to meet, or even to some extent violates, middle-class criteria for
its use. At its simplest, as worn by most fans it would never meet the
criteria of a Highland dress hire shop, nor could anyone attend a
graduation ceremony or a wedding in a kilt which is (by those norms)
often too long, combined with a variegated mixture of other non-
standard items, and frequently finished off with headgear which is –
quite deliberately – too broad, in one way or another 'incongruous'
and so on. In other words, what we are dealing with here, in keeping
with the Scottish discourse of the Tartan Army in general, is a
working-class appropriation of tartan, resignifying it as a defiant
marker of traditional working-class culture, putting two fingers up
to the strictures of middle-class rules and all that goes with them.

Within the European discourse, on the other hand, tartan has come
to mean something quite different, being absorbed into a grand,
almost timeless metaphysical framework of sporting ideals and the
quintessence of football. In the process tartan – like all signifiers –
reveals its polysemy, its ability to act as a vehicle not only for more
than one meaning, but meanings whose origins are quite different: a
Scottish meaning emerging from the relationship between Scottish
journalists and their readers (many of whom will also be fans) and
maintained and developed by the fans themselves in a range of often
highly creative ways as outlined above (see also Giulianotti 2005), and
a second 'European' meaning deriving not from any relationship
between those journalists and the Scottish fans (they have, needless
to say, no identifiable relationship with the Scottish fans as such) but
more from their relationships with a spectrum of official bodies
ranging from the police, through their own national football associations to high-level organisations such as Olympic Committees. As the

Figure 13.3 'It's tartan, Farquhar, but not quite as we know it.' Scottish fans in Amsterdam. © Daily Record

discourse of the 'Tartan Army' is uprooted from its home soil in this process, the most striking transformation in the meaning of tartan is its total divorce from notions of class. At the international level the place of class is taken over by notions of law and order and respect for (and recognition by) officialdom, and the meaning of tartan is effectively reversed as a result. Just as many chapters in this volume draw attention to the polysemy and variousness of meanings of tartan, so the Tartan Army itself embodies polysemy and variety.

Notes

1 For a Norwegian example, see http://www.dagbladet.no/sport/2005/09/ 07/ 442653.html
2 Taylor, 'When Wembley turned tartan', n.p.
3 See, for example, http://www.youtube.com/watch?v=M4Ez7T1y8Yc
4 http://www.electricscotland.com/history/tartan_army2.htm
5 Foucault, *The Archaeology of Knowledge*.
6 Ibid., p. 41.

7 See in particular Bradley, Giulianotti and Jarvie and Reid in the Bibliography.

8 Foucault, *The Archaeology of Knowledge*, p. 118.

9 Perhaps he cannot, but I (and no doubt many other readers) can. It was called 'Izal'. In other words, the complicity which Traynor is constructing with his readers has worked wonderfully in my case.

10 This is a reference to a small elevation within Wimbledon where fans without tickets to the Centre Court can watch the games on a giant screen. During Tim Henman's heyday it was called Henman Hill. When Andy Murray came to the fore it was renamed Murray Mound.

11 The missing word is 'poof'. When David Narey scored for Scotland against Brazil in the 1982 World Cup in Spain BBC commentator Jimmy Hill described the shot as a 'toe poke'. The Scottish fans subsequently responded in indignation by singing 'We hate Jimmy Hill, he's a poof' at international games, a song they sing to this day, getting on for thirty years later. Scarves containing these deathless lines can also still be bought at international matches. Again, the search for complicity with the readers – based on a shared collective memory – is obvious.

12 A small-scale but quite recognisable discourse on Izal is perfectly visible in British culture. An entertaining contribution appeared in *The Independent* of 4 July 2009, describing it as a 'minor British institution' which used to be 'routinely found in school toilets and public conveniences', and as a 'throwback to the age of austerity'. Expressing perplexity at the fact that this product is still available for purchase the article ended: 'Nostalgia, surely, has its limits: there's no need to scrape the bottom of the barrel.'

13 http://www.kinderfonds.nl/centre/nieuws/20090403/1_000_schotse_pond_voor_het_centre

14 See http://www.skeid.no/a-laget/nyhetsarkiv-a-laget/1483-were-skeid-and-we-know-we-are for many photographs of this event.

15 http://www.sis.pt/pt/actividades/hooliganismo.php

14

DON'T TAKE THE HIGH ROAD: TARTANRY AND ITS CRITICS

David Goldie

∾

If you were of a religious persuasion and had a sense of humour you might think tartan to be one of God's better jokes. To match up this gaudy, artificial, eye-strainingly irrational fabric with a countryside characterised by its mists and rains and a correspondingly rather dour people known throughout the world for canniness, pragmatism and rationality, seems a sublime piece of audacity and one that can hardly be explained by the normal historical means. It is true that there may be material historical reasons for tartan, that an impoverished people might weave a kind of textile bricolage from whatever stray fibres might come to hand, for example, and it is also plausible that muted tartans might have a practical role as an effective camouflage. But this is still quite far from explaining how a piece of such abstract and unwarranted extravagance as 'Ye principal clovris of ye clanne Stewart tartan' might have come into being.[1]

In a similar vein it is entirely credible to argue that the heady collision of Sir Walter Scott, King George IV and European Romanticism in Edinburgh in 1822 explains much about tartanry's sentimental vulgarity and its weird mixture of ostentation and supplication. But what remains seemingly beyond the range of explication (and what Scott already sensed in his fiction) is the fundamental, almost ridiculous mismatch between this impractical concoction and its symbolic importance to a nation seeking to build an international reputation on its hard practical skills in engineering, industrial chemistry and finance. It might be said that this strange, gauche inappropriateness of tartan is a symptom of Scotland's long-term inability to reconcile its Highland and Lowland cultures, or its rural and urban divisions. But such explanations fail to explain the extent to which tartan is and always was effectively a product of urbanism and Lowlandism – if not in its actual invention, then certainly in its definition and exploitation – and that the three groups who appear to have invested the most sentimental capital in it over the last century have been tourists, expatriates and the urban proletariat.[2] At these and several other levels tartanry has offered a real difficulty for high-minded Scottish critics. For twentieth-century critics especially, who sought to engineer social and cultural change, whether through the politics of the left or of nationalism, the discourse of tartan, with its connotations of couthy sentimentalism and provincialism on the one hand and low-brow music hall innuendo on the other, proved to be an aggravation and even a source of deep shame.

This, arguably, had been less of a problem in the nineteenth century, in spite of Balmorality and the vagaries of Victorian bourgeois taste that pushed tartan forcefully into the public gaze. The strength of the Union and, perhaps, a culture of deference meant that tartan had few ostensible negative connotations and tended to be celebrated rather than derided as a symbol of national Scottish and imperial British pride. The kilt might not be much worn but it was widely respected, not least as the identifier of the Highland soldier – a figure who loomed large in the Victorian popular imagination in a variety of guises, from the written accounts in the works of James Grant and the visualised heroics of Robert Gibb's 'The Thin Red Line' (1881) and Lady Butler's 'Scotland for Ever!' (1881) to the pathos of Philip Richard Morris's 'The Highland Laddie's Return' (1881).

That this view changed in the twentieth century was perhaps due to the development in the years surrounding the First World War of what we now recognise as the modern mass media: the large-circulation popular newspapers that followed the *Daily Mail* after 1896; a music hall transformed in the Edwardian era from marginal unrespectability to esteem and high popularity; and the newest and most truly inter-national medium, the cinema, which spread like a flu across the civilised world in the twenty years following its invention. These media in their very nature both threatened Scottish identity, by superseding the local networks through which regional and national cultural traditions had been formed, and offered it a hitherto unim-aginably large arena in which it might be expressed. Cultural products like tartan now had a wider geographical space in which they might be seen and also, with the appearance of the relatively affluent working-class consumer, a greater social depth to their consumption – offering greater reach, but to an arguably less discerning and discriminating audience. This, in a literal sense, vulgarised tartan. Now used as a brand to identify 'Scottishness', whether to promote loyalty within indigenous consumers in the ways exploited by the publications of the Thomson-Leng group or to signal romantic adventure to an international audience in Hollywood film, tartan had, in its mass-mediation, undergone a change – the line that might previously have separated tartan from tartanry had dissolved.[3] All, it seemed, was now tartanry.

This was perhaps most evident in cinema, where tartan had been visible almost from the moment of the medium's inception. Some of the earliest Scottish films, such as *The Gordon Highlanders Leaving Maryhill Barracks* (1896), screened at the Glasgow Skating Palace by Arthur Hubner and again in 1897, and William Walker's 1898 *Braemar Gathering at Balmoral*, featured tartan subjects, chosen presumably for their visual interest, as had one of the first experimental films in the British Kinemacolor process, *Tartans of the Scottish Clans* (1906).[4] Other early Scottish-made films drew not only on tartan's visual appeal but also on its connection to the romance traditions of high-land fiction, among them Britain's first three-reel feature film, United Films' Glasgow-made *Rob Roy* (1911).[5] International film-makers were similarly quick to see the romantic appeal of Scott's tartanry, with two more adaptations of *Rob Roy*, one English and one Amer-ican, before the First World War. This period also saw an American *Lochinvar*, *Kenilworth*, and *Bride of Lammermoor* in 1909; another American *Lochinvar* in 1911 and *Lady of the Lake* in 1913; and in 1914 an American and an English *Heart of Midlothian* (the American titled *A Woman's Triumph*) and another *Bride of Lammermoor*. The story of Mary, Queen of Scots had been of particular interest to French film-makers, who had produced seven separate versions before 1914. *Macbeth* was another favourite for international film-makers, with an American version in 1908, an Italian in 1909, a French in 1910, an English in 1911 and a German in 1914. There had even been an American *Scotland Forever* in 1913.[6] The early cinematic repre-sentation of Scotland, then, tended inevitably towards a tartan-draped vision of misty lochs and turbulent romance familiar to readers of nineteenth-century historical fiction, albeit interspersed with occa-sional comic representations of the Highlander in short films such as *The Adventures of Sandy MacGregor* (1904), *McNab's Visit to London* (1905) and *Sandy's New Kilt* (1914). The power of such Highland romance to draw both audiences and the emerging stars of Hollywood can be seen in the decision taken by 'America's Sweet-heart', the Canadian Mary Pickford, to expand her reputation for cutesy tempestuousness by taking on the role of Marget MacTavish, a chieftan's headstrong daughter, in *The Pride of the Clan* (1917).

If there was one home-grown figure who could be said to epitomise the kind of vulgar tartanry thrown up in this period it would almost certainly be Harry Lauder, the popular entertainer who for many years was Scotland's most visible embodiment on the world's stage: a kilted buffoon propped unsteadily on a ridiculously rustic walking stick, apt to dispense sly humour and easy sentiment to the tune of a cheery, well-sung song. Lauder was plainly never afraid of wrapping himself up in tartan for comic or sentimental effect, and was not averse either to exploiting it for more serious, if equally questionable, ends – not the least of which was making substantial sums of money for himself. Lauder is a pivotal figure, not just for his notorious caricatures of Scottishness, but because of the role he played in enlisting tartan to the allied effort in the First World War. He worked tirelessly throughout the war, drawing on his wide range of dramatic skills and on the recognition of his jaunty Highland image to entertain and cajole his audiences for the purposes of recruitment, troop entertainment and charitable fundraising.[7] He would gain a knighthood for this service in 1919, but in the eyes of some, he would win this by debauching the currency of Scottish culture, cheapening Scotland's markers of national identity and its martial tradition and letting them go for a sentimental song. Lauder was, of course, not an original. 'Scotch comics' like W. F. Frame had helped establish the genre from which Lauder would never deviate very far (although he had, in fact, begun as an Irish comic).[8] And music hall jingoism was hardly new – there had often been a noticeable connection between Scotch music hall comedy and the wider imperial mission.[9] Though the Scots martial tradition could sometimes be parodied too, as it was by the Scotch comic Harry Linn in his most celebrated number, 'The Fattest Man in the Forty-Twa', sung as he capered about in the costume of the 42nd Highland Regiment.[10] But Lauder's war efforts were particularly visible, caused at least partly by his promotion of the 'Harry Lauder Million Pound Fund' for wounded servicemen.

The popular-cultural context in which he was working during wartime was one that was particularly well disposed towards tartan. A series of early-war two-reelers, among them Barker's *A Daughter of Belgium* (Oct. 1914), Crusade's *A Daughter of France*, Barker's *Bravo Kilties!* and Samuelson's *A Son of France* (all Nov. 1914) had Highland soldiers playing the role customarily associated in cinema with the Seventh Cavalry: that of coming to the rescue of civilians imperilled by the depredations of marauding savages – in this case, those of the German military. Subsequent films, among them the Barker two-reeler, *24 Carat* (1914), the comedy, *Pimple in the Kilties* (January 1915) and Maurice Sandground's *Kilties Three: A Scottish Romance of the Great War* (1918), continued in this manner to portray the kilted soldier as a sentimentalised guarantor of British social stability. When, therefore, Lauder was performing in the revue *Three Cheers* in London's Shaftesbury Theatre in 1916–17, he pulled all the strings of Caledonian sentimentalism and brought the house down by singing 'The Laddies Who Fought and Won' as uniformed members of the Scots Guards marched on to the stage behind him.[11] This was much remarked upon at the time, but was, again, not unique. The revue *Razzle-Dazzle* at Drury Lane in 1916, for example, closed its first half with a 'Scotland For Ever' extravaganza that featured three hundred chorus girls in a chaotic variety of tartans leading a band of marching pipers down the representation of a Highland glen: not the most aesthetically tasteful way to celebrate Scottish martial achievement but it did affirm, as one commentator put it, 'the process by which an old feudal enemy had been claimed for the cause through those ever-popular Highland regiments'.[12]

In the years after the war such facile sentiments began to ring a little hollow. As wartime idealism turned to post-war disenchantment the wartime co-option of tartan came to seem like a trick, perhaps a grim joke played on a nation that had lost a higher proportion of its fighting men than almost all of the nations that had contested the war.[13] For the many people who saw things this way Lauder, as a visible symbol of this co-option, was particularly reviled. It comes as no surprise, then, to find the writers of the post-war Scottish Renaissance taking an active antipathy to everything that Lauder and his kilt appeared to stand for. In the eyes of the movement's driving force, and a man who had served in the war, Hugh MacDiarmid, tartanry joined the Burns cult and the literature of the Kailyard as pernicious expressions of a bastardised, inauthentic Scotland. MacDiarmid railed against Lauder frequently and vociferously, talking for example in 'The Scottish Muse' of 'the false trail of the Kailyard and Harry Lauder school' which 'demonstrably falsify and cheapen' the Scottish psychology, and the ways in which Scottish 'robustness and recklessness' are 'travestied into canniness and sickly sentiment' by popular literature and music hall tartanry.[14]

MacDiarmid, as his nom de plume indicates, was a Lowlander with an appreciation of the allure of the Celtic Highlands. Born and brought up much closer to Sunderland than Sutherland, his attempts to found a revived Scottish culture often drew substantially on a Highland cultural tradition to which he was alien by formation, and promoted a language, Gaelic, that he did not speak. On the one hand his efforts in this direction are plainly a generous gesture that seek to construct an inclusive new national culture, but on the other they suggest that MacDiarmid was perhaps as susceptible as other more credulously romantic souls to the Highland idea. He was ashamed of tartanry but himself wore the kilt, as if a careful line might be drawn between a purposive and a trivial use of tartan.[15] The argument for MacDiarmid was not about tartan itself, which he plainly considered an authentic, or at least suitably pragmatic, expression of nationhood, but of its vulgarisation in the hands of Harry Lauder, British imperialism and American-led popular culture.[16]

Those who followed MacDiarmid later in the century in criticising tartanry, and in linking it with the Kailyard as a twinned symbol of national degradation and false consciousness, were not on the whole kilt-wearers and so did not need to respect the ambiguous spaces between tartan and tartanry. George Blake was concerned mainly with the way the Kailyard had turned the focus of Scottish literature from the present to the past, and from the urban to the semi-rural, but could not resist seeing tartan as a malign ally in Kailyard fiction's flight from realism. For Blake, the Scottish novel's alternative modes of Highland romance and Lowland parochialism had made Scottish fiction evasive rather than engaged and had promoted 'a sort of national infantilism'.[17]

With the proliferation of tartan-tinged sentimentalism in mid-century, in the publications of D. C. Thomson and the frolics of *Brigadoon* and the *White Heather Club*, tartan and the Kailyard increasingly seemed – at least to serious cultural commentators – to be not so much naive ways of averting the public gaze from the real issues of the day as malign operators that monopolised the cultural infrastructure to the extent that alternative cultural discourse became impossible. This was the 'vast tartan monster' described with such a powerful mixture of gusto and disgust by Tom Nairn in *The Break-Up of Britain*, a devouring false consciousness that destabilised the Scottish psyche and reduced it not just to infantilism but to the point of neurosis.[18] According to Nairn, 'vulgar tartanry' lay at the root of both Kailyard's evasive nostalgia and what he described as 'cultural emigration'.[19] Nairn was shrewd enough to acknowledge the difficulty of resisting tartan's popular pull as he attempted to push Scottish culture in another direction. 'Tartanry,' he stated, 'will not wither away, if only because it possesses the force of its own vulgarity – immunity from doubt and higher culture'.[20] And he showed at least the beginning of a willingness to take it seriously as a source of real, as opposed to merely comic or trivial, disturbance in the Scottish mentality, arguing that if if 'the émigré-Kailyard dilemma can be taken to represent the plight of the nation's Ego,' then tartanry in the form of 'the Scott Monument, Andy Stewart and the *Sunday Post* [. . .] surely is the Id with which the intelligentsia has always had to wrestle'.[21]

Several of those who followed Nairn's lead were, however, less ready to treat tartanry as a proper subject for analysis, and chose instead to take the critical high road mapped out by MacDiarmid, adopting an attitude of *de haut en bas* and the weapons of ridicule. Nairn had noted in the argument quoted immediately above that tartan constituted 'a huge, virtually self-contained universe of *Kitsch*'. Barbara and Murray Grigor plainly agreed, and sought to expose that kitsch to mockery in their *Scotch Myths* exhibition in St Andrews and Edinburgh in 1981, which was followed up the next year by Murray Grigor's related Channel 4 film *Scotch Myths*, and his contribution 'From Scott-land to Disneyland' to Colin McArthur's book *Scotch Reels*. Grigor's approach here was primarily visual and not immediately analytical – the essay in McArthur's collection was a photomontage in the manner of John Berger's *Ways of Seeing* (1972). But the relentless concatenation of tartan images was, presumably, intended to be polemical, to invite mockery and perhaps shame that the Scots might allow themselves to be represented in this way. For people already suspicious of tartanry this was, one would guess, both hilarious and reinforcing. For those who were not above that culture, however – the very many unreconstructed readers of Highland romance and buyers of *People's Friend* calendars, those who innocently enjoyed Scottish Television's *Thingummyjig* in the 1970s and 1980s or who spent their weekends in Highland dancing or marching in pipe bands – the effect would presumably be quite different. These people might feel, with some justification, that their tastes and pleasures were being mocked by a self-appointed intelligentsia who might claim to speak for Scotland – whatever that might be – but who certainly did not speak for them.

This sense of superiorism, of a politicised intelligentsia primed on Gramsci and Althusser, confidently separating out the Scottish workerist sheep from the tartan goats is arguably what characterises many of the essays in *Scotch Reels*. There can be little doubt that the collection advances some thoughtful analysis of the limiting effects of both tartanry and Kailyard, and that it convinces in its major argument that these two discourses alone cannot fulfil the representational needs of a modern nation. But what is much less convincing is the argument, carried on from MacDiarmid and Nairn, concerning what McArthur describes as 'the seriously stunting effects Tartanry and Kailyard have had on the emergence of alternative discourses more adequate to the task of dealing with the reality of Scottish life'.[22] This argument, that two popular-cultural modes can effectively corner a national market and make alternative forms of expression impossible, is in itself extremely limiting and, to this reader at least, quite unpersuasive. Not only does it fail to account for the fact that a book like *Scotch Reels* has appeared out of that culture, which perhaps rather negates its own arguments, but it is an argument that also immediately places itself outside or above that culture. Put simply, *Scotch Reels* does not represent a discussion within Scottish culture but rather a solution for Scottish culture made by an enlightened group who have managed to escape its clutches. It is, then, paradoxically akin to Tom Nairn's notion of 'cultural emigration' – effectively an émigré account of a native culture made by those who have managed to free themselves from it or otherwise opt out.

This sense, that *Scotch Reels* does not speak within the culture but rather down to it, is reinforced by the book's sometimes supercilious tone. McArthur talks semi-facetiously at one point in his essay 'Scotland and Cinema: The Iniquity of the Fathers' about Loch Lomond and all it stands for, 'represented on scores of unspeakable postcards, shortbread tins and table mats'.[23] In the use of the word 'unspeakable' here McArthur arguably manifests an attitude that undoes much of his essay's good work in detailed ideological analysis. For all the essay's sophisticated dialectic, this kind of crude value judgement resembles nothing so much as straightforward snobbery – the simple distaste of an élite for the questionable preferences of the vulgar. Where Nairn had recognised the formidable power of vulgarity and had to that extent respected it, McArthur appears simply to dismiss it as that which cannot be spoken of in polite company. Ridicule is a valuable weapon and McArthur, like Grigor, uses it effectively as a means to underline the sheer daftness and occasional cynicism of tartanry. But the question remains whether they have in fact chosen the best way to interrogate the phenomenon.

Many of tartanry's critics in the twentieth century appear often to have proceeded without a full awareness of the ironies they generated in that criticism. Hugh MacDiarmid in kilt ranting at Harry Lauder for his inauthenticity comes to seem like Caliban raging at his own image in the mirror. Then there is the émigré Tom Nairn skewering tartanry and Kailyard as the fond products of distantiation and disengagement. The Grigors seek to expose tartanry's Kitsch, but reproduce it in their own form of critical Kitsch. Colin McArthur employs the analytical tools of socialism to assert the superiority of his tastes over those of the generality. And all the while tartan has continued rejoicing on its way. The Edinburgh Military Tattoo is more popular than ever, having consistently since the millennium sold out all its tickets in advance. The Scottish National Party gives guarded but tacit support to Braveheartism. Billy Connolly, once the great hope of a vibrant cultural Clydesideism, is now the laird of Canda- craig House in Strathdon and presides, 'decked head to toe in tartan' according to the *Press and Journal*, over the Lonach Gathering and Highland Games.[24]

This suggests that somehow these critics got it wrong about tar- tanry, that in dismissing it too easily they failed to understand its appeal and underestimated its continuing power. Had MacDiarmid and those critics who followed him shown a greater tolerance of tartanry, had they tried to understand a little more and condemn a little less, then they might have been able to enjoy a more productive relation with the phenomenon and with Scottish popular culture more generally. The faults of their critical approaches are arguably ones of perspective and can perhaps be described in a paradox – firstly, that they took tartan too seriously and secondly, that they did not take it seriously enough.

The way in which tartan was taken too seriously might be seen in the claims that tartan and Kailyard had driven more serious forms of national expression out of the marketplace. This was what MacDiar- mid accused the 'over-paid clown' Lauder of doing in effectively taking the bread out of the mouths of more serious entertainers and cultural workers.[25] This argument, that in promoting one very limited representation of Scotland Lauder was excluding all other views – that he was operating as a kind of cultural monopolist – surely overestimates his power. He was, after all, only a singer and popular entertainer working in a largely free cultural marketplace, which meant he earned only what the public chose to pay him out of their own pockets. One would surely have to have an extremely low opinion of either a nation or a popular audience to believe that it felt all its representational needs were exhausted by such a limited repertoire. All cultures have their Kitsch, but most are more relaxed in their attitudes towards it. Bollywood, for example, offers a version of Indian culture that is aesthetically dubious and perhaps even mildly embarrassing to some tastes, but it would be difficult to argue that it holds back other more serious representations of the nation or investment decisions in the Indian economy. In other words, it would be rare to find a serious person who thought any less of India because of it. Union Flag Kitsch – whether it's seen in Ginger Spice's dress, the roof of a Mini or in souvenir shops the length of Oxford Street – similarly attracts interest and embodies what some might consider a questionable aesthetic but causes little real anguish or damage to the national self-image. To that extent, then, perhaps cultural critics need simply to relax – to learn to stop worrying and love the bombast, the splendour and the folly of tartan. In this way they might put themselves in a better position to focus on the things that actually matter in the national culture and let the inessentials go. But there are also more troubling questions about tartanry that might repay deeper thought, and might make it more than the simple joke with which this chapter began.

For example, it is noticeable that few commentators other than Nairn have thought to interpret tartan as a manifestation of the Caledonian id – as an irrational technicoloured desire glimpsed momentarily and perhaps troublingly through the stifling hodden covers of the Scottish superego, like pink lace panties under a policeman's uniform. And that is because tartan (like a British policeman joke) is somehow always already below serious consideration. A joke to Freud was a means of venting the dark social unacceptabilities of sex, but that road of possibility seems always closed off to tartanry, which appears to exist only in a world of couthy sentiment or in a Donald McGill universe of buffoonery and mildly smutty innuendo. The subject of what lies beneath the kilt has for years been a reliable source of humour and speculation from the gently salacious 1815 post-Waterloo French prints of inquisitive Parisian women finding excuses to bend over to peer up oblivious Highland soldiers' kilts to twentieth-century seaside postcards, best man's speeches and films like *Carry on . . . up the Khyber*. Any attempt to analyse this further, though, to *really* look up the kilt and try to come to terms with exactly why it is considered so humorous and so embarrassing would, one guesses, only meet with more laughter or with hostility. Tartan provokes either a smile or a grimace; both are gestures that hold it at a distance.

This is unfortunate, because what is perhaps sometimes under-estimated is the intrinsic value of some of the things that have come to us wrapped in tartan. Harry Lauder may seem merely laughable at this distance, as the chief of a clan of 'tartan-clad Liberaces whom Billy Connolly has described as "singing shortbread tins" '.[26] But to think in this way is to disregard the very many contemporary opinions that recognised him as a highly skilled performer. MacDiarmid might gibe that Lauder was a purveyor of 'hokum, hokum, hokum', but there were many more who were prepared to take him seriously as an entertainer and actor.[27] Even when he was at his most mawkish there seems to have been, in some eyes at least, a saving quality in his performance that turned it into something very like art. This was certainly the case in the wartime performances of 'Laddies Who Fought and Won' at the Shaftesbury Theatre mentioned earlier. A reviewer in *The Times* who saw the show in early 1917 expressed his general belief that 'patriotic songs sung by actors in khaki are detestable', but nonetheless saw something exceptional in Lauder's performance. Lauder was, he wrote, in his example of personal sacrifice and the intensity of his performance, 'the very voice of all those' enduring life at the front.[28] H. V. Morton took up a similar refrain when he insisted that 'Lauder's genius is a thing apart' and talked of finding 'something essentially honest, good, pure, and simple' in his performance.[29] The great *Times* theatre critic James Agate discerned in Lauder 'an exceedingly fine feeling for character', and described him as a 'great actor', 'an evangelist whose tidings are of pure joy'.[30] Even one of Lauder's harsher Scottish critics, George Blake, had to admit that Lauder in his heyday was 'inspired by at least near-genius'.[31] So while MacDiarmid was content to see Lauder's performance as caricature and treat it as caricature, what he missed, and what audiences and many reputable theatre critics presumably did not, was the operation within this tartanry of a more complex aesthetic quality and humanity.

It would, of course, be pushing it a little to say that all manifesta-tions of tartanry can bear such scrutiny. There are plainly forms that most people would agree have very limited claim to serious aesthetic consideration. While there are occasions at which tartan is taken wholly seriously, as formal wear at weddings and funerals, for example, or in the performance of Highland music, there are many more others in which it is consumed not quite as Kitsch but certainly with a degree of irony and self-reflexiveness in the form of a kind of guilty pleasure. Margaret Munro has reminded us in her chapter that

Craig Hill's 2007 tour was entitled *Craig Hill's Kilty Pleasures.* An unsubtle critique of tartanry is one that fails to recognise that this is a fairly common and quite legitimate strategic use, and which fails to understand the complexity of this response. When Nairn talks of the 'vast tartan monster', he conjures an idea of tartanry as something along the lines of an Althusserian ideological state apparatus in which consumers of tartan are little more than interpellated subjects. Such a model offers no agency to the act of consumption itself, positing instead an individual who is made passive in the face of tartan's relentless hailing.[32] The evidence suggests, however, that tartanry is often consumed and actively remade by otherwise autonomous individuals. This is unarguably the case of Caroline Sullivan, the rock critic of *The Guardian.* Sullivan, an American, was in her youth a fan of the Bay City Rollers, and she recounts in her memoir *Bye Bye Baby: My Tragic Love Affair with the Bay City Rollers* the ways in which she and her friends, the self-named 'Tacky Tartan Tarts', both revelled in and appropriated for themselves the group's shameless tartanry. The way Sullivan tells it this was not an act of submission to a dominant discourse, but rather a playful, reflexive act of affiliation and ultimately rejection that was made almost entirely on her own terms – an act of empowerment rather than one of subjection. For Sullivan, tartanry offered a ground on which she might express her emerging identity as a young adult rather than an ideological straitjacket that constricted and narrowed her growth.[33] Craig Beveridge and Ronald Turnbull have written persuasively about the need to read popular culture, and particularly Scottish popular culture, in ways that recognise this mode of strategic, reflexive consumption. In their view, as Ian Brown has observed, criticism of tartanry has tended to

> overlook, or ignore a major postulate of cultural analysis: that meanings are never passively consumed, but always subject to selection and adjustment to other discourses. There is in reality, no *Sunday Post* reader waiting to soak up the messages conveyed by D. C. Thomson, but only *Sunday Post* readers, people who are also trade unionists, or Kirk-goers, or nationalists, or defenders of animal rights, and their response to tartanry is not uncritical assimilation, but a complex negotiation dependent on the beliefs and values which are bound up with these other concerns.[34]

This is surely the proper response towards tartanry. When Scotland's football fans, the so-called 'Tartan Army', pull on their jimmy wigs and drape themselves in lions rampant and outrageous tartans they are showing anyone with the eyes to see it a highly sophisticated idea of Scottishness that embodies both passion and humour – that signifies both a patriotic seriousness and generous expansive irony – they are flaunting the fact that they are not the victims of Scottish representational tradition but its masters. The problem with the higher critics of Scottish popular culture in the twentieth century was that they failed to see that in actively consuming and replicating tartanry in this way popular culture did not yield but effectively took ownership of it. This is a mistake that twenty-first-century criticism should not and probably will not make. Tartanry is, and should be seen as, something of a joke. But we should always remember that jokes are complex things, and remember too that you can do much more interesting things with jokes than simply laugh at them.

Notes

1 A designation offered by the Sobieski Stuarts in *Vestiarium Scoticum* (1842).
2 McCrone, *Understanding Scotland* (1992), p. 184.
3 McCrone, Morris and Kiely, *Scotland – the Brand*.
4 Peter, *100 Years of Glasgow's Amazing Cinemas*, p. 3.
5 Cloy, *Scotland in Silent Cinema*, p. 7. The only other feature produced in Scotland before the war was Inverness photographer Andrew Patterson's amateur film *Mairi – The Romance of a Highland Maiden* of 1913.
6 See the filmography in Cloy, *Scotland in Silent Cinema*, pp. 14–18.
7 See Lauder, *A Minstrel in France*.
8 Cameron and Scullion, 'W. F. Frame and the Scottish popular theatre tradition', pp. 39–61.
9 Summerfield, 'Patriotism and Empire', pp. 18–20.
10 House, *Music Hall Memories*, pp. 15–16.
11 See Lauder, *A Minstrel in France*, pp. 84–9.
12 Williams, *British Theatre in the Great War*, p. 47.
13 The only nation to suffer a higher proportion of casualties was Serbia. See Ferguson, *The Pity of War*. See also Montague, *Disenchantment*.
14 MacDiarmid, *The Raucle Tongue*, vol. 1, p. 187.
15 See, for example, his comment to Sorley MacLean in a letter of 22 May 1936, that 'I've taken to regular kilt wearing', Grieve, Edwards and Riach, *Hugh MacDiarmid: New Selected Letters*, p. 112. William Burroughs would later describe MacDiarmid at the now notorious 1962 International Writers' Conference in Edinburgh 'stalking around in his kilt with his knobby blue knees saying that Burroughs and Trocchi

belong in jail, not on a lecture platform, old jerk'. Campbell and Niel, *A Life in Pieces*, p. 159.

16 See Goldie, 'Hugh MacDiarmid, Harry Lauder and Scottish popular culture'.

17 Blake, *Barrie and the Kailyard School*, p. 9.

18 Nairn, *The Break-Up of Britain*, p. 162.

19 Ibid., p. 156.

20 Ibid., p. 165.

21 Ibid., p. 163.

22 McArthur, *Scotch Reels*, p. 3.

23 Ibid., p. 65.

24 *Press and Journal*, 24 August 2009. For McArthur's hope that Connolly might become 'a major subversive, and therefore progressive, force in Scottish cultural life', see *Scotch Reels*, p. 64.

25 See 'Special Correspondent' [Hugh MacDiarmid], 'Scottish People and Scotch Comedians', *Stewartry Observer*, 23 August 1928, in *The Raucle Tongue*, vol. 2, p. 115.

26 Gardiner, *Modern Scottish Culture*, p. 199.

27 *To Circumjack Cencrastus*, MacDiarmid, *Complete Poems*, vol. 1, pp. 252–4.

28 *The Times*, 4 January 1917, p. 11; quoted in Williams, *British Theatre in the Great War*, p. 32.

29 Morton, *In Search of Scotland*, pp. 155–6.

30 Agate, *Immoment Toys*, pp. 201–2.

31 Blake, *Barrie and the Kailyard School*, p. 81.

32 See Althusser, 'Ideology and ideological State apparatuses'.

33 Sullivan, *Bye Bye Baby*.

34 Beveridge and Turnbull, *The Eclipse of Scottish Culture*, p. 14.

BIBLIOGRAPHY

Adam, Frank, *The Clans, Septs and Regiments of the Scottish Highlands* (Edinburgh: W. & A. K. Johnston Ltd, 1908).

Agate, James, *Immoment Toys: A Survey of Light Entertainment on the London Stage, 1920–1943* (London: Jonathan Cape, 1945).

Althusser, Louis, 'Ideology and ideological State apparatuses', in *Lenin and Philosophy and Other Essays* (London: NLB, 1970).

Anderson, Benedict, *Imagined Communities: Reflections on the Origins and Spread of Nationalism* (London: Verso, 1992).

Ascherson, Neal, *Stone Voices: The Search for Scotland*, rev. edn (London: Granta, 2003).

Bachmann-Medick, Doris, *Cultural Turns: Neuorientierungen in den Kulturwissenschaften, rowohlts enzyklopädie*, 3rd edn (Reinbek: Rowohlt, 2009) [For a shorter version in English, see Doris Bachmann-Medick, 'Introduction: the translational turn', transl. Kate Sturge, *Translation Studies* 2.1 (2009), pp. 2–16.]

Banks, Jeffrey and Doria de la Chapelle (eds), *Tartan: Romancing the Plaid* (New York: Rizzoli, 2007).

Barker, Martin, *Comics: Ideology, Power and the Critics* (Manchester: Manchester University Press, 1989).

Barker, Martin, 'The lost world of stereotypes', in Tim O'Sullivan and Yvonne Jewkes, *The Media Studies Reader* (London: Arnold, 1997).

Barthes, Roland, *Mythologies*, selected and translated from the French by Annette Lavers (London: Jonathan Cape, 1972).

Bartley, James Orr, *Teague, Shenkin and Sawney* (Cork: Cork University Press, 1954).

Basu, Paul, *Highland Homecomings: Genealogy and Heritage Tourism in the Scottish Diaspora* (Abingdon: Routledge, 2007).

Berthoff, Rowland, 'Under the kilt: variations on the Scottish-American ground', *Journal of American Ethnic History* 1 (1982), pp. 5–34.

Beveridge, Craig and Ronald Turnbull, *The Eclipse of Scottish Culture: Inferiorism and the Intellectuals* (Edinburgh: Polygon, 1989).

Bhabha, Homi K., *The Location of Culture* (London: Routledge, 1994).

Black, Ronald, 'The Gaelic Academy: the cultural commitment of the Highland Society of Scotland', *Scottish Gaelic Studies* 14 (1986), pp. 1–38.

Blake, George, *Barrie and the Kailyard School* (London: Arthur Barker, 1951).

Bold, Alan, *Modern Scottish Literature* (London: Longman, 1983).

Boswell, James, *James Boswell: The Journal of his German and Swiss Travels, 1764*, ed. Marlies Danziger (Edinburgh: Yale and Edinburgh University Presses, 2008).

Bourdieu, Pierre, *Outline of a Theory of Practice* (Cambridge: Cambridge University Press, 1977).

Bradley, Joseph M., 'The patriot game: football's famous "Tartan Army" ', *International Review for the Sociology of Sport*, vol. 37: 2 (2002), pp. 177–97.

Bradley, Joseph M., 'Images of Scottishness and otherness in international football', *Social Identities*, vol. 9: 1 (2002), pp. 7–23.

Brogan, Colm, 'The Glasgow comedians', in J. R. Allan (ed.), *Scotland-1938* (Edinburgh: Oliver and Boyd, 1938).

Brogan, Colm, *The Glasgow Story* (London: Muller, 1952).

Brown, Ian, 'In exile from ourselves? tartanry, Scottish popular theatre, Harry Lauder and Tartan Day', *Études Écossaises* 10 (2005), pp. 123–41.

Bruce, Steve, 'A failure of the imagination: ethnicity and nationalism in Scotland's history', *Scotia: Interdisciplinary Journal of Scottish Studies*, vol. XVII (1993), pp. 1–16.

Bruford, Alan, 'Is tartan a Gaelic word?', in D. S. Thomson (ed.), *Gaelic and Scots in Harmony: Proceedings of the Second International Conference on the Languages of Scotland* (Glasgow: Department of Celtic, University of Glasgow, 1988), pp. 57–71.

Bruzzi, Stella, *Undressing Cinema: Clothing and Identity in the Movies* (London: Routledge, 1997).

Buxton, Ian, *The Enduring Legacy of Dewars: A Company History* (Glasgow: Neil Wilson Publishing, 2009).

Calder, Angus, 'Meditation on memorials', in *Disasters and Heroes: On War, Memory and Representation* (Cardiff: University of Wales Press, 2004).

Calloway, Colin, *White People, Indians and Highlanders* (New York: Oxford University Press, 2008).

Cameron, Alasdair and Adrienne Scullion, 'W. F. Frame and the Scottish popular theatre tradition', in Cameron and Scullion (eds), *Scottish Popular Theatre and Entertainment* (Glasgow: Glasgow University Library, 1996).

Cameron, James D., 'The university contribution to Canadian multiculturalism: a case study of St Francis Xavier University, Antigonish, Nova Scotia' (unpublished paper, 2005).

Campbell, Allan and Tim Niel (eds), *A Life in Pieces: Reflections on Alexander Trocchi* (Edinburgh: Rebel Inc., 1997).

Campbell, Patrick, *Travels in North America*, ed. William Ganong (Toronto: The Champlain Society, 1937).

Caughie, John, 'Scottish television: what would it look like?', in Colin McArthur (ed.), *Scotch Reels: Scotland in Cinema and Television* (London: BFI Publishing, 1982).

Caughie, John, 'Representing Scotland: new questions for Scottish cinema', in Eddie Dick (ed.), *From Limelight to Satellite: A Scottish Film Book* (Glasgow: Scottish Film Council and Polygon, 1990).

Chalmers, Thomas, *A Saga of Scotland: History of the 16th Battalion The Highland Light Infantry* (Glasgow: MacCallum, 1931).

Chapman, Malcolm, *The Gaelic Vision in Scottish Culture* (London: Croom Helm, 1978).

Charlesworth, Chris, 'The Bay City Rollers: kings of pop!', *Melody Maker*, 9 November 1974.

Cheape, Hugh, 'Researching tartan', *Costume. The Journal of the Costume Society* 27 (1993), pp. 35–46.

Cheape, Hugh, *Tartan. The Highland Habit*, 3rd edn (Edinburgh: National Museums of Scotland, 2006 [1991]).

Cheape, Hugh, 'A' lasadh le càrnaid: rhyme and reason in perceptions of tartan', *Journal of the Scottish Society for Art History* 13 (2008–9), pp. 33–8.

Cheape, Hugh and Anita Quye, 'Historical and analytical research of dyes in early Scottish tartans', in R. Janaway and P. Wyeth (eds), *The Scientific Analysis of Ancient and Historic Textiles* (London: Archetype Publications Ltd, 2005).

Cheska, Alyce Taylor, 'Antigonish Highland Games: a community's involvement in the Scottish festival of Eastern Canada', *Nova Scotia Historical Review* 3 (1983), pp. 51–63.

Chick, Stevie, 'Nirvana: with the lights out' (Geffen) [Album review], *The Stranger*, 18 November 2004.

Churchill, Winston S., *A History of the English Speaking Peoples: The Age of Revolution*, vol. 3 (London: Cassell, 1957).

Cloy, David, *Scotland in Silent Cinema: A Commemorative Catalogue to Accompany the Scottish Reels Programme at the Pordenone Silent Film Festival, Italy 1998*, ed. Janet McBain (Glasgow: Scottish Screen, 1998).

Clyde, Robert, *From Rebel to Hero: The Image of the Highlander, 1745–1830* (East Linton: John Donald, 1995).

Constable, Archibald, *A History of Greater Britain Compiled from the Ancient Authorities by John Major, 1521* (Edinburgh: Scottish History Society, 1892).

Coon, Caroline, 'Inside the Bay City Rollers' camp', *Melody Maker*, 13 September 1975.

Cozzens, Frederic, *Acadia, or, a Month with the Blue Noses* (New York: Derby & Jackson, 1859).

250   *From Tartan to Tartanry*

Craig, Cairns, 'Myths against history: tartanry and Kailyard in 19th-century Scottish literature', in Colin McArthur (ed.), *Scotch Reels: Scotland in Cinema and Television* (London: BFI Publishing, 1982).

Craig, Cairns, *Out of History: Narrative Paradigms in Scottish and English Culture* (Edinburgh: Polygon, 1996).

Craig, Cairns, 'National literature and cultural capital in Scotland and Ireland', in Liam McIlvanney and Ray Ryan (eds), *Ireland and Scotland: Culture and Society, 1700–2000* (Dublin: Four Courts Press, 2005).

Dalgleish, George and Dallas Mechan, *'I Am Come Home': Treasures of Prince Charles Edward Stuart* (Edinburgh: National Museum of Antiquities of Scotland, 1985).

Davidson, Julie, 'Heederum-Hoderum: Scottish Kitsch', in Arnold Kemp and Harry Reid (eds), *The Glasgow Herald Book of Scotland* (Edinburgh: Mainstream Publishing, 1990).

Dembling, Jonathan, 'Joe Jimmy Alec visits the Mod and escapes unscathed: the Nova Scotia Gaelic revivals' (unpublished masters thesis, Saint Mary's University, 1997).

Dembling, Jonathan, 'You play it as you would sing it: Cape Breton, Scottishness, and the means of cultural production', in Celeste Ray (ed.), *Transatlantic Scots* (Tuscaloosa: University of Alabama Press, 2005).

Devine, T. M., *The Scottish Nation 1700–2000* (London: Penguin, 1999).

Devlin, Vivien, *Kings, Queens and People's Palaces: An Oral History of the Scottish Variety Theatre, 1920–1970* (Edinburgh: Polygon, 1991).

Donaldson, William, 'The Jacobite song in eighteenth and early nineteenth-century Scotland' (unpublished PhD thesis, Aberdeen, 1974).

Donaldson, William, *Popular Literature in Victorian Scotland* (Aberdeen: Aberdeen University Press, 1986).

Donaldson, William, *The Jacobite Song* (Aberdeen: Aberdeen University Press, 1988).

Douglas, Mary, *Implicit Meanings* (London: Routledge and Kegan Paul, 1975).

Drummond-Norie, William, *Loyal Lochaber* (Glasgow: Morison Brothers, 1898).

Dunbar, John Telfer, *Two Centuries of Highland Dress* (Edinburgh: Edinburgh Public Libraries, 1951).

Dunbar, John Telfer, *History of Highland Dress* (Edinburgh: Oliver and Boyd, 1962).

Dunbar, John Telfer, *The Costume of Scotland* (London: Batsford, 1981).

Duncan, A. A. M., 'The dress of the Scots', *Scottish Historical Review* 29 (1950), pp. 210–12.

Duncan, Ian, 'Scott, the history of the novel, and the history of fiction', in Evan Gottlieb and Ian Duncan (eds), *Approaches to Teaching Scott's Waverley Novels* (New York: The Modern Language Association of America, 2009).

Dunn, Charles, *Highland Settler: A Portrait of the Scottish Gael in Cape Breton and Eastern Nova Scotia*, 2nd edn (Wreck Cove, Cape Breton: Breton Books, 1968).

Dyer, Richard, 'The role of stereotypes', in Jim Cook and Michael Lewington (eds), *Images of Alcoholism* (London: BFI Publishing, 1979).

The Economist, 21 December 1996, pp. 53–6.

Egoyan, Atom, DVD Sleeve Notes, *Exotica*, directed by Atom Egoyan, DVD (Miramax, 1994).

Epstein, Lawrence J., *The Haunted Smile: The Story of Jewish Comedians* (Oxford: PublicAffairs, 2002).

Faiers, Jonathan, *Tartan* (Oxford and New York: Berg, 2008).

Ferguson, Niall, *The Pity of War* (London: Penguin, 1998).

Ferguson, William, 'Samuel Johnson's views on Scottish Gaelic culture', *Scottish Historical Review*, vol. 77 (1998), pp. 183–98.

Ferguson, William, 'A reply to Professor Colin Kidd on Lord Dacre's contribution to the study of Scottish History and the Scottish Enlightenment', *Scottish Historical Review*, vol. 86 (2007), pp. 96–107.

Findlay, Bill, 'Scots language and popular entertainment in Victorian Scotland: the case of James Houston', in Alasdair Cameron and Adrienne Scullion (eds), *Scottish Popular Theatre and Entertainment* (Glasgow: Glasgow University Library, 1996).

Finlay, Richard J., 'Controlling the past: Scottish historiography and Scottish identity in the 19th and 20th centuries', *Scottish Affairs*, no. 9 (Autumn 1994), pp. 127–42.

Finlay, Richard J., 'Heroes, myths and anniversaries in Modern Scotland', *Scottish Affairs*, no. 18 (Winter 1997), pp. 108–25.

Fishman, Joshua A., 'An examination of the process and function of social stereotyping', *The Journal of Social Psychology*, no. 43 (1956), pp. 27–64.

Foucault, Michel, *The Archaeology of Knowledge*, trans. A. M. Sheridan Smith (London: Routledge, 2002) [French original published in 1969].

Frith, Simon, *Sound Effects: Youth, Leisure, and the Politics of Rock 'n' Roll* (New York: Pantheon, 1981).

Frith, Simon, *Performing Rites: On the Value of Popular Music* (Oxford: Oxford University Press, 1996).

Fuchs, Martin, 'Reaching out; or, nobody exists in one context only: society as translation', *Translation Studies* 2: 1 (2009), pp. 21–40.

Fyfe, J. G., *Scottish Diaries and Memories 1746–1843* (Stirling: Eneas Mackay, 1942).

Gaines, Jane, 'Costume and narrative: how dress tells the woman's story', in Jane Gaines and Charlotte Herzog (eds), *Fabrications: Costume and the Female Body* (London: Routledge, 1990).

Galt, Rosalind, *New European Cinema: Redrawing the Map* (New York: Columbia University Press, 2006).

Gardiner, Michael, *Modern Scottish Culture* (Edinburgh: Edinburgh University Press, 2005).

Gibson, John S., ' "The summer's hunting": historiography of Charles Edward's escape', in L. Scott-Moncrieff (ed.), *The '45: To Gather an Image Whole* (Edinburgh: The Mercat Press, 1988).

Gifford, Douglas and Alan Riach (eds), *Scotlands: Poets and the Nation* (Manchester: Carcanet Press and Edinburgh: Scottish Poetry Library, 2004).

Giulianotti, Richard, 'Football and the politics of carnival: an ethnographic study of Scottish fans in Sweden', *International Review for the Sociology of Sport*, vol. 30: 2 (1995), pp. 191–220.

Giulianotti, Richard, 'The sociability of sport: Scotland football supporters as interpreted through the sociology of Georg Simmel', *International Review for the Sociology of Sport*, vol. 40: 3 (2005), pp. 289–306.

Goldie, David, 'The British invention of Scottish culture: World War I and before', *Review of Scottish Culture*, no. 18 (2006), pp. 128–48.

Goldie, David, 'Hugh MacDiarmid, Harry Lauder and Scottish popular culture', *International Journal of Scottish Literature*, issue 1 (Autumn 2006).

Grange, Richard M. D., *A Short History of the Scottish Dress* (London: Burke's Peerage, 1966).

Grant, Alan (writer) and Frank Quitely (art), *Batman: Scottish Connection* (New York: DC Comics, 1998).

Grant, Isabel Frances and Hugh Cheape, *Periods in Highland History* (London: Shepheard-Walwyn, 1987).

Grieve, Dorian, Owen Dudley Edwards and Alan Riach (eds), *Hugh Mac-Diarmid: New Selected Letters* (Manchester: Carcanet, 2001).

Grigor, Barbara and Murray Grigor, *Scotch Myths – An Exploration of Scotchness* (Exhibition booklet: Edinburgh International Festival, 1981).

Grimble, Ian, *Scottish Clans and Tartans* (London: Lomond, 1997 [1973]).

Gunn, Rev. Adam, *Songs and Poems by Rob Donn Mackay* (Glasgow: Celtic Monthly Office, 1899).

Hagemann, Susanne, *Die Schottische Renaissance: Literatur und Nation im 20. Jahrhundert*, *Scottish Studies* 13 (Frankfurt am Main: Lang, 1992).

Hagemann, Susanne, 'Performative parodies: Scots and Americans in Compton Mackenzie's *The Monarch of the Glen*', in Klaus H. Schmidt and David Sawyer (eds), *Blurred Boundaries: Critical Essays on American Literature, Language, and Culture* (Frankfurt am Main: Lang, 1996).

Haldane, M. M., 'The great clan tartan myth', *The Scots Magazine*, vol. XV no. 6 (September 1931), pp. 448–62; vol. XVI no. 1 (October 1931), pp. 44–51; vol. XVI no. 2 (November 1931), pp. 139–47.

Hall, Stuart, David Held and Tony McGrew (eds), *Modernity and Its Futures* (Cambridge: Polity Press, in association with the Open University, 1992).

Harper, Sue, 'Bonnie Prince Charlie revisited: British costume film in the

1950s', in Robert Murphy (ed.), *The British Cinema Book*, 3rd edn (London: Palgrave Macmillan, 2009).

Harris, Bob, *Politics and the Nation: Britain in the Mid-Eighteenth Century* (Oxford: Oxford University Press, 2002).

Henderson, Diana M., *Highland Soldier: A Social Study of the Highland Regiments 1820–1920* (Edinburgh: John Donald, 1989).

Heylin, Clinton, *From the Velvets to the Voidoids: The Birth of American Punk* (London: Penguin, 1993).

Hill, Richard, 'The illustration of the Waverley Novels: Scott and popular illustrated fiction', *Scottish Literary Review* 1: 1 (2009), pp. 69–88.

Hogg, Brian, *All That Ever Mattered: The History of Scottish Rock and Pop* (London: Guinness, 1993).

House, Jack, *Comics in Kilts* (Glasgow: Scoop Books, 1945).

House, Jack, *Music Hall Memories* (Glasgow: Richard Drew, 1986).

J., C. R., 'A Scotch National Theatre', *Glasgow Herald*, 29 June 1907.

Jackson, John, *The History of the Scottish Stage* (Edinburgh: Peter Hill, 1793).

James, Lawrence, *Crimea 1854–1856: The War with Russia from Contemporary Photographs* (New York: Van Nostrand Reinhold Company, 1981).

Jarvie, Grant, *Highland Games: The Making of the Myth* (Edinburgh: Edinburgh University Press, 1991).

Jarvie, Grant and I. A. Reid , 'Sport, nationalism and culture in Scotland', *The Sports Historian*, vol. 19.1 (1999), pp. 97–124.

Jeffrey, Moira, 'Relics of rebellion', *In Trust* (Autumn/Winter 2008).

Keegan, John, *Six Armies in Normandy* (London: Jonathan Cape, 1982).

Keightley, Keir, 'Reconsidering rock', in Simon Frith, Will Straw and John Street (eds), *The Cambridge Companion to Pop and Rock* (Cambridge: Cambridge University Press, 2001), pp. 109–42.

Kennedy, Michael, *Gaelic Nova Scotia: An Economic, Cultural, and Social Impact Study* (Halifax: Nova Scotia Museum, 2002).

Kiely, Richard, Frank Bechhofer and David McCrone, 'Birth, blood and belonging: identity claims in post-devolution Scotland', *The Sociological Review*, 53: 1 (2005), pp. 150–71.

King, Elspeth, 'Popular culture in Glasgow', in R. A. Cage (ed.), *The Working Class in Glasgow 1750–1914* (London: Croom Helm, 1987).

Knights, Mark, *Representation and Misrepresentation in Later Stuart Britain* (Oxford: Oxford University Press, 2006 [2005]).

Laing, Dave, *One Chord Wonders: Power and Meaning in Punk Rock* (Milton Keynes: Open University Press, 1985).

Lauder, Harry, *Harry Lauder at Home and on Tour: By Ma'sel* (London: Greening & Co. Ltd, 1907).

Lauder, Harry, *A Minstrel in France* (New York: Hearst's International Library, 1918).

Lincoln, Andrew, *Walter Scott and Modernity* (Edinburgh: Edinburgh University Press, 2007).

Lindsay, Isobel, 'The uses and abuses of national stereotypes', *Scottish Affairs*, no. 20 (Summer 1997), pp. 133–48.

Linkletter, Michael, 'Bu dual dhà sin (that was his birthright): Gaelic scholar Alexander Maclean Sinclair (1840–1924)' (unpublished PhD thesis, Harvard University, 2006).

Logan, Jimmy, with Billy Adams, *It's a Funny Life* (Edinburgh: B&W Publishing, 1998).

Lynch, Michael, *Scotland: A New History* (London: Century Publishing, 1991).

M., A., 'The Gaelic Society of London', *The Celtic Magazine* 2 (1877), pp. 353–60.

MacDiarmid, Hugh, *Complete Poems*, ed. Michael Grieve and W. R. Aitken, 2 vols (Manchester: Carcanet, 1993).

MacDiarmid, Hugh (C. M. Grieve), *Lucky Poet: A Self-Study in Literature and Political Ideas*, ed. Alan Riach (Manchester: Carcanet, 1994 [1943]).

MacDiarmid, Hugh, *The Raucle Tongue: Hitherto Uncollected Prose*, ed. Angus Calder, Glen Murray and Alan Riach, 3 vols (Manchester: Carcanet, 1996).

MacDiarmid, Hugh, 'Scottish people and "Scotch comedians"', Special Correspondent, 23 August 1928, in Angus Calder et al (eds), *The Raucle Tongue: Vol II* (Manchester: Carcanet, 2000).

MacDonald, Angus and Archibald MacDonald, *The MacDonald Collection of Gaelic Poetry* (Inverness: The Northern Counties Publishing Company Ltd., 1911).

MacDonald, Myra and Jane Sillars, 'Gender, spaces, changes: emergent identities in a Scotland in transition', in Neil Blain and David Hutchinson (eds), *Media in Scotland* (Edinburgh: Edinburgh University Press, 2008).

Macdonald, Norman, 'Putting on the kilt: the Scottish stereotype and ethnic community survival in Cape Breton', *Canadian Ethnic Studies* 20 (1988), pp. 132–46.

MacDonald, Sharon, *Reimagining Culture: Histories, Identities, and the Gaelic Renaissance* (Oxford: Berg, 1997).

MacDonnell, A. C., *Lays of the Heather* (London: Eliot Stock, 1896).

Macdonell, Margaret, *The Emigrant Experience* (Toronto: University of Toronto Press, 1982).

Maceachen, Frances, 'What history?', *Am Bràighe* Winter 1994/5.

Macgeachy, Robert A. A., 'Captain Lauchlin Campbell and early Argyllshire emigration to New York', *Northern Scotland* 19 (1999), pp. 21–46.

Macinnes, Allan, 'Scottish gaeldom, 1638–1651: the vernacular response to the Covenanting dynamic', in John Dwyer, Roger Mason and Alexander Murdoch (eds), *New Perspectives on the Politics and Culture of Early Modern Scotland* (Edinburgh: John Donald, n.d. [1983]), pp. 59–94.

Macinnes, Allan, 'Scottish gaeldom and the aftermath of the '45: the creation of silence?', in Michael Lynch (ed.), *Jacobitism and the '45* (London: The Historical Association, 1995), pp. 71–83.

MacInnes, John, 'The panegyric code in Gaelic poetry and its historical background', in Michael Newton (ed.), *Dùthchas nan Gàidheal* (Edinburgh: Birlinn, 2006), pp. 265–319.

MacInnes, John, *Dùthchas nan Gàidheal: Selected Essays of John MacInnes*, ed. Michael Newton (Edinburgh: Birlinn, 2006).

Mackay, John George, *The Romantic Story of the Highland Garb and Tartan* (Stirling: Eneas Mackay, 1924).

Mackenzie, Annie M., *Òrain Iain Luim. The Songs of John MacDonald of Keppoch* (Edinburgh: Scottish Gaelic Texts Society, 1964).

Mackenzie, Compton, *The Monarch of the Glen* [1941], in Mackenzie, *The Highland Omnibus: The Monarch of the Glen – Whisky Galore – The Rival Monster* (Harmondsworth: Penguin, 1983).

MacKerlie, Peter Handyside, *An Account of the Scottish Regiments with the Statistics of Each from 1808 to March 1861* (Edinburgh: William P. Nimmo, 1862).

Mackie, Albert, *The Scotch Comedians* (Edinburgh: Ramsay Head Press, 1973).

MacKillop, Andrew, 'Military recruiting in the Scottish Highlands 1739–1815: the political, social and economic context' (unpublished PhD thesis, University of Glasgow, 1995).

MacKillop, Andrew, *'More Fruitful than the Soil': Army, Empire and the Scottish Highlands, 1715–1815* (East Linton: Tuckwell Press, 2000).

Maclean, Loraine, of Dochgarroch, *Indomitable Colonel: The Biography of Lieutenant-Colonel Sir Alan Cameron of Erracht* (London: Shepheard-Walwyn, 1986).

MacLeod, Angus, *The Songs of Duncan Bàn Macintyre* (Edinburgh: Scottish Gaelic Texts Society, 1952).

MacLeod, Angus, *The Songs of Duncan Bàn Macintyre* (Edinburgh: Scottish Gaelic Texts Society, 1978).

Maitland Hume, Ian, 'Tartan and the wearing of the kilt as a mark of changing concepts of identity in contemporary Scotland', *Review of Scottish Culture* 12 (1999–2000), pp. 59–68.

Maitland Hume, Ian, 'The contemporary role of the kilt and tartan in the construction and expression of Scottish American identity' (unpublished PhD thesis, University of Edinburgh, 2001).

Mäkelä, Janne, 'Tartan boys – Scottish popular music stardom in the 1970s', *Studia Celtica Fennica*, II (Helsinki: Finnish Society for Celtic Studies, 2005), pp. 110–17.

Maloney, Paul, *Scotland and the Music Hall, 1850–1914* (Manchester and New York: Manchester University Press, 2003).

Marr, Andrew, *The Battle for Scotland* (Hardmonsworth: Penguin, 1992).

Martin, Richard, 'From clan to punk: imputed meanings of the tartan', *Ars Textrina* 9 (1988), pp. 211–21.

Martin, Martin, *A Description of the Western Islands of Scotland*, ed. Charles W. J. Withers and R. W. Munro (Edinburgh: Birlinn, 1999 [1703]).

Mason, Roger, *Kingship and the Commonweal* (East Linton: Tuckwell Press, 1998).

Mason, Roger, 'Civil society and the Celts: Hector Boece, George Buchanan and the ancient Scottish past', in Edward J. Cowan and Richard J. Finlay (eds), *Scottish History: the Power of the Past* (Edinburgh: Edinburgh University Press, 2002).

Matheson, Trueman and Laurinda Matheson, *O Cheapaich nan Craobh / From the Keppoch of the Trees: The Poetry of the Keppoch Bard* (St Andrews, Nova Scotia: Sìol Cultural Enterprises, 2008).

May, Mona, in 'Fashion 101 – How the filmmakers invented the trend-setting fashions that defined the movie', *Clueless*, directed by Amy Heckerling, DVD (Paramount Pictures, 2005).

McArthur, Colin, 'Breaking the signs', *Cencrastus*, no. 7 (Winter 1981/2).

McArthur, Colin (ed.), *Scotch Reels: Scotland in Cinema and Television* (London: BFI Publishing, 1982).

McArthur, Colin, 'Scotland and cinema: the iniquity of the fathers', in Colin McArthur (ed.), *Scotch Reels* (London: British Film Institute, 1982).

McArthur, Colin, *Brigadoon, Braveheart and the Scots: Distortions of Scotland in Hollywood Cinema* (London: I. B. Tauris, 2003).

McClintock, Henry Foster et al., *Old Irish and Highland Dress*, 2nd edn (Dundalk: Dundalgan Press, 1950).

McCrone, David, *Understanding Scotland: The Sociology of a Stateless Nation* (London: Routledge, 1992).

McCrone, David, *Understanding Scotland: The Sociology of a Nation*, 2nd edn (London: Routledge, 2001).

McCrone, David, Angela Morris and Richard Kiely, *Scotland – the Brand: The Making of Scottish Heritage* (Edinburgh: Edinburgh University Press, 1995).

McDonald, Heather, *Postcard Records profile*, http://musicians.about.com/od/indielabels/p/postcardrecords.htm

Mckay, Ian, 'Tartanism triumphant: the construction of Scottishness in Nova Scotia, 1933–1954', *Acadiensis* 21 (1992), pp. 5–47.

McLaren, J. Wilson, *Edinburgh Memories and Some Worthies* (Edinburgh: Chambers, 1926).

Mclean, Craig, 'Big Country, but not big enough', *The Scotsman*, 26 May 2000, p. 17.

Mcmillan, John, 'The first settlers in Glengarry', *The Scottish Canadian* 9 (1904), pp. 167–76.

Meek, Donald, 'The sublime Gael: the impact of Macpherson's Ossian on literary creativity and cultural perception in Gaelic Scotland', in Howard Gaskill (ed.), *The Reception of Ossian in Europe* (London: Thoemmes Continuum, 2004).

Meek, Donald (ed.), *The Wiles of the World: Anthology of 19th Century Scottish Gaelic Verse* (Edinburgh: Birlinn, 2003).

Miller, Daniel, 'Artefacts and the meaning of things', in G. L. Pocius (ed.), *Living in a Material World: Canadian and American Approaches to Material Culture* (St John's: Memorial University of Newfoundland, 1991).

Moffat, Graham, *Join Me in Remembering: The Life and Reminiscences of the Author of 'Bunty Pulls the Strings'* (Camps Bay, Cape Province: Winifred L. Moffat, 1955) .

Monod, Paul Kléber, *Jacobitism and the English People* (Cambridge: Cambridge University Press, 1989).

Monro, Robert, *His Expedition, with the Worthy Scots Regiment called Mac-Keys* (London: William Jones, 1637).

Montague, Charles Edward, *Disenchantment* (London: Chatto and Windus, 1922).

Morton, Henry Vollam, *In Search of Scotland* (London: Methuen & Co., 1929).

Nairn, Tom, *The Break-Up of Britain*, 2nd edn (London: New Left Books, 1981).

Nairn, Tom, *After Britain: New Labour and the Return of Scotland* (London: Granta, 2000).

Neale, Steve, 'Masculinity as spectacle: reflections on men and mainstream cinema', *Screen* 24 (1983).

Newton, Michael, *We're Indians Sure Enough: The Legacy of the Scottish Highlanders in the United States* (Richmond: Saorsa Media, 2001).

Newton, Michael, 'In their own words: Gaelic literature in North Carolina', *Scotia* 25 (2001), pp. 1–28.

Newton, Michael, 'Jacobite past, Loyalist present', *e-Keltoi* 5 (2003), pp. 31–62.

Newton, Michael, ' "Becoming cold-hearted like the Gentiles around them": Scottish Gaelic in the United States 1872–1912', *e-Keltoi* 2 (2003), pp. 63–131.

Newton, Michael, 'The fiery cross: folklore, literature and fakelore', *History Scotland*, May/June 2005, pp. 34–9.

Newton, Michael, ' "This could have been mine": Scottish Gaelic learners in modern North America', *e-Keltoi* 1 (2005), pp. 1–37.

Newton, Michael, 'Gaelic literature and the diaspora', in Ian Brown, Thomas Clancy, Susan Manning and Murray Pittock (eds), *The Edinburgh History of Scottish Literature*, vol. 2 (Edinburgh: Edinburgh University Press, 2007), pp. 353–9.

Newton, Michael, *Warriors of the Word: The World of the Scottish Highlanders* (Edinburgh: Birlinn, 2009).

Newton, Michael, 'My bard is in the Highlands: Burns 2009 and a national Scottish literature', *The Bottle Imp* 5 (Spring 2009) http://www.arts.gla. ac.uk/ScotLit/ASLS/SWE/TBI/TBIIssue5/Bard.html

Nicholson, Robin, *Bonnie Prince Charlie and the Making of a Myth* (Lewisburg, PA: Bucknell University Press, 2002).

Okri, Ben, 'Diary', *New Statesman*, vol. 112, no. 2889 (8 August 1986), p.16.

Osborne, Brian, *The Last of the Chiefs* (Glendaruel: Argyll Publishing, 2001).

Parker, Anthony, *Scottish Highlanders in Colonial Georgia* (Athens: University of Georgia Press, 1997).

Percival, J. Mark, 'Britpop or Eng-pop?', in Andy Bennett and Jon Stratton (eds), *Britpop and the English Music Tradition* (Farnham: Ashgate, 2010).

Perkins, Tessa, 'Rethinking stereotypes', in Michèle Barrett, P. Corrigan, A. Kuhn and J. Wolff, *Ideology and Cultural Production* (London: Croom Helm, 1979).

Peter, Bruce, *100 Years of Glasgow's Amazing Cinemas* (Edinburgh: Polygon, 1996).

Peterson, Richard A., *Creating Country Music: Fabricating Authenticity* (Chicago: University of Chicago Press, 1997).

Petrie, Duncan, *Contemporary Scottish Fictions: Film, Television and the Novel* (Edinburgh: Edinburgh University Press, 2004).

Philip, James, *The Grameid*, ed. Alexander D. Murdoch (Edinburgh: Scottish History Society, 1888 [1691]).

Pitt, William, *The Speeches of the Right Honourable the Earl of Chatham in the Houses of Lords and Commons: With a Biographical Memoir and Introductions and Explanatory Notes to the Speeches* (London: Aylott and Jones, 1848).

Pittock, Murray, *Jacobitism* (Basingstoke: Macmillan, 1998).

Pittock, Murray, *Celtic Identity and the British Image* (Manchester: Manchester University Press, 1999).

Pittock, Murray, 'Material culture in modern Scotland', in Ian Brown, Thomas Clancy, Susan Manning and Murray Pittock (eds), *The Edinburgh History of Scottish Literature*, vol. 3 (Edinburgh: Edinburgh University Press, 2007), pp. 64–8.

Pittock, Murray, 'Patriot dress and patriot games: tartan from the Jacobites to Queen Victoria', in Caroline McCracken-Flesher (ed.), *Culture, Nation and the New Scottish Parliament* (Lewisburg: Bucknell University Press, 2007), pp. 158–74.

Pittock, Murray, *Scottish and Irish Romanticism* (Oxford: Oxford University Press, 2008).

Pittock, Murray, *The Myth of the Jacobite Clans: The Jacobite Army in 1745*, 2nd and rev. edn, (Edinburgh: Edinburgh University Press, 2009).

Pittock, Murray, 'To see ourselves as others see us', *European Journal of English Studies*, 13: 3 (2009), pp. 293–304.

Pitt-Rivers, Augustus Lane-Fox, *The Evolution of Culture and other Essays*, ed. John Linton Myers (Oxford: Clarendon Press, 1906).

Porter, James, 'The folklore of Northern Scotland: five discourses on cultural representation', *Folklore* (1998).

Prebble, John, *The King's Jaunt: George IV in Scotland, August 1822* (London: Collins, 1988).

Purser, John et al., *The Music of Scotland* (Hamilton, New Zealand: University of Waikato Scottish Studies Association Avizandum Editions no. 2, 1994).

Quye, Anita and Hugh Cheape, 'Rediscovering the Arisaid', *Costume: The Journal of the Costume Society* 42 (2008), pp. 1–20.

Ramsay, Allan, *The Works of Allan Ramsay*, ed. Burns Martin and John Oliver (New York and London: Scottish Text Society, 1972).

Rankin, Effie, *As a' Bhràighe / Beyond the Braes: The Gaelic Songs of Allan the Ridge MacDonald 1794–1868* (Sydney: UCCB Press, 2004).

Rankin, Ian (writer) and Werther Dell'Edera (art), *Dark Entries* (New York: DC Comics / Vertigo Crime, 2009).

Ray, Celeste, *Highland Heritage: Scottish Americans in the American South* (Chapel Hill, NC: University of North Carolina Press, 2001).

Redmond, Gerald, *The Caledonian Games in Nineteenth-Century America* (Rutherford: Fairleigh Dickinson University Press, 1971).

Renn, Joachim, *Übersetzungsverhältnisse: Perspektiven einer pragmatistischen Gesellschaftstheorie* (Weilerswist: Velbrück, 2006).

Reynolds, Simon, 'Guns N' Roses: danger lurks beyond The Doors', *The Observer*, 25 August 1991.

Riach, Alan, *Representing Scotland in Literature, Iconography and Popular Culture: The Masks of the Modern Nation* (Basingstoke: Palgrave Macmillan, 2005).

Rimmer, Dave, *Like Punk Never Happened: Culture Club and the New Pop* (London: Faber and Faber, 1985).

Rimmer, Dave, *New Romantics: The Look* (London: Omnibus, 2003).

Roberts, David, *British Hit Singles and Albums*, 19th edn (London: Guinness, 2006).

Robertson, James Irvine, *The First Highlander: Major-General David Stewart of Garth CB* (East Linton: Tuckwell Press, 1998).

Royle, Trevor, *Flowers of the Forest: Scotland and the First World War* (Edinburgh: Birlinn, 2006).

Sabin, Roger (ed.), *Punk Rock: So What? The Cultural Legacy of Punk* (London: Routledge, 1999).

Samuel, Raphael and Paul Thompson (eds), *The Myths We Live By* (London: Routledge, 1990).

Sassi, Carla, *Why Scottish Literature Matters* (Edinburgh: Saltire Society, 2005).

Savage, Jon, *England's Dreaming: The Sex Pistols and Punk Rock* (London: Faber and Faber, 1991).

Scarlett, James D., *Tartan: The Highland Textile* (London: Shepheard-Walwyn, 1990).

Schlereth, Thomas J., 'Material culture in material life', in G. L. Pocius (ed.), *Living in a Material World: Canadian and American Approaches to Material Culture* (St John's: Memorial University of Newfoundland, 1991).

Schlesinger, Philip, *Media, State and Nation. Political Violence and Collective Identities* (London: Sage Publications, 1991).

Shaw, John, 'Brief beginnings: Nova Scotian and Old World bards compared', *Scottish Gaelic Studies* 17 (1996), pp. 342–55.

Shaw, John, 'The collectors: John Francis Campbell and Alexander Carmichael', in Ian Brown et al. (eds), *The Edinburgh History of Scottish Literature*, vol. 2 (Edinburgh: Edinburgh University Press, 2007), pp. 347–52.

Sinclair, Alexander Maclean, *Clàrsach na Coille* (Glasgow: Archibald Sinclair, 1881).

Sinclair, Alexander Maclean, *Filidh na Coille* (Charlottetown, Prince Edward Island: The Examiner Publishing Company, 1901).

Sinclair, Sir John, of Ulbster, *An Account of the Highland Society of London* (London: B. McMillan, 1813).

Skene, William F., *The Highlanders of Scotland*, ed. Alexander Macbain (Stirling: Eneas Mackay, 1902 [1837]).

Snyder, Robert, *The Voice of the City: Vaudeville and Popular Culture in New York* (Oxford: Oxford University Press, 1989).

Spiers, Edward M., *The Scottish Soldier and Empire 1854–1902* (Edinburgh: Edinburgh University Press, 2006).

Spring, Ian, 'Lost Land of Dreams: Representing St Kilda', *Cultural Studies* 4 (1990).

Stevenson, David, *Alasdair Mac Colla and the Highland Problem in the Seventeenth Century* (Edinburgh: John Donald, 1980).

Stewart, David, of Garth, *Sketches of the Character, Manner and Present State of the Highlanders of Scotland, with Details of the Military Service of the Highland Regiments* (Edinburgh: Constable, 1822).

Stewart, Donald Calder, *The Setts of the Scottish Tartans* (Edinburgh: Oliver and Boyd, 1950; rev. edn London: Shepheard-Walwyn, 1974).

Stewart, Donald Calder and J. Charles Thompson, *Scotland's Forged Tartans* (Edinburgh: Paul Harris, 1980).

Stewart, Donald William, *Old and Rare Scottish Tartans* (Edinburgh: George P. Johnston, 1893).

Stiùbhart, Domnhall Uilleam, 'Highland rogues and the roots of Highland romanticism', in Christopher MacLachlan (ed.), *Crossing the Highland Line* (Glasgow: Association for Scottish Literary Studies, 2009).

Storaas, Randi, 'Clothes as an expression of counter-cultural activity', in *Ethnologica Scandinavica* (Lund: Royal Gustav Adolf Academy, 1986).

Sullivan, Caroline, *Bye Bye Baby: My Tragic Love Affair with the Bay City Rollers* (London: Bloomsbury, 1999).

Summerfield, Penny, 'Patriotism and Empire: Music-Hall Entertainment 1870–1914', in John M. MacKenzie (ed.), *Imperialism and Popular Culture* (Manchester: Manchester University Press, 1986).

Sweeting, Adam, 'Obituary: Stuart Adamson, Big Country founder whose songs were suffused with the sense of the great outdoors', *The Guardian*, 20 December 2001.

Szechi, Daniel, 'The Jacobite theatre of death', in Jeremy Black and Eveline Cruickshanks (eds), *The Jacobite Challenge* (Edinburgh: John Donald, 1988).

Tasker, Yvonne, *Spectacular Bodies: Gender, Genre and the Action Cinema* (London: Routledge, 1995).

Taylor, Julian, 'When Wembley turned tartan', http://news.bbc.co.uk/sport1/hi/scotland/669029.stm (2007).

Tonkin, Elizabeth, 'History and the myth of realism', in Raphael Samuel and Paul Thompson (eds), *The Myths We Live By* (London: Routledge, 1990).

Trevor-Roper, Hugh, 'The invention of tradition: the Highland tradition of Scotland', in E. Hobsbawm and T. Ranger (eds), *The Invention of Tradition* (Cambridge: Cambridge University Press, 1983).

Trevor-Roper, Hugh, *The Invention of Scotland* (New Haven and London: Yale University Press, 2008).

Turner, Roger, *Manchester in 1745*, Royal Stuart Society Paper XLIX (London, n.d.).

Vance, Michael, 'A brief history of organized Scottishness in Canada', in Celeste Ray (ed.), *Transatlantic Scots* (Tuscaloosa, AL: University of Alabama Press, 2005).

Vinache, William E., 'Stereotypes as social concepts', *The Journal of Social Psychology*, no. 46 (1957), pp. 229–43.

Wall, Max, *The Fool on the Hill* (London: Quartet, 1975).

Wall, Mick, *W. Axl Rose: The Unauthorized Biography* (London: Pan, 2008).

Wallace, Gavin, 'Compton Mackenzie and the Scottish popular novel', in Cairns Craig (ed.), *The History of Scottish Literature: Twentieth Century* (Aberdeen: Aberdeen University Press, 1987).

Watson, Roderick, 'Maps of desire: Scottish literature in the twentieth century', in T. M. Devine and R. J. Findlay (eds), *Scotland in the Twentieth Century* (Edinburgh: Edinburgh University Press, 1996).

Watson, William J., *Bàrdachd Ghàidhlig. Specimens of Gaelic Poetry, 1550–1900*, 2nd edn (Stirling: An Comunn Gàidhealach, 1932 [1918]).

Whitehead, Maurice, *Held in Trust: 2008 Years of Sacred Culture* (Stonyhurst: St Omer's Press, 2008).

Whitt, Laurie Anne, 'Cultural imperialism and the marketing of Native America', in Devon Mihesuah (ed.), *Natives and Academics: Researching and Writing about American Indians* (Lincoln, NE: University of Nebraska Press, 1998).

Williams, Gordon, *British Theatre in the Great War: A Revaluation* (London: Continuum, 2003).

Williamson, John, Martin Cloonan and Simon Frith, *Mapping the Music Industry in Scotland: A Report* (Glasgow: Scottish Enterprise, 2003) http://www.scottish-enterprise.com/publications/scottishmusicmappingreport.pdf

Womack, Peter, *Improvement and Romance: Constructing the Myth of the Highlands* (Basingstoke: Macmillan, 1989).

Wood, Stephen, *The Scottish Soldier* (Manchester: Archive Publications, 1987).

Wright, Gordon, *MacDiarmid: An Illustrated Biography of Christopher Murray Grieve (Hugh MacDiarmid)* (Edinburgh: Gordon Wright, 1977).

RECORDED INTERVIEWS

Interview with Alex Frutin by Ben Braber, AUD OHP 0001, Glasgow Jewish Archive Centre

University of Edinburgh School of Scottish Studies Sound Archives (abbreviated SSS: SA).

BROADCASTS

Ronnie Corbett Tickles Your Fancy, STV, 31 December 1999

Hoots, BBC1, 10 February 2000.

Myleene's Musical Tour, Episode 5: 'A Scottish Soldier' by Trevor Royle, *The One Show*, BBC1, 30 April 2008.

Edward VII – The Prince of Pleasure, BBC 2, 23 March 2010.

DISCOGRAPHY

Albums

Big Country, *The Crossing* (Mercury, 1983).

Big Country, *Steeltown* (Mercury, 1984).

Guns N' Roses, *Appetite For Destruction* (Geffen, 1987).

Nirvana, *Nevermind* (DGC Records, 1991).

Outkast, *Speakerboxxx / The Love Below* (La Face, 2003).

Andy Stewart's Scotland (VITV 563, Scotdisc, BGS Productions Ltd, Kilsyth).

Andy Stewart, 'A Scottish Soldier', *The Very Best of Andy Stewart* (EMI Records, 1961).

Singles

The Skids, *Into The Valley* (Virgin Records, 1979).

VIDEOGRAPHY

Big Country, *Live at Barrowland 1983: The Home Coming* (CD & DVD, 2009).

FILMOGRAPHY

Annie Laurie (United States, John S. Robertson, 1927).
Attack Girls' Swim Team Versus The Undead (Japan, Kôji Kawano, 2007).
Auld Lang Syne (United Kingdom, George Pearson, 1929).
Austin Powers: The Spy Who Shagged Me (United States, Jay Roach, 1999).
Babel (United States, Alejandro González Iñárritu, 2006).
Bande à Part (France, Jean-Luc Godard, 1964).
Battle of the Sexes (United Kingdom, Charles Crichton, 1959).
Bonnie Prince Charlie (United Kingdom, Charles Calverts, 1923).
Bonnie Prince Charlie (United Kingdom, Anthony Kimmins, 1948).
Bonnie Scotland (United States, James W. Horne, 1935).
Braveheart (United States, Mel Gibson, 1995).
Brigadoon (United States, Vincente Minnelli, 1954).
Brothers, The (United Kingdom, David MacDonald, 1947).
Carry on . . . up the Khyber (United Kingdom, Gerald Thomas, 1968).
Clueless (United States, Amy Heckerling, 1993).
Dewar's It's Scotch (United States, Edison Manufacturing Company, 1898).
Effects of Too Much Scotch, The (United Kingdom, Alf Collins, 1903)
End of the Road, The (United Kingdom, Alex Bryce, 1936).
Exotica (Canada, Atom Egoyan, 1994).
51st State (United Kingdom, Ronny Yu, 2001).
Ghost Goes West, The (United Kingdom, René Clair, 1935).
Ghost World (United States, Terry Zwigoff, 2001).
Harry Lauder in a Hurry (United Kingdom, Alf Collins, 1908).
Huntingtower (United Kingdom, George Pearson, 1927).
Kidnapped (United Kingdom, Robert Stevenson, 1960).
Kidnapped (United Kingdom, Delbert Mann, 1971).
Kill Bill: Volume 1 (United States, Quentin Tarantino, 2003).
Local Hero (United Kingdom, Bill Forsyth, 1983).
Love Story (United States, Arthur Hiller, 1970).
Macbeth (United States, Orson Welles, 1948).

Machine Girl, The (Japan, Noboru Iguchi, 2008).

Maggie, The (United Kingdom, Alexander Mackendrick, 1953).

Mairi – The Romance of a Highland Maiden (United Kingdom, Andrew Patterson, 1913).

Mary of Scotland (United States, John Ford, 1936).

Mary Queen of Scots (United Kingdom, Edwin Greenwood, 1922).

Master of Ballantrae, The (United Kingdom, William Keighley, 1953).

Music in the Air (United States, Joe May, 1934).

Nina's Heavenly Delights (United Kingdom, Pratibha Parmar, 2006).

On a Clear Day You Can See Forever (United States, Vincente Minnelli, 1970).

Pardon my Scotch (United States, Del Lord, 1935).

Pretty in Pink (United States, Howard Deutch, 1986).

Prime of Miss Jean Brodie, The (United Kingdom, Ronald Neame, 1969).

Pulp Fiction (United States, Quentin Tarantino, 1994)

Rob Roy (United Kingdom, Arthur Vivian, 1911).

Rob Roy (United Kingdom, W. P. Kellino, 1922).

Rob Roy (United States, Michael Caton-Jones, 1995).

Rob Roy – The Highland Rogue (United Kingdom/United States, Harold French, 1953).

Scotch Myths (United Kingdom, Murray Grigor, 1983).

Trainspotting (United Kingdom, Danny Boyle, 1996).

Whisky Galore (United Kingdom, Alexander Mackendrick, 1948).

Yo Yo Girl Cop (Japan, Kenta Fukasaku, 2006).

NOTES ON THE CONTRIBUTORS

Ian Brown is playwright, poet and Professor in Drama at Kingston University. General Editor of *The Edinburgh History of Scottish Literature* (2007), he is joint series editor of *The Edinburgh Companions to Scottish Literature*, co-editing with Alan Riach the volume on *Twentieth-Century Scottish Literature* (2009) and editing that on *Scottish Drama* (2011). A visiting professor at Glasgow and Glamorgan Universities, he writes on theatre, literary and cultural topics.

Richard Butt is Head of Media, Communication and Performing Arts at Queen Margaret University, Edinburgh. His research interests include screen adaptation and Scottish media. His publications include 'Scottish Mass Media in the Twentieth Century', in *The Edinburgh History of the Book in Scotland, Vol. 4* (2007) and 'Literature and Screen Media, 1918 to date', in *The Edinburgh History of Scottish Literature, Vol. 3* (2007).

Hugh Cheape teaches a post-graduate programme at Sabhal Mòr Ostaig and holds a Research Chair in the University of the Highlands and Islands. He was formerly Principal Curator in the National Museums Scotland and collaborated on research into tartans and dye-analysis between 1996 and 2007. He has published widely in the fields of regional ethnology and musicology.

David Goldie is a senior lecturer in the Department of English Studies at the University of Strathclyde. He is the author of *A Criticial Difference: T S Eliot and John Middleton Murry in English Literary Criticism* (1998) and editor, with Gerard Carruthers and Alastair Renfrew, of *Beyond Scotland: New Contexts for Twentieth-Century Scottish Literature* (2004) and the forthcoming *Scotland in the Nineteenth-Century World*.

Susanne Hagemann teaches at the University of Mainz, Germany. She has written extensively on Scottish literature and on translation. Her latest book, *Deskriptive Übersetzungsforschung: Eine Auswahl* (2009), is a volume of German translations of classical texts from the field of descriptive translation studies.

Ian Maitland Hume achieved a First Class Honours degree in Scottish Ethnology and Scottish History, followed by a PhD at the School of Scottish Studies in the University of Edinburgh. He has lectured in Britain and America on his main field of interest, identity and Highland dress, and led specialist tours of Scotland for selected groups of Americans.

Paul Maloney is Research Associate on Pantomime in Scotland: 'Your other national theatre', an AHRC-funded research project based at the Department of Theatre, Film and Television Studies at the University of Glasgow. He recently completed a PhD on the Britannia Music Hall and the development of urban popular entertainments in Glasgow, and is author of *Scotland and the Music Hall, 1850–1914* (2003).

Margaret Munro was awarded a PhD by Queen Margaret University for a thesis entitled *Language and Cultural Identities in the Scots Comic Tradition.* She is a local history researcher, joint author of a popular volume of old photographs of Portobello and Duddingston and a founder Director and Chairperson of the newly established Portobello Heritage Trust.

Michael Newton is Assistant Professor in Celtic Studies at St Francis Xavier University, Nova Scotia. His PhD is from Edinburgh University in 1998. He has written widely on many aspects of Highland tradition and history in Scotland and North America. He edited *Dùthchas nan Gaidheal: Selected Essays of John MacInnes* (Saltire Research Book of the Year, 2006) and wrote *Warriors of the Word: The World of the Scottish Highlanders*, nominated for the 2009 Katharine Briggs Award for folklore research.

Hugh O'Donnell is Professor of Language and Popular Culture at Glasgow Caledonian University. He specialises in cross-cultural analysis of a range of popular-cultural topics, in particular sport and national identity, soap operas and representations of monarchy, and has also carried out large-scale cross-cultural analyses of television news.

J. Mark Percival lectures in Media and Culture at Queen Margaret University, Edinburgh. His academic writing includes work on the relationship between radio and the music industry, and on the local production of indie and alternative popular music. A member of the Mercury Music Prize judging panel in the award years 1999 and 2000, his broadcasting includes presenting alternative rock and electronic music radio shows at BBC Radio Scotland.

Murray Pittock is Bradley Professor of English Literature and Dean of the Faculty of Arts at the University of Glasgow. His most recent books include *Loyalty and Identity* (2010), *The Myth of the Jacobite Clans* (2nd edn, 2009) and *Scottish and Irish Romanticism* (2008). He is a Fellow of the Royal Society of Edinburgh and a prizewinner of that Society and the British Academy. Currently he is Principal Investigator of the AHRC Beyond Text grant, 'Robert Burns: Inventing Tradition and Securing Memory'.

Alan Riach is the Professor of Scottish Literature at Glasgow University, whose most recent critical books include *Representing Scotland in Literature, Popular Culture and Iconography* and, co-authored with Alexander Moffat, *Arts of Resistance: Poets, Portraits and Landscapes of Modern Scotland*. His poetry is collected in five books: *This Folding Map, An Open Return, First & Last Songs, Clearances* and *Homecoming*. With Ian Brown, he co-edited the *Edinburgh Companion to Twentieth-Century Scottish Literature*.

Trevor Royle is an Honorary Fellow in the School of History, Archaeology and Classics at the University of Edinburgh. He is also an Associate Editor of the *Sunday Herald*. Recent works include *The Road to Bosworth Field: A New History of the Wars of the Roses* (2009) and the concise histories of the eight pre-1968 Scottish infantry regiments (2007–9).

INDEX